Hands-On KornShell93
Programming

Hands-On KornShell93 Programming

Barry Rosenberg

ADDISON–WESLEY

Boston • San Francisco • New York • Toronto • Montreal
London • Munich • Paris • Madrid
Capetown • Sydney • Tokyo • Singapore • Mexico City

The publisher offers discounts on this book when ordered in quantity for special sales. For more information, please contact:

Pearson Education Corporate Sales Division
One Lake Street
Upper Saddle River, NJ 07458
(800) 382-3419
corpsales@pearsontechgroup.com

Visit AW on the Web: www.awl.com/cseng/

Library of Congress Cataloging-in-Publication Data

Rosenberg, Barry
    Hands-on KornShell93 programming / Barry Rosenberg.
        p.   cm.
    Includes bibliographical references and index.
    ISBN 0-201-31018-X (alk. paper)
    1. KornShell (Computer program language). I. Title.
QA76.73.K67R67   1998
005.13'3--DC21   98-29949
                                                          CIP

Text printed on recycled and acid-free paper.

ISBN 020131018X

4 5 6 7 8 9 MA   04 03 02 01

4th Printing   March 2001

To Marilyn, Rachel, and Danny

Contents

3   Data Types   25

4   Math   43

5

Pattern Matching 57

6

Conditions 73

7   Loops   103

10 Functions   163

11 Start-Up Scripts and Environments   197

12 Input and Output 209

13 Manipulating Strings 255

14 KornShell Reserved Variables 283

15   Foreground, Background, and Signaling   309

16 Command Line Editing and the History File   325

17 Writing CGI Scripts   335

Appendixes

List of Tables

List of Figures

Preface

... That No One Will Ever Read

Research indicates that virtually no one actually reads prefaces in computer books. In fact, this preface could be about the Loch Ness Monster for all that most readers care.

But why don't people read prefaces? Is it because prefaces sometimes get too personal? ("...and I want to thank Sal, who made this book possible.") Is it because the sentiments of nerdy authors can be a bit repulsive? ("...Sal, my SparcStation, was always there when I needed her.") Is it because they are predictably self-deprecatory in an ironic way? ("...and I want to thank: [list of 250 noted experts goes here] for reviewing drafts of this manual. Naturally all mistakes are my own.") No, when it comes right down to it, people avoid prefaces because they're boring.

It is also *de rigueur* for the nerdish author to explain, folksinger style, why he or she decided to write this piece. I guess this book sort of came to me while I was camping out in the glorious Rocky Mountains. I was gazing at pristine waterfalls and awe-inspiring sunsets when I said to myself, "This land must be preserved: I shall write a KornShell book." Possessed by a demonic ecological fervor, I roared down that mountain in a snowmobile, fired up a 1200-watt workstation, and wrote it all down for you. I only ask that you use the power of the KornShell for good, rather than evil.

Through the years, I've been lucky enough to get lots of feedback from my readers. What do you think they ask for? More text? No. More syntax? Definitely not. When it comes right down to it, readers consistently ask for only one thing: *more examples.*

So, I listened to them and based this tutorial entirely on examples.

I feel that short, focused examples are more valuable than long, detailed examples, and I've written the book accordingly. The purpose of the book is not to make me look clever; it is to make you look clever. Nevertheless, I've sprinkled a few lengthy examples into the mix for those of you who enjoy that sort of thing.

When I was a mere lad, my family doctor pointed to a massive encyclopedia of pharmaceuticals and told me that he could treat 90 percent of all patients with only six different medicines. Similarly, although the KornShell is a very rich language, my goal is to focus on the common script ailments and to leave the beriberi treatment to specialists.

Beginners may be wondering, "Is this book too hard for me?" No, probably not. Programmers experienced in various languages, though not in the KornShell, are probably wondering, "Is this book too wimpy for me?" No, probably not. To help guide both kinds of readers through the book, I've marked certain sections as being more appropriate for one group or the other. Many beginners need an explanation of loops, while experienced programmers need to know how KornShell loops differ from loops in other languages.

Since the KornShell runs on all sorts of operating systems, I've tried to keep operating system dependencies to a bare minimum. Nevertheless, I do assume that readers are either working directly on the UNIX[1] operating system or indirectly on UNIX through a package like U/WIN.

My three primary reviewers were KornShell gurus David Korn, Steve Sommars, and Glenn Fowler, all of whom gave fantastic and diplomatic criticism.

I also received important criticism and help from Tom Barstow, Dave Beckedorff, Bart Hanlon, Warren Johnson, Ed Johnston, Mark Keil, Mike Kong, Alice Lynch, Dave Penfield, Will Roaf, Frank Rubinsky, John Weiss, Daryl Winters, Teri Witham, and other people whose names I have no doubt forgotten to list. Eric Eldred and Quentin Sullivan found so many bugs in early drafts that, and I mean this as a compliment, they should have a brand of insecticide named after them.

Judy Tarutz is my long-suffering editor. In person, Judy is a kind, gentle soul with an outrageous sense of humor. Give her a red pen, though, and she turns into Conan the Barbarian. Her savage red pen cut a bloody swath through early drafts of this book. If we should chance to meet up one day, dear reader, I'll tell you all the "weak" jokes she made me take out.

I'd also like to thank the members of the Academy.

A consortium of great minds—those minds owned and operated by Ted Ricks, John Wait, Jack Danahy, and Steve Spicer—led me to the KornShell and helped me define the material for this book.

Finally, I'd like to thank the person who really made this book possible: my wife and best friend, Marilyn.

Whoops, almost forgot. Naturally, all mistakes are my own.

Author's Note Regarding the ksh93 Edition

It has been a very long time since I wrote the ksh88 edition, entitled *KornShell Programming Tutorial*. I began to suspect as much when I noticed that of all the people acknowledged in this Preface, and I'm sure they were capital reviewers—intelligent, meticulous, helpful—the only familiar name was my wife's.

But how to resurrect a vanished book? All traces of the ksh88 edition had disappeared until 1997, when a fragment was found suspended in a piece of amber at a Chinese restaurant in Palo Alto. Working round the clock, scientists at Addison

---

1. UNIX is a registered trademark of UNIX System laboratories, Inc.

Wesley Longman were able to piece together most of the old book. When gaps were found, DNA sequences from Kernighan and Ritchie were substituted.

After reading *KornShell Programming Tutorial*, many readers asked me important questions such as, "How does a joke get to be in your book?" or "Couldn't you just write a preface next time and skip the rest of the stuff that came after it?" or "Did you hear the one about the traveling KornShell salesman and the system administrator's daughter?"

Actually, creating humor for this book is not as haphazard as it may seem. All jokes are put through a rigorous five-step Beta testing procedure. I need to ensure that a joke is just as funny on the tenth reading as it is on the first. Although not all Beta testers installed the jokes, I did get enough feedback to toss out a ridiculous amount of material, for example, the original start of Chapter 1 went like this:

"I first saw David Korn writing shell scripts in a small club in the Village in 1946. The post-War euphoria was contagious and it wasn't long before the whole room was up and swaying to a pounding UNIX beat."

In a second edition, the author is obliged to correct the occasional error or two that cropped up in the first edition. (A special note to all of you at the Strategic Air Command—you're absolutely right guys, it *was* supposed to be a comma, *not* a semicolon.) A pair of translators, Hideyuki Hayashi and Masataka Isoya, get the credit for finding the most mistakes in the ksh88 edition. These two were incredibly rigorous and could not have been more diplomatic. (*"Barry-San, every word on page 233 appears to be a typo."*) Yep, the truth is out there, but a lot of it failed to work its way into the ksh88 edition. To improve accuracy, Sarah Tuttle wrote a validation suite that tests most of the sample KornShell scripts appearing in this book.

When I wrote the *KornShell Programming Tutorial* book, KornShell88 was beginning to make KornShell86 obsolete. As I go to press with this book, *Hands-On KornShell93 Programming*, KornShell93 is starting to overtake KornShell88. The KornShell93 scripts are far richer than KornShell88, and I've focused this book completely on KornShell93. If you liked KornShell88, you're going to love KornShell93.

Several reviewers strongly suggested a chapter on CGI programming with KornShell. As an avid CGI programmer, I happily agreed.

The CD accompanying this book contains the U/WIN package, created by David Korn and a cast of thousands, and now commercially marketed by Global Technologies Development. The package contains all the popular UNIX utilities—the grep's and awk's and diff's you know and recognize—all ready to run on your Windows 95 machine.

Table P-1 on the next page shows how I've organized the book.

Table P-1. Chapter by Chapter

Chapter	Describes
1	How the KornShell stacks up against other programming languages.
2	Writing simple KornShell scripts, executing them, debugging them, and so on.
3	Data types like strings, integers, floats, structures, arrays, and such.
4	Mathematics, which is surprisingly rich for a shell language.
5	Pattern matching, including the five uniquely KornShell wildcards.
6	Conditional evaluation.
7	Looping. You'll want to read it over and over and over again.
8	Creating simple menus with the **select** statement.
9	Passing arguments on the command line.
10	Functions, including regular KornShell functions, autoloaded functions, and extension functions written in C.
11	Start-up files, environments, exporting variables, and the like.
12	Input and output.
13	Manipulating strings—an area in which the KornShell excels.
14	Reserved variables like **PATH** and **PS1**. There are dozens of these.
15	Sending and trapping signals; running scripts in the background.
16	Command line editing, repeating previous commands, and such.
17	CGI scripting tutorial. The KornShell is a terrific choice for your next CGI program.
App. A	A quick reference of all statements in the KornShell. This appendix will become more valuable to you as your KornShell experience increases.
App. B	A very short HTML tutorial; this is just enough HTML to help understand what's going on in Chapter 17.

Primary reviewers for this book include John Allen, Chris Baron, Dave Beckedorff, Ann Hall, Bobby Higgins, Ollie Jones, Jeff Korn, David Korn, Charlie Northrup, and Bob Weil. Thanks also to Jason Jones, Mike Hendrickson, Marina Lang, and Marilyn Rash at Addison Wesley Longman. There's a saying in Japan that goes something like, "Everybody should climb Mt. Fuji once, but only a fool would climb it a second time." Dave Beckedorff—thanks for reviewing my book a second time. Thanks to the wonderful staff at Open Market, Inc. for their collective Web expertise.

The success of *KornShell Programming Tutorial* was primarily due to the collective "tough love" of its reviewers. Thank you again. Special thanks to Judy Tarutz for an editorial job that still amazes me seven years later.

And to my wife Marilyn—your love, support, and amazing patience is what really made this book.

Hands-On KornShell93
Programming

1 Before Writing Your First KornShell Scripts

Some people learn best from pure reference material. These people like a meticulous, dirt-free, syntactic representation of all known program features. These people prefer their world broken down into squiggly braces and italicized symbols. These people not only can spell "Backus Naur" correctly, they can pronounce it correctly, too.

Avoid these people.

This book, on the other hand, is a tutorial for people who prefer to learn through examples. In fact, the book is approximately 50 percent examples.[1]

Warning! This book does not detail every single amazing nuance of the KornShell. The KornShell is very rich in features, but my intention is to focus on what I have found to be the most useful features at the expense of the more obscure.

I will now answer a few of the more common beginner's questions.

"What is a shell?"

Just about every operating system provides at least one shell. Typically, the operating system invokes a shell when you log in. After the shell starts up, it waits for you to enter commands. For example, if you were a UNIX user who wanted to know the names of the files in a directory, then you would probably type the command ls inside a UNIX shell. The UNIX shell will *interpret* the ls command, which means that it will figure out what command you typed ("oh, you want to execute an ls command") and then invoke the command. By contrast, Apple Macintosh users typically don't use a shell program; instead, they interact with the operating system by clicking a mouse button.

For many users, the only purpose of a shell is to enter operating system commands or to start programs.

"Can a shell do anything besides executing operating system commands?"

Yes. Most shells support a shell programming language. Some of these shell programming languages are fairly primitive. Others rival high-level languages such as C or FORTRAN in their complexity.

---

1. This book is sold by weight, not by volume. Some settling of examples may occur during shipping.

One way of looking at a shell is that it is a high-level language from which it is very easy to invoke operating system utilities.

"What can I do with a shell programming language?"

That really depends on the shell programming language you're using and on your skill as a programmer. The KornShell's programming language lets you perform many of the same feats that you can in C. And often you can often write a KornShell *script* faster than you could write a comparable C program. A KornShell script is a program, stored in a text file, written in the KornShell's special shell programming language.

"What is the KornShell?"

The KornShell is a shell invented by David Korn of Bell Laboratories.

"How does the KornShell compare to other UNIX shells?"

The Bourne shell is the original UNIX shell. It was invented by Stephen Bourne in the early 1970s. The syntax of the Bourne shell programming language resembles the syntax of an old language called ALGOL.

The C shell was invented in the late seventies by Bill Joy, one of the founders of Sun Microsystems. It contains many features not found in the Bourne shell. The syntax of the C shell programming language resembles that of the C programming language.

The KornShell was invented in the mid-1980s. It is a superset of the Bourne shell, meaning that it supports every feature of the Bourne shell plus many new ones. In addition, the KornShell incorporates some of the best features of the C shell.

Many other shells, such as `bash` or `tcsh`, are currently floating around the Internet. Most of these shells are hybrids of the Bourne shell, C shell, or KornShell.

"If I already know the Bourne shell, why should I bother learning the KornShell?"

Because Bourne shell scripts will run without modification under the KornShell, Bourne shell users may be tempted to ignore the KornShell. However, that's kind of like saying, "I already know how to ride a tricycle. Why should I bother learning how to ride a bicycle?" True, both the Bourne shell and KornShell will get you to the same place, but you'll arrive there faster and more comfortably in the KornShell.

"If I already know the C shell, why should I learn the KornShell?"

We don't mean to get your ponytails all frizzy, but you long-time C shell diehards really ought to consider the superior string handling, stronger data typing, and broader capabilities of the KornShell. Yep, the C shell had its heyday, but, then again, so did disco.

"Which revision of the KornShell does this book describe?"

David Korn customarily releases a new revision of the KornShell every few years. KornShell fans identify these revisions by the year in which Korn releases them. This book describes the KornShell revision that came out in 1993, popularly known as KornShell 93 (or, more simply, ksh93). Each KornShell revision builds on the features of the previous ones. So, the next version of the KornShell will contain the features described in this book plus a few new ones.

If you aren't sure which revision of the KornShell you are currently using, issue the following command:

```
$ print ${.sh.version}
```

If the output of this command contains the number 93, then you have a KornShell 93. For example, my KornShell replies:

```
Version M-12/28/93f
```

If your KornShell prints a blank line, then you have an earlier version of the KornShell, and many of the examples in this book won't work.

"How do I obtain a KornShell?"

All major commercial versions of UNIX—including Solaris, HP/UX, AIX, Digital UNIX, and IRIX—come with versions of the KornShell. Some of these UNIX versions are still offering KornShell 88. To upgrade to KornShell 93, see `http://www.kornshell.com`. Several UNIX vendors provide KornShell 93 through a program called the Desktop KornShell. The Desktop KornShell usually is located at pathname `/usr/dt/bin/dtksh`.

The shareware versions of UNIX, such as linux and bsdi, mainly offer KornShell imitations (such as `pdksh`) rather than true KornShells. These imitations can be frustrating to use; many of the examples in this book will not work on them.

Microsoft does not currently ship a KornShell with Windows 98 or Windows NT. However, the CD at the back of this book contains the complete U/WIN package. This package, developed by David Korn and AT&T, contains a KornShell 93 and more than 180 popular UNIX commands. You can download a version of U/WIN that is free-for-noncommercial-use by directing your browser to `http://www.research.att.com/sw/tools/uwin`. To purchase a supported commercial version of this package, contact Global Technologies, Ltd. of Old Bridge, New Jersey, USA. Finally, the venerable MKS Toolkit has been filling the UNIX-utilities-on-Windows niche for a very long time. Unfortunately, though, as of this writing, the KornShell that currently accompanies the MKS Toolkit is a KornShell 88 hybrid.

"Are KornShell scripts portable?"

A script or program that is *portable* can run without modification on different operating systems and different hardware. For example, a truly portable program runs exactly the same under Windows NT as on Solaris or HP/UX.

KornShell scripts can consist of any combination of KornShell statements and operating system commands. KornShell scripts that consist solely of KornShell statements are, in theory, completely portable. In practice, such KornShell scripts are portable across different UNIX systems, though some differences in behavior do occasionally pop up when you port the script to a Windows-based system.

KornShell scripts that contain operating system commands may or may not be portable, and the smart money usually is on them being nonportable. However, if you are on a POSIX-compliant system and are *very* careful to use POSIX commands only, then you do have a fighting chance of producing a portable script.

By the way, if portability is paramount, you can eliminate many calls to operating system commands by rewriting them as KornShell scripts.

"What is the best way to use this book?"

In general, people remember only a small percentage of what they read but a high percentage of what they do. Therefore, I'd like to encourage you to play with the examples. That is, use them as a springboard for your own experiments. You'll get frustrated from time to time, but I do hope that you'll have fun.

"Do I have to be a programmer to use this book?"

Well, to be honest, the more you know about programming, the more you'll get out of this book. Nevertheless, even rank beginners should be able to get through at least the first nine chapters.

"If I'm still hungry for more KornShell after I digest this book, what else can I chew on?

You can read the definitive KornShell reference manual, which is:

> Bolsky, Morris, and David Korn. *The New KornShell Command and Programming Language*. Upper Saddle River, New Jersey: Prentice Hall, 1995.

2 Getting Started

This chapter shows you how to write and execute very simple KornShell scripts.

A KornShell script is simply a text file. To create a text file you'll need a text editor. You can use any ASCII text editor on your system. For example, UNIX users may wish to use vi or emacs. Windows users could employ Notepad or some other editor. Choose whatever text editor you like as long as the text editor does not place formatting characters inside the file. Do not, for example, save your KornShell script in Microsoft Word or FrameMaker format.

Here is a KornShell script to help get you started. Use your text editor to open a new file named first.ksh. Then, enter the following single line of text into this file:

```
echo $RANDOM
```

When you've finished entering this text, save the file.

Executing This Script

Start a KornShell. (More about this follows.) When you start a KornShell, the Korn-Shell will display a prompt. The default prompt for users is $; the default prompt for the superuser (root) is #. Assuming you aren't root, here's what you'll see:

```
$
```

By the way, you can define any KornShell prompt you want (see page 296), but I use a bland old dollar sign just for the sake of capitalistic simplicity.

At the prompt, enter the pathname of the file in which the script is stored. For example, assuming that file first.ksh is stored in your current directory, you'd execute it by typing:

```
$ ./first.ksh
12752
$
```

Notice the dot and slash (./) preceding the filename first.ksh. The dot refers to the current directory and the slash is a pathname separator. So, ./first.ksh means the file named first.ksh stored in the current directory.

If the system outputs a random integer, then you are in the KornShell and are ready to go. If the system does *not* display an integer, read the next section.

What Shell Is Executing My Script?

To start a KornShell from a Windows 95 or Windows NT system, you merely click the KornShell icon, choose the KornShell from the start menu, or type the pathname of the KornShell into a Run menu.

Your system may support more than one kind of shell. For example, a typical UNIX workstation comes with at least three different shells: the KornShell, the Bourne shell, and the C shell. Because so many different shells are available, you have to ensure that it is the KornShell, and not one of these other shells, that is executing your KornShell scripts. Unfortunately, the shell in which you are working is rarely willing to scream out its identity without some prodding.

The `first.ksh` script, simple as it is, can help you identify the type of shell that is executing your script. As I mentioned before, if the script outputs a random integer, then the KornShell is executing the script. If, however, the script outputs a blank line, for example:

```
$ ./first.ksh

$
```

then the Bourne shell is probably executing your script.

If executing the script produces an error message like this:

```
$ ./first.ksh
RANDOM: undefined variable
```

then the C shell or some other shell probably is executing your script.

When you log in to a UNIX system, UNIX will start up a login shell for you. But which one? Typically, your system administrator picks a starting shell for you, and then you can use a UNIX command (such as `passwd` or `chsh`) to change the system administrator's pick.

Suppose you can't figure out how to specify the KornShell as your login shell. In this case, you usually can start up the KornShell from within the other kind of shell. To do this, you have to remember that the KornShell itself is simply a program file named `ksh`. If you're in a UNIX shell, you can execute the program by typing its pathname; for example:

```
% ksh
$
```

If you're lucky, this simple command will snap you into the KornShell. However, if it doesn't work, you may have to specify the full pathname at which the `ksh` program is stored. For example, the `ksh` program is often stored in pathname `/bin/ksh`, so here's a possibility:

```
% /bin/ksh
$
```

Now for the confusing part: you can execute a KornShell script without actually being in a KornShell. There are two ways to do this.

One way is to specify `ksh` followed by the pathname of your KornShell script. For example, suppose you are in a C shell but want to execute the KornShell script stored at pathname `./first.ksh`. In this case, you'd issue the following command:

C Shell Prompt: **ksh ./first.ksh**

There is a second way to execute a KornShell script without actually being in a KornShell, but this second way isn't standard. That is, although some operating systems use the following convention, I can't guarantee that yours will. This method should, however, work on all modern UNIX systems. In this method, you specify the pathname of the executing shell on the first line of the script. Precede the name of the executing shell with the two characters `#!`; place these two characters flush left. So, for example, if you add the `#!` preamble to script `first.ksh`, the script will consist of:

```
#!/bin/ksh
echo $RANDOM
```

Thanks to its new top line, you can now execute `first.ksh` from any kind of shell. For example, suppose you are working in the C shell. When you type:

C Shell Prompt: **./first.ksh**

the operating system will read the `first.ksh` line of the script, then have the Korn-Shell stored at pathname `/bin/ksh` execute the remainder of the script.

Operating System Commands in a Shell Script

Suppose that you execute two UNIX commands, date and df, from the KornShell command line as follows:

```
$ date
Mon Sep 15 17:43:22 EST 1997
$ df .
Filesystem          Type   blocks      use    avail  %use  Mounted on
/dev/dsk/dks033s7    efs   5537050  4483072 1053978   81%  /home/ghar
```

The date command prints the current date and time, and the df command tells you how much disk space you have available. (The df command generates slightly different results on different implementations of the UNIX operating system, so the output format you see may not look exactly like the above.)

Instead of issuing these two commands individually on the command line, you can bundle them into a KornShell script. KornShell scripts often contain one or more operating system commands. The following script consists solely of operating system commands. Please use your text editor to type this script into a file named starting.ksh.

```
date
df .
```

Executing This Script

Assuming that you are working in a KornShell, you execute a KornShell script by entering the pathname of the file in which it is stored. For example, assuming that starting.ksh is stored in your current directory, you would type:

```
$ starting.ksh
Mon Sep 15 17:43:22 EST 1997
Filesystem          Type   blocks      use    avail  %use  Mounted on
/dev/dsk/dks033s7    efs   5537050  4483072 1053978   81%  /home/ghar
$
```

(If typing starting.ksh doesn't work, try typing ./starting.ksh instead.)

When a script finishes, the KornShell will display a new prompt (here represented as $) and await your next command.

BEWARE: Are You Allowed to Execute This Script?

UNIX and Windows NT permit users to deny other users the chance to execute a script. There may be good reasons to prevent certain secret scripts from falling into the wrong hands. However, at this point we're more interested in preventing our own frustration than in preventing some nefarious plot.

Suppose you try to execute a KornShell script named `sample.ksh`, but the operating system returns an error message similar to the following:

```
$ sample.ksh
ksh: sample.ksh: cannot execute
```

or perhaps this:

```
$ sample.ksh
ksh: sample.ksh: cannot open
```

The preceding messages tell you that you don't have permission to execute this script. If you are working on the UNIX operating system or have the UWIN package on Windows NT, fix the problem by typing the following command:

```
$ chmod 755 sample.ksh
```

The preceding command will give you permission to read and to execute the script *if* you are the owner of file `sample.ksh`. If you don't own the file, you cannot change a file's permissions. A possible way to circumvent this restriction is to copy the script into a directory that you do own and then give yourself the appropriate permissions.

To invoke a script by typing its name, you usually need both read and execute permission.

```
$ sample.ksh      # need both read and execute permission
```

An alternate way of invoking a KornShell script is by specifying the pathname of the KornShell itself followed by the script name; for example:

```
$ /bin/ksh sample.ksh  # need read permission only
```

To invoke a script this way, you only need read permission. That is, you don't need execute permission.

Commenting Your Code

Here is an example that shows how to put comments into your script. Using a text editor, type the following into a file named comments.ksh:

```
# The KornShell permits you to write comments that take up an entire
# line or just part of a line. To tell the KornShell that you are
# making a comment, precede your comment with a # sign.

# Some scripts begin with an operating system directive like this:
#      #!/bin/ksh
# In that special situation, the # does not indicate
# a comment; it indicates the name of the shell program that will
# process the script.

 date          # this UNIX command returns the date and time
 df .          # this UNIX command tells you how much disk space is
               # currently available on the current partition

# This script contains some blank lines. The KornShell ignores blank
# lines. Use blank lines and other white space to make your program
# easier to read.

# We're going to place comments at the start of every sample shell
# script in the book. These comments will explain what the script is
# demonstrating.
```

Executing This Script

Assume that this shell script is stored in file comments.ksh. To invoke this script, issue the following command:

```
$ comments.ksh
Mon Sep 15 17:43:22 EST 1997
Filesystem        Type    blocks       use     avail   %use  Mounted on
/dev/dsk/dks033s7  efs    5537050   4483072  1053978    81%  /home/ghar
$
```

From now on, I'm going to omit the trailing $ prompt.

BEWARE: Picking a Bad Name for Your Script

Sometimes you will write the perfect KornShell script, invoke it, and then NOTHING HAPPENS! Worse yet, perhaps you invoke the script and SOMETHING TOTALLY UNEXPECTED HAPPENS! What now?

If you are absolutely certain (and you never will be) that your coding is good, you might try to change the filename of the script. Perhaps you've inadvertently given the script a name reserved for some other KornShell use. For example, suppose you put your script in a file named `test`. If you type `test` at the shell prompt, the KornShell will not invoke your shell script; rather the KornShell will try to perform a `test` statement because, by coincidence, `test` also is the name of a KornShell statement. You can find a list of KornShell statements in Appendix A.

Another possibility is that your script name matches an operating system command name. For example, suppose you name a script `cat`. That name is perfectly legal; however, `cat` also happens to be the name of a UNIX command. So, if you type `cat` on the command line, which `cat` will get executed—your script or the UNIX command? I'll answer that in a moment, but it should be clear to you by now that you don't want to get into that situation. Avoid script names that match other command names on the system.

Now, which cat gets executed? That depends on your **PATH** variable, which is described on page 294. To find out what your **PATH** directories are, type:

```
$ print $PATH
```

Briefly, the KornShell starts looking for a file named `cat` in the ordered list of **PATH** directories. If the directory that contains your shell script (for instance, `./`) precedes the directory containing the `cat` command (for instance, `/bin`), the KornShell executes your script. However, if the directory containing your shell script comes after the directory containing the `cat` command, the KornShell executes the `cat` command. Incidentally, a way to ensure that your `cat` script gets executed is to specify its full pathname when you execute it; for example:

```
$ cat              # too vague
$ ./cat            # right
$ /usr/newmar/cat  # right again
```

A good convention to follow is to append the suffix `.ksh` to every filename that contains a KornShell script. So, for example, instead of naming the file `cat`, you might name it `cat.ksh` instead. Not only will you avoid trouble, it will also make it easier for you to identify files containing KornShell scripts.

The Usage Line

Every KornShell script from here on out will contain a *usage* line. A usage line describes how to invoke the script. You don't *have to* put a usage line in your scripts—the KornShell itself won't care whether you supply one—but script mavens consider such an omission to be bad form, a red-wine-with-fish kind of mistake.

In the early chapters of this book, the usage line usually will be pretty bland, but in later chapters we'll demonstrate some fairly elaborate usage lines. For example, a more complex usage line might specify the names of possible options to enter on the command line. We'll also see scripts that print the usage line if the user invokes the script improperly.

```
USAGE="usage: sample.ksh" # this line tells you how to start the script

date     # this UNIX command returns the date and time
df .     # this UNIX command tells you how much disk space is
         #   currently available on the current partition
```

Executing This Script

Assume that this shell script is stored in file `sample.ksh`. To invoke it, you issue the following command:

```
$ sample.ksh
Mon Sep 15 17:43:22 EST 1997
Filesystem       Type   blocks      use     avail  %use  Mounted on
/dev/dsk/dks033s7  efs  5537050  4483072 1053978   81%  /home/ghar
```

By the way, specifying a usage line has a hidden benefit; namely, a user can issue a `grep` command to find out how to invoke the script. `grep` is a UNIX command that finds occurrences of specified words inside a specified file. For example, if the user wants to find out how to run `sample.ksh` without resorting to trial-and-error, the user can type the following UNIX command:

```
$ egrep ^USAGE sample.ksh
USAGE="usage: sample.ksh"   # tells you how to start the script
```

The preceding `grep` command displays all lines in `sample.ksh` that starts with USAGE.

Simple Output

The KornShell supports three output statements: **echo**, **print**, and **printf**. The **echo** statement is passe; don't use it. Use **print** or **printf** instead. We'll hit the difference between **print** and **printf** in Chapter 12; for now, let's concentrate on **print**.

```
USAGE="usage: output1.ksh" # simple uses of the print statement

 echo   "Hello world"      # the last echo in the book
 print                     # prints a blank line

# Use print to output text. Although you don't have to surround your
# text in single or double quotes, it is a good idea to get into that
# habit. That's because the double quotes will preserve all white
# space within your output. See "Beware: The Quotes from Hell" at the
# end of this chapter.
 print Hi        earth.    # okay
 print "Hi       earth."   # better

# By default, the print statement ends each line with a newline
# character. In other words, the output of two consecutive print
# statements will appear on separate lines. If you don't want the
# print statement to end each line with a newline, use the -n option.
 print -n "Bon"       # -n inhibits the newline here...
 print -n "jour"      # ... and here
 print    " le monde."   # no -n; therefore, print a newline

# The \n is an explicit order to print a newline character.
 print "hi\nto\nyou"    # print a single word on each line

# Use \t within your text to print a tab.
 print "\tBuenos dias al mundo."
```

Executing This Script

```
$ output1.ksh
Hello world.

Hi earth.
Hi              earth.
Bonjour le monde.
hi
to
you
        Buenos dias al mundo.
```

Variables

As in algebra, a KornShell variable is a symbol that represents a value. For example, the variable **x** might represent a numerical value such as 365 or a textual value such as "`earth cycle.`" Actually, naming a variable **x** isn't very evocative. It's better to pick descriptive names for your variables, such as **length_of_a_year**.

Variable names can contain any combination of

- Letters (uppercase or lowercase)

- Digits

- Underscores (_)

In certain cases, you also can place dots in variable names; see page 40 for details.

A variable name cannot begin with a digit or have spaces between words. Here are some examples of legal and illegal variable names:

```
tears_of_a_clown   # legal variable name
tears of a clown   # illegal because of white space between words
eighty_six         # legal variable name
86                 # illegal because it starts with a digit
eighty6            # legal
```

Variable names can be as long or as short as you want.

You can create as many variables as you like within a KornShell script. In addition to the variables that you create, the KornShell reserves quite a few variables of its own. (See Chapter 14 for an explanation of the KornShell's reserved variables.) To get a list of all variables, whether set by you or set by the KornShell, just type **set** at the prompt; for example:

```
$ set
.sh.version='Version M-12/28/93f'
CMDLINE=WIN
EDITOR=vi
ENV=/udir/rosenber/.kshrc
...   # lots of variables omitted for space reasons
x=7
```

BEWARE: Variable Names Are Case Sensitive

Variable names are case sensitive. For example, the KornShell views **DOG**, **dog**, and **Dog** as three distinct variable names. By convention, the variables that the KornShell reserves have names consisting of all uppercase letters. To avoid conflicts with these reserved variables, you should avoid creating all uppercase variable names. For example, **dog** or **Dog** are better choices for a variable name than is **DOG**.

Simple Input

Use the **read** statement to perform input. The **read** statement is very versatile; you can use it to gather entered numbers or entered text. The syntax of **read** is simpler than comparable input statements of other high-level languages. You don't need to supply any fancy **A7** directives (as in FORTRAN) or **%d** specifiers (as in C). See Chapter 12 for complete details on input.

```
USAGE="usage: input1.ksh" # read statement

# The read statement gathers one line of input and assigns it to one or
# more variables.
 print -n "Enter a number, letter, word, phrase, or sentence: "
 read user_input

# Here, the read statement gathers one line of input and assigns it to
# three different variables.
 print -n "Enter three numbers: "
 read first second third
# If the user enters 10 15 20, then read will assign 10 to variable
# first, 15 to variable second, and 20 to variable third.
```

Executing This Script

When you invoke input1.ksh, the script will pause whenever it reaches a **read** statement and wait for you to type something. After you type some information and press the **<RETURN>** key, the script will assign your input to the appropriate variable or variables. By the way, sample input appears in **boldface** so that you can distinguish it from the script's output.

```
$ input1.ksh
Enter a number, letter, word, phrase, or sentence: Rachel Elisa
Enter three numbers: 10 15 20
```

The KornShell will assign the value "Rachel Elisa" to variable **user_input.** Then the KornShell will assign the value 10 to variable **first,** the value 15 to variable **second,** and the value 20 to variable **third.**

Obtaining the Value of a Variable

Use the following syntax to represent the value of a variable:

$variable

That is, you put a dollar sign $ in front of the variable name. For example, the following command outputs the value of a variable named **counter**:

```
print "$counter"
```

Do not put *any* white space between the dollar sign and the variable name.

The following script demonstrates how to output the value of a variable. See Chapter 12 for more information about the **print** statement.

```
USAGE="usage: var_out.ksh" # writing the value of a variable

 print -n "Enter a number, letter, word, phrase, or sentence: "
 read x            # assign to x whatever user enters
 print             # print a blank line

# contrast the following three print statements:
 print "x"         # prints the letter x
 print "$x"        # prints the value of variable x
 print "x = $x"    # prints x = and then the value of variable x
```

Executing This Script

```
$ var_out.ksh
Enter a number, letter, word, phrase, or sentence: Lyon is in France

x
Lyon is in France
x = Lyon is in France
```

BEWARE: The Dollar Sign in read Statements

Do not put the dollar sign in front of the variable name in a **read** statement. For example, compare the following:

```
read sentence     # right
read $sentence    # wrong
```

Newlines, Semicolons, White Space, and Columns

Anybody who has been around the block a few times with programming languages wants to know the answers to several fundamental questions.

"Can I put more than one command on the same line?"

You can put multiple commands on the same line if you separate the commands with semicolons; for example:

```
date  df        # wrong
date; df        # right
```

"Can I spread a single command over more than one line?"

In general, commands should start and end on the same line. However, some commands can span more than one line; for example, the following is okay because the newline appears inside a pair of quotes:

```
print "hi
there"          # writes "hi" on one line and "there" on the next
```

"Do I need to put white space between different parts of a command?"

The KornShell is obsessive about *white space* (space, tab, and newline). Sometimes, white space is required; sometimes, white space is forbidden. In general, you should place white space between the different parts of a command; for example:

```
print -n "Hi"    # right
print-n "Hi"     # wrong, need white space between print and -n
```

However, there are plenty of exceptions, which will be described throughout this book. For example, certain assignment statements forbid white space:

```
x=10             # right
x = 10           # wrong, can't have white space
```

"Do commands have to start in a particular column?"

FORTRAN and many assembly languages require certain kinds of commands to start at certain columns. In the KornShell, the column at which you start a command has absolutely no influence on how the KornShell will execute that command.

BEWARE: Confusing + and -

Many beginners expect the + to turn something on and the - to turn something off. However, the KornShell sees the + and - the other way around.

Assigning a Value to a Variable

The KornShell supports many ways of assigning a value to a variable. The easiest method is to specify the name of a variable, then the equal sign **=**, and then the value you are assigning to the variable. So, for example, the following line assigns the value 100 to variable **test_score**:

```
test_score=100
```

```
USAGE="usage: assign.ksh" # assigning values to variables

# Here are four ways to assign a numerical value to a variable.
 n=100           # white space is illegal before and after equal sign
 let n=100       # let statement is old-fashioned
 let "n = 100"   # white space is legal before and after equal sign
 ((n = 100))     # white space is legal before and after equal sign
 print "The value of n is $n"

# You can assign a letter, word, or phrase to a variable by specifying
# the variable name, an equal sign, and the value; for example:
 letter="Q"
 word="elephant"
 phrase="The rain in Spain."
 print "letter = $letter;  word = $word;  phrase = $phrase"

# Use the equal sign to assign the value of one variable to another
# variable; for example:
 x=$n            # assign the value of variable n to variable x
 print "x = $x"

# While we're on the subject, let's print out the usage line
 print "$USAGE"
```

Executing This Script

```
$ assign.ksh
The value of n is 100
letter = Q;  word = elephant;  phrase = The rain in Spain.
x = 100
usage: assign.ksh
```

BEWARE: Common Mistakes When Assigning Variables

Variable assignment often frustrates beginning KornShell programmers because the KornShell is so sensitive to white space. For example, consider the following two variable assignments:

```
y = 100
title = "Mountains of Norway"
```

They both look wholesome enough; however, both will cause a KornShell error because of improper use of white space. For example, the first assignment might cause an error like this:

```
y: not found
```

The correct way to write these assignments is as follows:

```
y=100
title="Mountains of Norway"
```

Don't put any white space on either side of the equal sign. The only proper place for white space in an assignment statement is within the quotes.

Now consider another kind of variable assignment mistake, one involving improper use of the dollar sign. The following lines assign the value 50 to variable **dog** and then show the right and wrong ways to assign the value of **dog** to another variable named **bear:**

```
dog=50          # assign 50 to variable dog
bear=dog         # mistake 1: assigns the word "dog" to bear
$bear=$dog       # mistake 2: don't put a $ in front of bear
bear=$dog       # right: assigns value of dog to bear
```

Mistake 1 is particularly bothersome because the KornShell will not warn you about it. The KornShell thinks you want to assign the string "dog" to a variable named **bear** and sees nothing wrong with that. (The KornShell cannot guess your intentions.) Mistake 2, on the other hand, will cause the following KornShell error message:

```
=50:  not found: [No such file or directory]
```

Finding Your Mistakes

If your KornShell script isn't working properly, you can figure out what's wrong by:

- Staring intently at the terminal until large vats of sweat pour down your brow, or

- Running the entire script (or part of it) in debug mode.

To run the entire script in debug mode, invoke it like this:

    $ ksh -x name_of_script

For example, to run the script input1.ksh in debug mode, issue the following command:

```
$ ksh -x input1.ksh
+ USAGE=usage: input1.ksh
+ print -n Enter a number, letter, word, phrase, or sentence:
Enter a number, letter, word, phrase, or sentence: [6]+ read
user_input
Rachel Elisa
+ print -n Enter three numbers:
Enter three numbers: + read first second third
22 33 57
```

The + is the default debug mode indicator. As the KornShell executes a command, it prints the + followed by the command itself, allowing you to trace the progress of your program. The lines not preceded by a + are the script's input and output. In other words, if you ran the script normally (not in debug mode), you'd see every line not preceded by a +.

A script running in debug mode often runs very slowly and produces volumes of output. To diminish these negatives you can limit the range of debug mode. That is, you can run regions of the script in debug mode and other regions in normal mode. Place the directive set -x just before the line at which you want debug mode to start. To stop debug mode, place the directive set +x at the point where you want normal mode to start. You can place any number of set -x and set +x pairs in your script. In the following script, the debug region covers the two assignment statements between set -x and set +x. Statements outside of the debug region run in normal mode.

```
print "hello there."    # normal mode (not in debug mode)
set -x                  # start debug mode
y=10                    # in debug mode
z=$y                    # in debug mode
set +x                  # stop debug mode, start normal mode
print "bon jour la"     # normal mode (not in debug mode)
```

Ordinarily, if you've placed at least one set -x inside the script, then you shouldn't specify ksh -x when you invoke the script; instead, just type the name of the script.

Can I Quote You on That?

The final pages of this chapter are devoted to *quoting*, a topic that has ruined many a fine day of shell scripting. In this section, I'll explain the difference between the single quote and the double quote. Plus, I'll get into related topics such as the backslash.

Quotes influence the way that the KornShell interprets *special characters*. The following are the special characters of the KornShell:

```
$ \ # ? [ ] * { } + & | ( ) ; " ' < > ~ `
```

For example, consider the almighty dollar sign. It obviously has a special meaning to the KornShell. Notice how the presence or absence of a dollar sign makes a big difference in the following two statements:

```
print x    # output the letter x
print $x   # output the value of variable x
```

In most instances, you will want the special characters to act in their special ways; after all, the KornShell provides the special characters to simplify programming. However, there are some instances in which you will want the KornShell to *turn off* the special significance of these characters. For example, there may come a time when you will want the dollar sign to mean just a plain old dollar sign rather than "the operator that evaluates variables."

You can turn off the meaning of the special characters by supplying either of the following:

- A pair of single quotes, which turns off the special significance of *all* special characters enclosed by the single quotes.

- A pair of double quotes, which turns off the special significance of all special characters enclosed by the double quotes, except for

  ```
  $ ' " \
  ```

For example, suppose you want to print the value of variable **y.** In the following example, the single quote turns off the special significance of the dollar sign, but the double quote does not:

```
y=50
print $y    # right;        Output -- 50
print "$y"  # right again;  Output -- 50
print '$y'  # wrong;        Output -- $y
```

Suppose you want to use the UNIX command rm to delete a file named stain. Since filename stain contains no special characters, quotation marks are irrelevant and the following three commands are synonymous:

```
rm stain
rm 'stain'
rm "stain"
```

Suppose, however, that the file was named `$stain` rather than just plain `stain`. In this case, you must tell the KornShell to turn off the special significance of the dollar sign. If you don't turn it off, the KornShell will interpret `$stain` as meaning the value of variable `stain`. Here are a few good and bad ways to remove filename `$stain`:

```
rm $stain   # wrong, because KornShell will try to evaluate stain
rm '$stain' # right
rm '$'stain # right also
rm "$stain" # wrong, because the value of "$stain" is null.
```

The backslash character (\) is a cousin of the quotes. Unlike the quotes, which can influence many characters, the backslash influences only a single character, namely, the character immediately to the right of the backslash. Thus, yet another way to remove filename `$stain` is:

```
rm \$stain  # right, backslash shuts off special meaning of $
```

The backslash character is often called the *escape character*. The character following the backslash is often called the *escaped character*.

You can use either single or double quotes to preserve white space within a string. If you don't enclose a string within single or double quotes, then the KornShell will eliminate all extra blanks spaces between the words and convert all tab characters to blank spaces.

```
print hi       there    # output -- hi there
print 'hi      there'    # output -- hi        there
print "hi      there"    # output -- hi        there
```

Since the single quotes and double quotes themselves have special meaning, you may be wondering how to print them. Consider the following examples:

```
print 'Welcome 'Home''     # output -- Welcome Home
print 'Welcome "Home"'     # output -- Welcome "Home"
print "Welcome 'Home'"     # output -- Welcome 'Home'
print "Welcome "Home""     # output -- Welcome Home
print "Welcome \"Home\""   # output -- Welcome "Home"
```

Do not confuse the grave accent ` (also known as the backtick or the backquote) with the single quote '. Although they look similar, they have different meanings. As a rule of thumb,[1] you can usually find the single quote on the same key as the double quote ". And while you're at it, don't confuse the backslash \ with the forward slash /.

Remember to pair your quotes. For every unescaped double quote, there must be an opposite and equal closing double quote. And for every unescaped single quote, there must be a closing single quote. Failure to pair quotes in a script will lead to errors. Such omissions sometimes can be difficult to spot. Failure to pair quotes on the KornShell command line typically causes the KornShell to display the line con-

---

1. Actually, it's more a rule of right pinky if you're a touch typist.

tinuation prompt. For example, the following line looks perfectly correct until you notice that there's only one double quote instead of the requisite two:

```
$ print "Let me introduce a man who needs no introduction
>
```

The > is the default KornShell line continuation prompt. It means that the Korn-Shell could not see the end of the command on the previous line. To end it, you must provide a second double quote; for example:

```
$ print "Let me introduce a man who needs no introduction
> "                # end the print statement
```

For the *coup de grace*, KornShell 93 actually adds *two more* ways to quote. The first newbie is just like a pair of single quotes except that you put a dollar sign in front of the first single quote. This quoting operator acts just like a pair of single quotes, except that escape sequences (such as \n and \t) inside this quoting operator do not lose their special meaning. This quoting operator is useful when assigning escape sequences to variables; for example:

```
$ x=$'\t\n' # assign a tab and newline to variable x
```

The second new quoting mechanism introduced by KornShell 93 looks just like a pair of double quotes except that you put a dollar sign in front of the first double quote. The purpose of this kind of quoting is to turn on translation. This kind of quoting acts exactly like a pair of double quotes unless the system holds a message catalog for the language indicated by the current value of the **LANG** variable. For example, suppose a message catalog for Spanish exists and you set **LANG** to a value that corresponds to the Spanish message catalog. In this case, the KornShell will look up the value of whatever string is inside the quotes and try to translate it to Spanish.

```
$ LANG=sp-sp
$ print $"duck"
pato
```

Yep, there are an awful lot of "ifs" in this mechanism, but it is pretty nifty when it works.

3   Data Types

This chapter explains data types in the KornShell.

If You're New to Programming . . .

Every variable holds a value. The *data type* of a variable specifies the kind of values that the variable is allowed to hold. That is, a variable with a certain data type can hold only certain kinds of data. If you assign the wrong kind of data to a variable, the KornShell will issue an error.

If you don't explicitly declare the data type of a variable, the KornShell automatically assumes that the variable has the *string* data type. A string variable can hold zero or more letters, numbers, punctuation marks, white spaces, tabs, or newlines. For example, here are eight different string values:

```
elephant
Q
Cat in the Hat
/usr/users/einstein
537
8.2
^#@2Y
Call me at 555-1212
```

A string is the least restrictive data type. A string variable can hold any sort of value. The KornShell won't issue an error message even if you assign something bizarre to a string variable. The vast majority of variables used in KornShell scripts have the string data type. For this reason, most beginners need only a cursory understanding of data types.

The *integer* data type indicates that a variable can hold only an integer value. If you intend to use a certain variable in mathematical calculations, you should consider declaring it as an integer data type. If you're a little rusty on math, let me remind you that an integer is a number without a fractional (decimal) part. (Numbers with fractional parts are called *real numbers*.) For example, the following numbers are integers:

```
    8        537         -9000        125
```

but the next group are real numbers:

```
8.2     537.914    -9000.529    125.0
```

The *float* data type indicates that a variable can hold any kind of number, including real numbers. Older versions of the KornShell do not provide a float data type, but KornShell 93 does.

By the way, did you notice that 537 appears as an example of both an integer and a string? Remember: A string variable can hold any sort of values, even integers and real numbers.

Another data type, the *array*, is a collection of values, where each value has the same data type. For example, you could create an array of integers or an array of strings. Each value in the collection is stored in a separate cell. That is, the array is made up of multiple cells, each cell containing one value. Each cell is numbered. The first string value is stored in array cell number 0, the second string value is stored in array cell number 1, and so on. Because the cells are numbered, you can easily store and retrieve specific values. An array is a great place to store related information. For example, Table 3-1 illustrates an array that holds city names in France. The first cell of the array, cell number 0, holds the value Paris, the second cell holds the value Aix en Provence, and so on. This array consists of five cells.

Table 3-1. An Array Is a Way of Organizing Related Information

Cell number	String value stored in this cell
0	Paris
1	Aix en Provence
2	Biarritz
3	Nice
4	Marseilles

Finally, you can specify *constants*. A constant is like a variable in that each has a name and each holds a value. However, unlike a true variable, the value of a constant can never change. You assign a value to a constant when you declare it, and from that point on, you cannot change its value.

If You're an Experienced Programmer . . .

Programming in many compiled high-level languages is, to a large extent, an exercise in declaring data types and then using them correctly. By contrast, most shell scripting languages don't support any data types.

Programming in the KornShell falls somewhere between these two extremes. That is, the KornShell supports some data types; however, you usually do not have to explicitly declare the data type of any variable before using it. Good data type declaration can make your KornShell scripts run faster.

As an experienced programmer, you probably have certain expectations about data types. Please be warned that KornShell data types do not always work the same as data types in other high-level languages. In fact, data types in the KornShell have a certain *laissez-faire* edge to them. For example, in a KornShell script, you can declare a variable as an integer and then change the data type, mid-script, into a string.

The KornShell supports the following three fundamental data types:

- Strings

- Integers

- Floats

By default, all variables are strings. In other words, if you do not specify the data type of a particular variable, the KornShell implicitly types it as a string. KornShell strings are a little different from strings you may be familiar with in other programming languages. For example, in the KornShell, you can do mathematical operations on strings. You do not ordinarily specify the length of a string when you declare it, so KornShell strings can be of arbitrary length. Chapter 13 describes several string *attributes;* for example, you can specify that a string cannot contain any uppercase letters or that a string is always right-justified.

The KornShell provides an integer data type and a float data type. Unlike the C programming language, the KornShell does not provide various lengths of integers or floats. For example, in the C programming language, you can specify short or long ints; in the KornShell, you can only specify one length (**integer**). In the C programming language, you can declare single or double floats; in the KornShell, only floats. The KornShell stores all integer variables in 32 bits and all float variables as double-precision values on your system (usually 64 bits). Nevertheless, the KornShell does offer something called *type attributes* that have no true parallel in the C programming language.

As in most high-level languages, the KornShell supports arrays. You can create arrays of strings (the default), arrays of integers, or arrays of floats. Arrays can have numerical subscripts or string subscripts. Arrays with string subscripts are called associative arrays. Unlike most high-level compiled languages, you do not specify the number of elements in the array.

By default, all variables are global; however, it is possible to declare a local variable within a KornShell function (see Chapter 10).

Declaring Strings

By default, every variable has the *string* data type. That is, unless you tell the Korn-Shell otherwise, every variable that you use in your script is automatically considered a string. In the following script, the variables **letter, sentiment, book, numerical_string,** and **phone_message** are all strings, simply because you don't declare them. See Chapter 13 for more details on string attributes.

```
USAGE="usage: decl_string.ksh" # how to declare strings

# Assign values to five different string variables.
 letter="A"
 sentiment="always"
 book="Cat in the Hat"
 numerical_string="537"
 phone_message="Call me at 555-1212"

 print "Here are some string values: "
 print "$letter, $sentiment, $book, $numerical_string, $phone_message"

 print -n "Enter anything -- "
 read z
 print "Here is another string: $z"

# For clarity, you can explicitly declare a variable as a string with
# the typeset statement.
 typeset st
 st=$z
```

Executing This Script

```
$ decl_string.ksh
Here are some string values:
A, always, Cat in the Hat, 537, Call me at 555-1212
Enter anything -- concrete noun
Here is another string: concrete noun
```

Declaring Integers

You can declare an integer variable in either of the following equivalent ways:

typeset **-i** *variable_name*

integer *variable_name*

The following script explores the integer data type.

```
USAGE="usage: decl_int.ksh" # how to declare integers

integer y        # declare variable y as an integer
y=100            # assign an integer value to variable y
print "y = $y" # output the value of variable y

# Now that y is an integer, you cannot assign a string value to it.
# y="Cat in the Hat"   # will usually cause an error

# Put an integer value into a string variable.
x=150            # x is a string because you didn't declare it otherwise
print "x = $x"
x="Cat in the Hat"  # okay to assign non-numerical value to x
print "x = $x"
```

Executing This Script

```
$ decl_int.ksh
y = 100
x = 150
x = Cat in the Hat
```

What's the difference between **y** (the integer) and **x** (the string)? Basically, **y** can hold only a collection of digits, but **x** can hold any character. On the other hand, doing math with **y** is faster than doing math with **x**. (Chapter 4 details math.) So, a rule of thumb is to declare a variable as an integer if you intend to use this variable's value in integer math operations. Otherwise, let the variable stay a string.

Binary, Octal, Hex, and So On

By default, when you specify an integer value, the KornShell assumes that the value is in base 10. To specify a different integer base, use the following syntax:

   base#value

where *base* is a number between 2 and 64, inclusive. For example, here are values in a few different common bases:

```
2#11010001    # base 2 (binary) value
8#73425173    # base 8 (octal) value
16#FA79B029   # base 16 (hexadecimal) value
```

By default, the KornShell outputs integer values in base 10. To get the KornShell to use a different base when outputting a variable, declare the variable with the following syntax:

   typeset -i*base variable*

where *base* is a number between 2 and 64 inclusive.

```
USAGE="usage: base.ksh" # integers in different bases
  typeset -i   x      # declares x as a base 10 integer (default)
  typeset -i2  y      # declares y as a base 2 (binary) integer
  typeset -i8  z      # declares z as a base 8 (octal) integer
  typeset -i16 h      # declares h as a base 16 (hexadecimal) integer

  print -n "Enter an integer: "
  read x
# Note the absence of dollar signs in front of variable names on
# the following line. This works only when all four variables are
# explicitly declared.
  h=z=y=x  # assign the value of x to y, z, and h
  print "Translated into base 2, $x is $y"
  print "Translated into base 8, $x is $z"
  print "Translated into base 16, $x is $h"
```

Executing This Script

```
$ base.ksh
Enter an integer: 125
Translated into base 2, 125 is 2#1111101
Translated into base 8, 125 is 8#175
Translated into base 16, 125 is 16#7d

$ base.ksh    # notice on next line that user inputs a binary value
Enter an integer: 2#11011
Translated into base 2, 2#11011 is 2#11011
Translated into base 8, 2#11011 is 8#33
Translated into base 16, 2#11011 is 16#1b
```

Declaring Floats

A variable declared as a **float** can hold a real number. To declare a variable as a **float**, use one of the following syntaxes:

> **typeset** -E*n* *variable_name*   *default is 10*
>
> **typeset** -F*n* *variable_name*   *presion decimal places*
>
> **float** *variable_name*

The first syntax tells the KornShell to print *n* significant digits when printing the value of *variable_name*. The second syntax tells the KornShell to print *n* digits past the decimal point when printing the value of *variable_name*. The third syntax provides no output precision control. By the way, your choice of -**E** or -**F** will modify the behavior of the **printf** statement (see Chapter 10).

```
USAGE="usage: decl_float.ksh" # how to declare floats

# Declare r as a float.
 float r=8.482561
 print "r = $r"

# Declare s as a float that displays 4 significant digits.
 typeset -E4 s=8.482561
 print "s = $s"

# Declare s as a float that displays 4 digits past the decimal point
 typeset -F4 t=8.482561
 print "t = $t"

# You can change the output precision at any time.
# Changing the output precision to 9 causes trailing zeros to be printed.
 typeset -F9 t
 print "t = $t"
```

Executing This Script

```
$ decl_float.ksh
r = 8.482561
s = 8.483
t = 8.4826
t = 8.482561000
```

You can use scientific notation to represent a floating-point number; for example:

```
float x=6.27E6      # assign 6270000 to x
float y=3.781E-4    # assign 0.0003781 to y
```

Declaring Constants

You can initialize a variable when you declare it; for example:

```
int x=7  # declare x as an integer and set x's starting value as 7
float j=4.2  # declare j as a float and set j's starting value as 4.2
```

The 7 and the 4.2 are only initial values; you can change these values later in the script. However, in many cases, the initial value should never change. For example, suppose you declare:

```
float pi=3.14159
```

It would be a bad idea to change the value of **pi** later in the script. Fortunately, the KornShell lets you mark **pi** or any other variable as a constant. A *constant* is a variable whose value, once set, can never change. Use either of the following syntaxes to declare a constant:

> **typeset -r**[*data type*] *variable_name=value*

> **readonly** [*data type*] *variable_name=value*

If you do not specify a data type, the string data type is implied. When declaring a constant, notice that you must specify an initial value for it. Once you declare a constant, the KornShell will issue an error if you try to assign a new value to it.

```
USAGE="usage:decl_con.ksh"  # how to declare constants

# Declare legs_per_dog as an integer constant.
 readonly integer legs_per_dog=4
 print "legs_per_dog = $legs_per_dog"
# legs_per_dog=6              # illegal to reassign its value

# Declare greeting as a constant; since no data type is specified,
# the KornShell assumes that greeting is a string constant
 readonly greeting="Ohio"
 print "greeting = $greeting"

# It is illegal to reassign the value of a constant, but let's try it
# anyway just to see what happens.
 greeting="Kohneecheewa"
```

Executing This Script

```
$ decl_con.ksh
legs_per_dog = 4
greeting = Ohio
decl_con.ksh: line 14: greeting: is read only
```

Declaring nameref Variables

A *nameref* variable is a synonym for another variable. The nameref variable will always have the same value as its partner. If either variable becomes unset, the partner also becomes unset. C++ programmers may recognize the similarity between KornShell nameref variables and C++ reference variables. Nameref variables are very useful in function calling, which is described Chapter 10.

To create a nameref variable, use either of the following synonymous syntaxes:

> **nameref** *nameref_variable=regular_variable*

> **typeset -n** *nameref_variable=regular_variable*

Any variable can have multiple nameref variables attached to it.

```
USAGE="usage: decl_nameref.ksh"      # how to declare nameref's

integer sister=82            # declare a regular integer variable
nameref brother=sister       # make brother a nameref for sister
# The fortunes of brother and sister are now tied together
print "sister = $sister"
print "brother = $brother"   # brother has the same value as sister

# Changing the value of sister will also change the value of brother.
sister=93
print "brother = $brother"

# Changing the value of brother will also change the value of sister.
brother=104
print "sister = $sister"

# Deleting (unsetting) either variable will also unset its partner.
unset sister
print "brother = $brother"
```

Executing This Script

```
$ decl_nameref.ksh
sister = 82
brother = 82
brother = 93
sister = 104
brother =
```

If you somehow forgot who **brother** was attached to, you could type:

```
print ${!brother}   # output: sister
```

However, typing `print ${!sister}` will simply return `sister`.

Declaring Arrays

You can create a one-dimensional array of strings, integers, or floats. Unlike most languages, you do not explicitly declare arrays. Rather, when you use array syntax to assign a value to a variable, that variable automatically becomes an array.

By default, all arrays are arrays of strings. To create an array of integers, you must declare an integer variable and then use array syntax to assign a value to that integer variable. Similarly, you create an array of floats by declaring a float variable and then assigning a value to it.

In most languages, when declaring an array, you must specify the number of elements it contains. By contrast, you never specify the number of elements in a Korn-Shell array. The KornShell allows you to add elements until the system-defined capacity is reached. In KornShell 93, this capacity is guaranteed to be at least 4,096 elements. Obviously, you do not have to use up the entire capacity of each array.

Like the C programming language, KornShell arrays begin at subscript number 0, not subscript number 1. Therefore, in most KornShells, array subscripts range from 0 to 4095.

```
USAGE="usage: decl_array.ksh" # declaring arrays and filling them

# Create an array of strings and assign some values to it.
 animal[0]="dog"         # the KornShell creates an array named animal
                         # and puts the string value "dog" in cell #0
 animal[1]="horse"       # put "horse" into cell #1
 animal[2]="pigeon"      # put "pigeon" into cell #2
# You don't have to assign values to all cells in the array.
# You can skip cells 3, 4, and 5, and then assign a value to 6.
 animal[6]="monkey"      # put "monkey" into cell #6
# Cells 3, 4, and 5 of animal are unset.  Come to think of it, cells
# 7 through 4,095 are also unset.

# Create an array of integers and assign some values to it.
 integer test_scores    # test_scores is now an integer
 test_scores[0]=100      # test_scores just became an array of integers
 test_scores[1]=95       # put 95 into cell #1
 test_scores[2]=97       # put 97 into cell #2
 print -n "Enter the score on the final exam: "
 read test_scores[3]     # assign value of cell #3 at runtime
# test_scores[4]="pigeon" # illegal because "pigeon" is not an integer
```

Executing This Script

```
$ decl_array.ksh
Enter the score on the final exam: 96
```

Declaring Arrays with set -A

An alternate way to declare an array is to use the **set** **-A** statement. The advantage of declaring an array this way is that you get to declare and initialize the elements of an array in one statement. The KornShell assigns the elements in order, starting with subscript 0.

When you use **set** **-A**, the resulting array is always an array of strings. You cannot declare an array of integers or floats with **set** **-A**.

```
USAGE="usage: decl_array_with_set.ksh" # initializing arrays with set -A

# The following line creates an array of strings named
# flowers and assigns values to the array's first three elements.
 set -A flowers gardenia "bird of paradise" hibiscus

# The preceding statement is equivalent to the following three
# statements:
#    flowers[0]="gardenia"
#    flowers[1]="bird of paradise"
#    flowers[2]="hibiscus"
```

Executing This Script

```
$ decl_array_with_set.ksh
```

This script is the strong silent type. For more interesting examples, we need to learn how to output the values of arrays.

Printing Array Values

The following script illustrates how to print the contents of an entire array or just one cell of an array. It also demonstrates the **-A** option to the **read** statement, which gathers an entire array.

```
USAGE="usage: print_array.ksh"  # printing array values

# Create an array of strings and assign four values to it:
 set -A flowers gardenia "bird of paradise" hibiscus rose

# Print individual cells of the array:
 print "Cell #0 contains ${flowers[0]}"
 print "Cell #1 contains ${flowers[1]}"
 cell_number=2
 print "Cell #$cell_number contains ${flowers[$cell_number]}"
 print        # blank line

# Print all the elements of an array like this:
 print "The entire array contains -- ${flowers[*]}"
# or like this:
 print "The entire array contains -- ${flowers[@]}"
# See Chapter 9 for the distinction between these two ways of printing
# all the elements of an array.

# Let the user provide values for an array:
 print   # blank line
 print -n "Enter your favorite vegetables: "
 read -A vegetable
 print "The vegetable array contains -- ${vegetable[*]}"
```

Executing This Script

```
$ pr_ary.ksh
Cell #0 contains gardenia
Cell #1 contains bird of paradise
Cell #2 contains hibiscus

The entire array contains gardenia bird of paradise hibiscus rose
The entire array contains gardenia bird of paradise hibiscus rose

Enter your favorite vegetables: celery carrots peppers
The vegetable array contains -- celery carrots peppers
```

Notice how hard it is to tell from the output that "bird of paradise" is a single entry. Later in the book, we'll see how to place separators (such as commas or semicolons) between the output elements.

BEWARE: Common Array Mistakes

The pair of braces {} confuses a lot of array users. Don't use the braces when the name of the array appears on the left side of the assignment operator (=); for example:

```
array[2]="tulip"       # right
${array[2]}="tulip"    # wrong
```

However, you must use the braces when the name of the array appears on the right side of the assignment operator; for example:

```
flower=${array[2]}     # right
flower=array[2]        # wrong
```

Putting the two sides together, the following statement assigns one element of an array to another:

```
array[3]=${array[2]}   # right
```

In general, you should use the braces when printing an array element. For example, suppose you assign the value "tulip" to **array[2]**. Here are the right and wrong ways to print that value:

```
array[2]="tulip"       # assign a value to array[2]
 print "${array[2]}"   # right; the KornShell will print "tulip"
# print "array[2]"     # wrong
# print "$array[2]"    # wrong
```

By the way, the expression $array means the value of the first element of **array.** In other words, $array is a synonym for ${array[0]}. So, consider the following sequence:

```
# Create an array named fruit and assign three values to it
set -A fruit grapes bananas pears
fruit="carambola"  # assign "carambola" to fruit[0]
```

The three elements of fruit are now carambola, bananas, and pears.

Declaring Associative Arrays

So far, all the arrays we've seen have had numerical subscripts, such as `my_array[0]`, `my_array[1]`, and so on. The KornShell also supports a special kind of array known as an *associative array* in which the subscripts are strings rather than integers. For example, an associative array could have element names such as `my_array["howdy"]` and `my_array["doody"]`.

To declare an associative array, use the following syntax:

> **typeset -A** *associative_array_name*

You can supply additional arguments to **typeset** to describe the data type of the values that the associative array will hold; for example, the following statement declares an associative array named **vectors** that will hold integer values only:

> typeset -Ai vectors

The following synonymous syntaxes return a list of subscripts in the associative array:

> `${!name[*]}`   or   `${!name[@]}`

Associative arrays are a nice way to store glossaries.

```
USAGE="usage: decl_associative_arrays.ksh"  # associative arrays

# Declare lakes as an associative array that will hold float values.
typeset -AE lakes
# Assign values to four elements of lakes.
lakes["Walden"]=5.7
lakes["Erie"]=6.8
lakes["Okeechobee"]=7.4
lakes["Michigan"]=6.6

print "Here are the lakes for which there is data:"
print "${!lakes[*]}"   # list the names of all subscripts
print -n "Enter the name of a lake: "
read chosen
print "The value in this lake is ${lakes[$chosen]}"
```

Executing This Script

```
$ decl_associative_array.ksh
Here are the lakes for which there is data:
Walden Michigan Erie Okeechobee
Enter the name of a lake: Erie
The value in this lake is 6.8
```

Notice that the script assigns subscripts in one order (Walden, Erie, Okeechobee, Michigan), but the **print** statement outputs the subscripts in a different order (Walden, Michigan, Erie, Okeechobee).

Probing Arrays

The KornShell provides several interesting ways to probe arrays. For example, the following two synonymous syntaxes return the number of values assigned to *array_name*:

> ${#*array_name*[*]} or ${#*array_name*[@]}

Because sometimes there are gaps in arrays (for instance, there are values for subscripts 4 and 6, but not for subscript 5), the number of values assigned to *array_name* is not necessarily the highest subscript used in the array.

To get a list of the subscripts for which there are array values, use the syntax:

> ${!*array_name*[*]}   or ${!*array_name*[@]}

To get values for a section of an array, use either of the following syntaxes:

> ${*array_name*[*]:*starting_subscript*:*number_of_elements*} or

> ${*array_name*[@]:*starting_subscript*}

For example, given an array named **ar**, the statement ${ar[*]:70:10} starts at element ar[70] and gets the next ten values stored in the array. If there are no gaps in **ar**, the preceding statement would return the values of elements ar[70] through ar[79]. If there are some gaps, the preceding statement continues forward through **ar** until it has gathered 10 elements or until the array ends.

```
USAGE="usage: array_probing.ksh"    # cute array tricks

# A teacher put test scores in "grade", but half of the eight scores
# are missing.
 grade[1]=95;   grade[3]=97;   grade[6]=92;   grade[8]=75

 num_of_tests_recorded=${#grade[*]}
 which_tests_are_recorded=${!grade[*]}
 test_scores_for_last_half_of_course=${grade[*]:5:4}

 print "This student took the following $num_of_tests_recorded tests:"
 print "$which_tests_are_recorded"
 print "The scores for the second half of the course are: "
 print "$test_scores_for_last_half_of_course"
```

Executing This Script

```
$ array_probing.ksh
This student took the following 4 tests:
1 3 6 8
The scores for the second half of the course are:
92 75
```

Declaring Structures Part I

In various computer languages, a *structure* or *record* is a data type that holds a collection of related values, each of which could have a different data type. For example, a student structure might hold a student's name (which is a string), ID number (an integer), and grade point average (a float). Structures provide a nice way to organize this related data.

The KornShell does not actually provide a classic structure data type; however, using a few tricks, it is easy to simulate a structure. The trick is to create a bunch of variable names, each having a common prefix followed by a dot, and then ending with a different suffix.

The following syntax will return a list of all variable names beginning with string:

> ${!*string**}

```
USAGE="usage: decl_structures.ksh"  # how to simulate a structure

# Create a pseudo-structure named student containing three fields.
 student=    # required in order to use student as a pseudo-structure
 typeset student.name  # field "name" will hold a string
 integer student.id    # field "id" will hold an integer
 float   student.gpa   # field "gpa" will hold a float

# Enter values for the fields.
 print -n "Enter student's name: "
 read student.name
 print -n "Enter student's ID number: "
 read student.id
 print -n "Enter student's grade point average: "
 read student.gpa

# Print fields of a structure as you would print any variable.
 print "${student.name} has a grade point average of ${student.gpa}"

# Get a recap on this data type.
 fields=${!student.*}
 print "The fields of student are: $fields"
```

Executing This Script

```
$ decl_structure.ksh
Enter student's name: Fenster Macher
Enter student's ID number: 1470
Enter student's grade point average: 3.25
Fenster Macher has a grade point average of 3.25
The fields of student are: student.gpa student.name student.id
```

Declaring Structures Part II

The KornShell supports a programming construct called a *compound variable*, which is akin to a structure. The syntax of a compound variable is:

> *compound_variable_name=(*
>   *[datatype] field1_name[=initial_value]*
>   ...
>   *[datatype] fieldN_name[=initial_value]*
> *)*

Use the syntax **${***compound_variable_name.field_name***}** to get the value of the specified field.

```
USAGE="usage: decl_compound_variable.ksh"  # how to simulate a structure

# Create a student structure
student=(                    # structure is named student
   typeset name   # field name will hold a string
   integer id     # field "id" will hold an integer
   float   gpa    # field "gpa" will hold a float
)

# Enter values for the fields
print -n "Enter student's name: "
read student.name
print -n "Enter student's ID number: "
read student.id
print -n "Enter student's grade point average: "
read student.gpa

# Get a recap on this data type
print "$student"
```

Executing This Script

```
$ decl_compound_variable.ksh
Enter student's name: Kerry
Enter student's ID number: 1380
Enter student's grade point average: 3.7
(
        typeset -i id=1380
        name=Kerry
        typeset -E gpa=3.72
)
```

A field in a compound variable can itself be a compound variable. Thus, phrases such as ${owner.name.first} are legal.

Arrays of Structures

It is possible to create an array of pseudo-structures (described on page 40) or an array of compound variables (described on page 41). Such arrays could hold information not just on a single student but on an entire university. The following example is a bit of a plodder; to use such arrays efficiently, you would need one of the looping constructs described in Chapter 7.

```
USAGE="usage: decl_structures.ksh"  # how to simulate a structure

# Create a student structure
 student=               # structure is named student
 typeset student.name   # field name will hold a string
 integer student.id     # field "id" will hold an integer
 float   student.gpa    # field "gpa" will hold a float

# Enter values for the first student.
 print -n "Enter a student's name: "; read student.name[0]
 print -n "Enter student's ID number: "; read student.id[0]
 print -n "Enter student's average: "; read student.gpa[0]
 print

# Enter values for the second student.
 print -n "Enter a student's name: "; read student.name[1]
 print -n "Enter student's ID number: "; read student.id[1]
 print -n "Enter student's average: "; read student.gpa[1]
 print

# Print some values for both students.
 print "\n${student.name[0]} has an average of ${student.gpa[0]}"
 print "${student.name[1]} has an average of ${student.gpa[1]}"
```

Executing This Script

```
$ decl_array_of_structures.ksh
Enter a student's name: Rachel
Enter student's ID number: 1380
Enter student's average: 3.61

Enter a student's name: Danny
Enter student's ID number: 1552
Enter student's average: 3.48

Rachel has an average of 3.61
Danny has an average of 3.48
```

4   Math

This chapter explains how to do math in the KornShell.

If You're New to Programming . . .

The KornShell gives you nearly every feature available on a decent hand-held calculator, from addition through sines and cosines. As you'll see later in the book, you also can supplement the KornShell's offerings by writing your own mathematical functions.

By the way, don't get overly polite and use commas (periods in some countries) to chop up large integers. For example, here are some right and wrong ways to represent the integer ten thousand:

```
10000    # right
10,000   # wrong
10.000   # wrong
10 000   # wrong
```

The KornShell is no speed demon when it comes to math. If you need to average a few million numbers, you should use a compiled language such as C or FORTRAN rather than the KornShell. On the other hand, averaging a hundred integers might take a KornShell script only a fraction of a second longer than a comparable C program. And since you can usually code and debug KornShell scripts faster than you can code C programs, the extra fraction might be well worth it.

If You're an Experienced Programmer . . .

If you're still chugging along with KornShell 88, you'll find only primitive integer math functionality. However, if you're cruising with KornShell 93, you can do integer or floating-point calculations and a boatload of trigonometric and transcendental functions. Yep, you can do square roots, cosines, left shifts, bitwise AND's—you name it.

By default, all math operations are done in floating-point, which often leads to sluggish performance. You can, however, declare operands as integers, which will definitely speed up things.

Double Parentheses

Put all math operations inside a pair of double parentheses; for example:

```
((answer = 15 + $x))  # assign the sum of 15 and x to variable answer
```

You can place any amount of white space inside the pair of double parentheses. Extra white space can make your code easier to read. For example, the following statements are synonymous:

```
(( answer = 15 + $x ))              # right
((answer=15+$x))                    # right
((      answer=   15    +   $x ))   # right
```

Inside a pair of double parentheses, the dollar sign is optional. The preceding operation could have been written as:

```
(( answer = 15 + x ))
```

Despite the absence of the dollar sign, the KornShell cleverly understands that the second operand is the value of variable **x** rather than the literal value x.

Integer Addition, Subtraction, and Multiplication

The following script declares all its math operands as integers and then demonstrates some fundamental integer math operations.

```
USAGE="usage: math_int.ksh"   # demonstrates +, -, and *
# Declare variables x, y, and z as integers.
 integer x=5           # assign 5 as the starting value of x
 integer y=7           # assign 7 as the starting value of y
 integer z             # declare z as an integer, but don't initialize it

((z = x + y))         # add x and y and assign the sum to z
print "$x plus $y is $z"

((z = x - y))         # subtract y from x and assign the sum to z
print "$x minus $y is $z"

((z = x * y))         # multiply x and y and assign the product to z
print "$x times $y is $z"

# You can embed a math operation inside the print statement.
 print "$x times $y is still $((x * y))"
```

Executing This Script

```
$ math_int.ksh
5 plus 7 is 12
5 minus 7 is -2
5 times 7 is 35
5 times 7 is still 35
```

If I had not explicitly declared a data type for **x**, **y**, and **z**, the KornShell would have assumed that these variables were strings. That would not have been a tragedy because the KornShell still would have been clever enough to calculate the correct results. However, failing to provide an explicit data type for **x**, **y**, and **z** would have hurt performance (interminable microseconds!). Waste enough microseconds and pretty soon you're throwing away entire milliseconds. Later in the book, though, we will see scripts that do thousands of math operations, and data typing will carve off noticeable amounts of time when these scripts run.

In general, providing data types for your variables is a good discipline that can simplify debugging and maintenance.

Integer Division

Do you remember learning long division in elementary school? Before you knew anything about fractions and decimals, you learned that each division problem yielded a two-part answer: a quotient and a remainder. For example, if your teacher asked you what 16 divided by 3 was, you answered, "The quotient is 5 and the remainder is 1."

The KornShell has a similarly simplistic view of integer division. Because each division answer has two parts, the KornShell provides two division operators: one for the quotient (/) and one for the remainder (%). The % operator is also called the *modulo division operator*.

```
USAGE="usage: division.ksh" # two kinds of division operations

 integer distance kilometers remaining_meters

 print -n "How far did you run (in meters)? "
 read distance

 ((kilometers = distance / 1000))
 ((remaining_meters = distance % 1000))

 print "You ran $kilometers kilometers and $remaining_meters meters."
```

Executing This Script

```
$ division.ksh
How far did you run (in meters)? 2700
You ran 2 kilometers and 700 meters.

$ division.ksh
How far did you run (in meters)? 700
You ran 0 kilometers and 700 meters.
```

Floating-Point Math

You can perform addition, subtraction, multiplication, and division on floating-point operands. The following script declares all its math operands as floats and runs through a few computations.

Modulo division on floating-point operands returns an integer result. It is rarely used.

```
USAGE="usage: math_real.ksh"   # demonstrates +, -, and *
# Declare variables x, y, and z as integers.
 float x=5.8        # assign 5.8 as the starting value of x
 float y=3.7        # assign 3.7 as the starting value of y
 float z            # declare z as an integer, but don't initialize it

((z = x + y))       # add x and y and assign the sum to z
print "$x plus $y is $z"

((z = x - y))       # subtract y from x and assign the difference to z
print "$x minus $y is $z"

((z = x * y))       # multiply x and y and assign the product to z
print "$x times $y is $z"

((z = x / y))       # divide x by y and assign the quotient to z
print "$x divided by $y is $z"
```

Executing This Script

```
$ math_real.ksh
5.8 plus 3.7 is 9.5
5.8 minus 3.7 is 2.1
5.8 times 3.7 is 21.46
5.8 divided by 3.7 is 1.567567568
```

Later in the book, we'll see how to control the output precision when printing floating-point values.

Mixing Floating-Point and Integer Math

If both operands in a mathematical operation are integers, the KornShell uses integer math rules. If either operand or both operands are floating-point numbers, the KornShell uses floating-point math rules.

For example, in the following statement, both operands are integer constants; therefore, integer math rules apply, and the KornShell will print the integer 2:

```
print $(( 11 / 4 )) # both operands are integer constants
```

In the following statement, one of the operands is a floating-point constant; therefore, floating-point math rules apply, and the KornShell will print the floating-point value 2.75:

```
print $(( 11 / 4.0 )) # second operand is a floating-point constant
```

Each mathematical operation produces a result. If the result is assigned to a floating-point variable, floating-point math rules apply even if both operands are integers. For example, in the following statement, both operands are integer constants. However, because the result is assigned to floating-point variable **q**, the KornShell will assign the floating-point value 2.75 to **q**:

```
typeset -E q
(( q = 11 / 4 ))
```

Conversely, suppose that **q** is declared as an integer variable but one of the operands is a floating-point value. In this case, the KornShell uses floating-point math rules to do the calculation, but then converts the result to an integer in order to assign it to **q**. The KornShell converts by truncating (chopping off the entire fractional part), not by rounding. Therefore, the KornShell will assign the value 2 to **q** even though 3 is a closer estimate:

```
integer q
(( q = 11 / 4.0 ))
```

By the way, notice how forgiving (maybe too forgiving) the KornShell is. Some other languages complain when you try to fit a floating-point value into an integer. Not the KornShell. This can lead to apparent miscalculations, for example:

```
integer x
float y
print -n "Enter a value: "
read x
(( y = $x + $x ))
print "$y"
```

Executing the preceding code produces the following:

```
Enter a value: 7.9
14        # But wouldn't 15 or 16 been a more appropriate answer?
```

Grouping Mathematical Operations

As in algebra, you can use a pair of single parentheses to group mathematical operations. Using the parentheses removes potential ambiguities and makes code easier to understand.

Consider the following statement:

```
((centigrade = fahrenheit - 32 * 5 / 9))     # wrong
```

The problem with the preceding statement is that it is not obvious which of the three math operations (-, *, or /) the KornShell should execute first. In fact, the KornShell will perform the multiplication first, the division second, and the subtraction third, which will produce an erroneous result.

Let's try it again, this time using parentheses to clarify our intentions:

```
((centigrade = ((fahrenheit - 32) * 5) / 9))  # right
```

By using pairs of parentheses, we forced the correct order of operations. That is, the KornShell performed the subtraction first, the multiplication second, and the division third.

```
USAGE="usage: math_grouping.ksh"  # grouping math operations

 integer tigers
 integer lions
 readonly integer legs_per_cat=4

 print -n "How many tigers are roaming the city? "
 read tigers
 print -n "How many lions are roaming the city? "
 read lions

# Tell the KornShell to add tigers and lions together and then multiply
# that sum by 4.
(( cat_legs = (tigers + lions) * legs_per_cat ))
 print "There are $cat_legs cat legs loose in the city."
```

Executing This Script

```
$ math_grouping.ksh
How many tigers are roaming the city? 22
How many lions are roaming the city? 8
There are 120 cat legs loose in the city.
```

BEWARE: Common Mistakes in Math Operations

Here are antidotes for a few common mathematical poisons.

First, don't forget that you have to enclose the entire mathematical operation within a double pair of parentheses. A single pair of parentheses has a completely different meaning to the KornShell.

```
(z = x + y)        # wrong; run this command in a subshell
((z = x + y))      # right
```

Second, if you do use pairs of single parentheses to group mathematical expressions, make sure that the number of opening parentheses equals the number of closing parentheses. For example, carefully count the opening and closing parentheses in the following two operations:

```
((z = (x + y) * (a + b))     # wrong, missing one closing paren.
((z = (x + y) * (a + b) ))   # right
```

Don't be afraid to use extra white space inside the double parentheses to clarify your intentions.

Third, for variables declared as **integer**, the KornShell cannot hold an infinitely high positive integer or an infinitely low negative integer. The legal range of integer values is $-2,147,483,648$ to $+2,147,483,647$ (a tad over two billion). The KornShell will not issue an error message if you exceed one of these limits; however, peculiar values will result. For example, suppose you declare variable **debt** as an **integer** and then issue the following statement:

```
((debt = 2000000000 * 3))
```

You'd expect variable **debt** to hold the value 6000000000; however, the actual value stored in **debt** will be the overflowed nonsensical 1705032704.

Fourth, printing negative numbers is a little tricky; for instance, consider:

```
((loss = 5 - 7))
print "$loss"       # wrong
```

You'd expect the KornShell to print out the value of **loss** (-2), but the KornShell instead prints the following error message:

```
ksh: print: bad option(s)
```

The root of this puzzler is that all KornShell options start with a minus sign; therefore, the KornShell thinks that you are trying to specify -2 as an option to the **print** statement. Use **print** **-R** instead of just plain **print** to correct this problem; for example:

```
print -R "$loss"       # right
```

Finally, note that = is an assignment operator, not a comparison operator. Don't use = to compare two numbers. (For details on comparing two numbers, see Chapter 6.)

Mathematical Assignment Operators

KornShell 93 borrowed most of its math operators from the C programming language. This is a big win for KornShell programmers who already know C, but can be annoying for others forced to deal with the impeccable "logic" of C.

The += operator tells the KornShell to add a value to a variable and then assign the sum back to the variable. For example, the following statements are synonymous. Both add 5 to the current value of **reg** and assign the new sum back to **reg**:

```
(( reg = reg + 5 ))   # add 5 to reg, then assign sum to reg
(( reg += 5 ))        # add 5 to reg, then assign sum to reg
```

The += assignment operator is a kind of programmer's shorthand. The C attitude (and now the KornShell attitude) is, hey, why bother typing the variable name (**reg**) twice.

Variables often need to be incremented by 1. Now, you could use the following statement to increment variable **reg** by 1:

```
(( reg += 1 ))  # add 1 to reg, store sum in reg
```

However, even the += operator is too much typing. (I'm getting writer's cramp just thinking about it.) The culturally correct way to increment by 1 is through the ++ operator, to wit:

```
(( reg++ ))  # add 1 to reg, store sum in reg (post-increment)
```

The ++ operator comes in two flavors: pre-increment and post-increment. In the preceding example, the ++ operator appears after the variable name, so it is a post-increment operator. The pre-increment operator goes before the variable name; for example:

```
(( ++reg ))  # add 1 to reg, store sum in reg (pre-increment)
```

What's the difference between the post-increment operator and the pre-increment operator? In the preceding examples, there is no difference. However, the ++ operator can be used in more complex statements in which the differences will be noticeable; for example:

post-increment operator	pre-increment operator
integer z=7	integer z=7
((y = z++))	((y = ++z))
Results: y=7, z=8	Results: y=8, z=8

In the post-increment form, the KornShell assigns the value of **z** to **y** *and then* increments **z**. In the pre-increment form, the KornShell first increments the value of **z** and then assigns the incremented value of **z** to **y**.

The KornShell also provides a -- operator, which decrements a variable by one. It comes in two flavors—a pre-decrement form (*--variable*) and a post-decrement form (*variable--*). For a rundown on the other assignment operators, see Table 4-2 on page 55.

The Triggy Stuff

The KornShell provides lots of trigonometric and transcendental functions. For the complete list, see Table 4-3 on page 56. To call any of these functions, use the following syntax:

((*result* = *function*(*argument*)))

for example:

```
(( y = sqrt(37.5) ))  # y is the result, sqrt is
                      # the function, 37.5 is the argument
```

All trigonometric and transcendental functions return a floating-point value.

```
USAGE="usage: trig.ksh"

typeset -Er pi=3.14159265359    # declare pi as a constant
typeset -E radians degrees s c t

 print -n "How many degrees (0-360): "
 read degrees

# Convert degrees to radians because the trig functions expect their
# arguments in radians.
 (( radians = (degrees / 360) * (2 * pi) ))

# Call trigonometric functions.
 (( s = sin(radians) ))
 (( c = cos(radians) ))
 (( t = tan(radians) ))
 print "Sine: $s\tCosine: $c\tTangent: $t"
```

Executing This Script

```
$ trig.ksh
How many degrees (0-360): 45
Sine: 0.7071067812   Cosine: 0.7071067812   Tangent: 1
```

BEWARE: Math Functions Inside Double Parentheses

The special math functions can be called only from within a pair of double parentheses. The absence of double parentheses causes an error. Compare the following:

```
y=sqrt(37.5)      # wrong
(( y=sqrt(37.5) )) # right
```

A Practical Math Example

Just to demonstrate that you really can write a real-world practical mathematical program in KornShell, here's a simple program to calculate the monthly payment on an American-style mortgage:

```
USAGE="usage: mortgage.ksh"   # practical math application
# Simple interest, interest compounded monthly.

 float principal
 print -n "Enter the principal of the loan (for example, 70000): "
 read principal

 float annual_rate
 float monthly_rate
 print -n "Enter the interest rate (for example, 7.25): "
 read annual_rate
 (( monthly_rate = (annual_rate / (12 * 100)) ))

 float years
 print -n "Enter the number of years of the loan: (for example, 30): "
 read years
 float months
 (( months = years * 12 ))

# Calculate the monthly payment.
 (( numerator = principal * monthly_rate ))
 (( denominator = (1 - exp((-1 * months) * log(1 + monthly_rate)))  ))
 (( monthly_payment = numerator / denominator ))
 print "The monthly payment is \$$monthly_payment"
```

Executing This Script

```
$ mortgage.ksh
Enter the principal of the loan (for example, 70000): 82500
Enter the interest rate (for example, 7.25): 6.875
Enter the number of years of the loan (for example, 30): 15
The monthly payment is $735.779825495
```

The KornShell does not supply a built-in function to calculate regular exponents; for instance, there is no built-in function to calculate 4.25. However, you can still calculate regular exponents by using the following formula:

$$a^u = exp^{(u)log(a)}$$ # Note that log calculates natural logarithms

For instance, to calculate 4.2^5 and store the result in variable **answer**:

```
(( answer = exp(5 * log(4.2)) ))
```

Math Operator Summary

Table 4-1 contains a list of all the math operators in the KornShell, except for those operators that also perform assignment. Table 4-2 lists all the KornShell math operators that assign its results to the first variable in the operation.

Table 4-1. Math Operators

Operation	What it does	Example	Resulting value of y
x + z	Adds **x** and **z**.	((y = 7 + 10))	17
x – z	Subtracts **z** from **x**.	((y = 10 – 3))	7
x * z	Multiplies **x** and **z**.	((y = 5 * 6))	30
x / z	Divides **x** by **z**; if both **x** and **z** are integers, the result is the truncated quotient.	((y = 37 / 5))	7
x % z	Modulo divides **x** by **z**; if both **x** and **z** are integers, the result is a remainder; if either or both operands are real, the result is undefined.	((y = 37 % 5))	2
x << n	Shifts **x**'s bits **n** spaces to the left. No wraparound.	((y = 2#1011 << 2))	2#101100
x >> n	Shifts **x**'s bits **n** spaces to the right. No wraparound.	((y = 2#1011 >> 2))	2#10
x & z	Returns the bitwise AND of **x** and **z**.	((y = 2#1010 & 2#1100))	2#1000
x ^ z	Returns the bitwise EXCLUSIVE OR of **x** and **z**.	((y = 2#1010 ^ 2#1100))	2#0110
x | z	Returns the bitwise OR of **x** and **z**.	((y = 2#1010 | 2#1100))	2#1110

Table 4-2. Math Assignment Operators

Operation	What it does	Example	Resulting value of y
y++	Post-increment operator. Adds 1 to **y**, stores result in **y**. If **y++** is used on the right side of an assignment operation, the KornShell uses the old value of **y** (the value before one was added).	`((y = 7))` `((y++))`	8
++y	Pre-increment operator. Adds 1 to **y**, stores result in **y**. If **y++** is used on the right side of an assignment operation, the KornShell uses the new value of **y** (the value after one was added).	`((y = 7))` `((++y))`	8
y--	Subtracts 1 from **y**, stores result in **y**. If y-- is used on the right side of an assignment operation, the KornShell uses the old value of **y** (the value before one was subtracted).	`((y = 7))` `((y--))`	6
--y	Subtracts 1 from **y**, stores result in **y**. If y-- is used on the right side of an assignment operation, the KornShell uses the new value of **y** (the value after one was subtracted).	`((y = 7))` `((y--))`	6
y += x	Adds **x** to **y**, stores result in **y**.	`((y = 7))` `((y += 2))`	9
y -= x	Subtracts **x** from **y**, stores result in **y**.	`((y = 7))` `((y -= 2))`	5
y *= x	Multiplies **x** and **y**, stores result in **y**.	`((y = 7))` `((y *= 2))`	14
y /= x	Divides **y** by **x**, stores result in **y**.	`((y = 7))` `((y /= 2))`	3
y %= x	Modulo divides **y** by **x**, stores result in **y**.	`((y = 7))` `((y %= 2))`	1
y <<= x	Shifts **y**'s value **x** places to the left, stores result in **y**. No wraparound of excess bits.	`((y = 2#11001))` `((y <<= 3))`	2#11001000
y >>= x	Shifts **y**'s value **x** places to the right, stores result in **y**. No wraparound of excess bits.	`((y = 2#11001))` `((y >>= 2))`	2#110
y &= x	Performs a bitwise AND on **x** and **y**, stores result in **y**.	`((y = 2#0101))` `((y &= 2#1100))`	2#0100
y ^= x	Performs a bitwise XOR on **x** and **y**, stores result in **y**.	`((y = 2#0101))` `((y ^= 2#1100))`	2#1001
y |= x	Performs a bitwise OR on **x** and **y**, stores result in **y**.	`((y = 2#0101))` `((y |= 2#1100))`	2#1101

Table 4-3 lists all built-in math functions, including all trigonometric functions.

Table 4-3. Built-In Math Functions

Function	What it returns	Example	Resulting value of y
abs(x)	Absolute value of **x**	((y = abs(-7)))	7
acos(x)	Arc cosine of **x**	((y = acos(3.14159/6)))	1.02
asin(x)	Arc sine of **x**	((y = asin(3.14159/6)))	0.551
atan(x)	Arc tangent of **x**	((y = tan(3.14159/6)))	0.482
cos(x)	Cosine of **x**	((y = cos(3.14159/6)))	0.866
cosh(x)	Hyperbolic cosine of **x**	((y = cosh(3.14159/6)))	1.14
exp(x)	e^x, where **e** is 2.71828182846	((y = exp(2)))	7.389
int(x)	Integer component of **x** (truncation)	((y = int(3.85)))	3
log(x)	Natural logarithm of **x**	((y = log(exp(2))))	2
sin(x)	Sine of **x**	((y = sin(3.14159/6)))	0.500
sinh(x)	Hyperbolic sine of **x**	((y = sinh(3.14159/6)))	0.548
sqrt(x)	Square root of **x**	((y = sqrt(40)))	6.325
tan(x)	Tangent of **x**	((y = tan(3.14159/6)))	0.577
tanh(x)	Hyperbolic tangent of **x**	((y = tanh(3.14159/6)))	0.48

5   Pattern Matching

This chapter explains how to specify patterns that you can use in certain KornShell commands or statements.

If You're New to Programming . . .

Computers are supposed to be these heartlessly exacting creatures that don't allow for fuzziness. For example, a computer program ought to be able to tell that the word *elephant* obviously matches the word *elephant*. But the KornShell allows you to be a little less exact than that. For example, you could tell the KornShell that the words *elephants* and *elephantine* also are sufficiently close enough to *elephant* to count as matches. You might even tell the KornShell that any word starting with the letter *e* counts as a match.

You use *wildcards* to express this fuzziness. The term *wildcard* should remind you of card games such as poker. If deuces are wild in a poker hand, you can pretend that the deuce is some other card. Similarly, the KornShell wildcard ? matches any single character. Unlike poker, though, KornShell wildcards come with varying levels of power. For example, the KornShell wildcard [a-m] will match only a lowercase letter from a to m.

A *pattern* is any collection of wildcards and constants.

If You're an Experienced Programmer . . .

Suppose you had to write code to answer the following question: Given a variable-length string, does the string start with the letters **ch**, contain at least one digit, and end with a consonant?

You probably would find it rather difficult to answer that question with your average workaday high-level language. Oh sure, you might be able to call a library routine that would search for substrings. That might help a little. But, admit it, unless you're using a special-purpose pattern-matching language, you'd probably be better off with a shell language than with FORTRAN or C. Among the shell languages, the KornShell is particularly rich in pattern-matching constructs.

Table 5-1. Five KornShell-Only Wildcards

Pattern	Matches
?(*subpattern1 | subpattern2... | subpatternN*)	Zero or one of the specified subpatterns
@(*subpattern1 | subpattern2... | subpatternN*)	Exactly one of the specified subpatterns
*(*subpattern1 | subpattern2... | subpatternN*)	Zero, one, or more of the specified subpatterns
+(*subpattern1 | subpattern2... | subpatternN*)	One or more of the specified subpatterns
!(*subpattern1 | subpattern2... | subpatternN*)	Any subpattern except one of the specified subpatterns

Longtime UNIX users will be comforted to learn that the KornShell supports the familiar *, ?, and [ ] wildcards of other UNIX shells. However, the KornShell also supports the five additional wildcard forms shown in Table 5-1.

Table 5-1 shows a | symbol separating the different subpatterns. However, you can put an & symbol between subpatterns instead of a | symbol. The & symbol means Boolean AND. Therefore, if you place an & between two subpatterns, both subpatterns must match in order for the pattern to match. If you place a | between two subpatterns, either subpattern (or both subpatterns) must match in order for the whole pattern to match. If a pattern contains a mix of & and | separators, the & operator takes precedence over the | separator, which means that the KornShell will perform the & operations before the | operations.

For a practical example that uses the & symbol, see "Matching Multiple Strings on the Same Line" on page 272.

For Everyone

Wildcards are building blocks of other statements and commands described later in the book. More specifically, you can use wildcard(s):

- As arguments to certain operating system commands (such as the UNIX commands rm and ls).

- Within a **case** statement or a [[...]] condition to compare a string to a pattern. See Chapter 6 for examples.

- Within a **for** or **select** statement to expand a pattern into a set of pathnames. See Chapter 7 and Chapter 8 for examples.

- Within a **set** statement to expand arguments into the set of positional parameters. See Chapter 9 for examples.

- Within string manipulation statements. See Chapter 13 for details.

The ? Wildcard

The ? wildcard matches exactly one character. The character could be any single ASCII value.

Pattern: car?
Matches: any four-character string whose first three characters are car
Possible Matches: card, cart, cara, carA, car2
Does Not Match: car, carts, car54

Pattern: ca?e
Matches: any four-character string whose first two letters are ca and last letter is e
Possible Matches: cave, ca3e, cabe, caRe
Does Not Match: cae, ca54e, caves

Pattern: ?ab?e
Matches: any five-character string whose second and third letters are ab and last letter is e
Possible Matches: cable, table, 5abTe
Does Not Match: abe, babe, tables

Pattern: ???
Matches: any three-character string
Possible Matches: act, now, 532, NBA, N5t
Does Not Match: am, acts

The [char1char2...charN] Wildcard

The square brackets wildcard matches any *one* of the characters inside it.

Pattern:	car[det]
Matches:	the three letters car followed by d, e, or t
Only Matches:	card, care, cart

Pattern:	[aeiouAEIOU]
Matches:	any one vowel, whether lowercase or uppercase
Only Matches:	a, e, i, o, u, A, E, I, O, U

Pattern:	[0-9]
Matches:	one digit; that is, this pattern matches any character from 0 to 9
Only Matches:	0, 1, 2, 3, 4, 5, 6, 7, 8, 9

Pattern:	[2-9][0-9][0-9]
Matches:	any integer between 200 and 999
Possible Matches:	235, 762, 987
Does Not Match:	185, 2000

Pattern:	[a-z][a-z][a-z][a-z]s
Matches:	any five-letter lowercase string ending in s
Possible Matches:	cards, lakes, boats, glbxs
Does Not Match:	CARDS, Lakes, BOATs

Pattern:	[a-zA-Z][a-zA-Z][a-zA-Z]
Matches:	any three-letter alphabetic string
Possible Matches:	rat, Rat, RAT, raT
Does Not Match:	123, r3t

Pattern:	car[!det]
Matches:	any four-character string whose first three letters are car and whose last character is anything other than d, e, or t (the ! means don't match these characters)
Possible Matches:	cars, carb, cara, carn, car3, carD
Does Not Match:	card, care, cart

Pattern:	st[\-\]\!\\]
Matches:	any three-character string whose first two letters are st and whose last character is -,], !, or \ (the \ preceding each of these characters is the escape character that turns off the special meaning of the character that follows it)
Only Matches:	st-, st], st!, st\

Character Classes

A character class is a highly readable (though slightly verbose) way of expressing the category to which a character must belong. For example, the following two patterns are equivalent ways of requiring that a particular character be a letter:

```
[a-zA-Z]
[[:alpha:]]
```

Table 5-2 lists the supported character classes.

Table 5-2. Supported Character Classes

Character class	Equivalent [...] pattern	Meaning
[[:alnum:]]	[a-zA-Z0-9]	A letter or a digit
[[:alpha:]]	[a-zA-Z]	A letter
[[:blank:]]	[ ]	A blank space or a tab
[[:cntrl:]]	no equivalent	A control character
[[:digit:]]	[0-9]	A digit
[[:graph:]]	[!]	Anything but a blank space or tab
[[:lower:]]	[a-z]	A lowercase letter
[[:print:]]	[a-zA-Z0-9`~!@#$%^&*()-_=+[{]}|;:'",<.>/?]	A letter, digit, or punctuation mark
[[:punct:]]	[`~!@#$%^&*()-_=+[{]}|;:'",<.>/?]	A punctuation mark
[[:space:]]	[ ]	A blank space, tab, or carriage return
[[:upper:]]	[A-Z]	An uppercase letter
[[:xdigit:]]	[0-9a-fA-F]	A hexadecimal digit

Pattern: `[[:digit:]][[:upper:]][[:digit:]]`
Matches: any three-character string starting and ending with a digit and having an uppercase letter as its second character
Possible Matches: `7B6, 9R3`
Does Not Match: `77B6, 9RR33`

Pattern: `[[:digit:]]*`
Matches: any string starting with a digit
Possible Matches: `47352359, 7up, 3.14`
Does Not Match: `555-1212, x942`

The * Wildcard

Matches zero or more characters. That is, the * matches a null string or any other pattern.

Pattern: `car*`
Matches: the three letters **car** followed by no characters, one character, or many characters
Possible Matches: `car, cars, car54, carbohydrate, carOB`

Pattern: `*`
Matches: just about anything (see bottom of page for exceptions); this is the wildest of wildcards
Possible Matches: `care, 15adfaseEEAS, 154, Tedwardo`

Pattern: `*.bak`
Matches: any string ending in `.bak`
Possible Matches: `153.bak, card.bak, Apple.bak`

Pattern: `c*r*s`
Matches: any string starting with `c`, ending with `s`, and containing `r`
Possible Matches: `crs, cars, cr3s, cards, chairs, charbroilers, c3r35234s`

BEWARE: Matching Filenames

To the KornShell, just about everything is a string. For instance, a pathname is a string. You can use wildcards to match any kind of string. For example, the pattern `A*` would match any string, pathname or not, beginning with uppercase A. However, the rules for matching a pattern to a pathname are slightly different from the rules for matching a pattern to a string that isn't a pathname. In particular, when you're comparing patterns to pathnames:

- Wildcards do not match pathnames that start with a dot (.). For example, the pattern `*` (by itself) would not match pathname `.startup` because `.startup` begins with a dot. To match the dot portion of the pathname, you must explicitly specify a dot as part of the pattern. Therefore, the pattern `.*` would match `.startup`.

- Wildcards do not match pathnames containing the slash (/) character. To match the slash portion of the pathname, you must explicitly specify a slash as part of the pattern. For example, the pattern `*` would not match pathname `flo/jo`; however, the pattern `*/*` would.

The ?(pattern1|pattern2... |patternN) Wildcard

Matches zero or one of the specified patterns. You can specify any number of patterns between the parentheses. If you specify more than one pattern, you have to separate the patterns with the | operator.

Pattern: `car?(t)`
Only Matches: `car, cart`

Pattern: `car?([ted])`
Only Matches: `car, cart, care, card`

Pattern: `care?(ful|less|free)`
Only Matches: `care, careful, careless, carefree`

Pattern: `car?(bohydrate|ob|[a-z])`
Matches: the words `car`, `carbohydrate`, and `carob`, plus any four-letter
                  lowercase word whose first three letters are `car`
Possible Matches: `car, carbohydrate, carob, cara, carb, carc, cars`
Does Not Match: `carA, car3, carzbohydrate, carobs`

Pattern: `car?(?|??)`
Matches: any three-, four-, or five-character string whose first three characters
                  are `car`
Possible Matches: `car, card, carob, car54, car2z`
Does Not Match: `carbon, cave`

BEWARE: White Space Within Patterns

If you specify any white space within a pattern, the KornShell will treat the white space literally. In other words, the KornShell will treat the white space as part of the pattern. This can be a problem for many users who sprinkle white space liberally in order to make scripts more readable. For example, the following pattern:

```
care?(ful | less| free)
```

matches `"careful "`, `"care less"`, and `"care free"`.

The moral: don't put white space into a pattern unless you really mean it to be part of the pattern.

The @(pattern1|pattern2... |patternN) Wildcard

Matches exactly one of the specified patterns. This pattern is identical to the pattern on the previous page except that this pattern does not match the null string.[1] The previous pattern does.

Pattern:	car@(t)
Matches:	car followed by t; this is functionally identical to the pattern car[t]
Only Match:	cart
Does Not Match:	car

Pattern:	car@([ted])
Only Matches:	cart, care, card
Does Not Match:	car

Pattern:	care@(ful|less|free)
Only Matches:	careful, careless, carefree
Does Not Match:	care

Pattern:	@(orange|lemon|lime|grapefruit)
Only Matches:	orange, lemon, lime, grapefruit

(This pattern is similar to an enumerated data type declaration in C or Pascal.)

Pattern:	car@(?|??)
Matches:	any four- or five-character string whose first three characters are car
Possible Matches:	card, carob, car54

---

1. Unless you explicitly list the null string "" as one of the patterns.

The *(pattern1|pattern2... |patternN) Wildcard

Matches zero or more of the specified patterns.

Pattern: `car*(t)`
Matches: `car` or a string starting with `car` followed by one or more t's
Possible Matches: `car, cart, cartt, carttt, cartttt`
Does Not Match: `caret, carttt3t`

Pattern: `car*([ted])`
Matches: `car` or a string starting with `car` followed by any combination of t's, e's, and d's
Possible Matches: `car, cart, care, card, carte, carted, caret, careteeted`
Does Not Match: `ted, carets`

Pattern: `*([a-z])`
Matches: the null string or any string containing only lowercase letters
Possible Matches: `zoo, keeper, tiger`
Does Not Match: `3, qb7, Kyoto`

Pattern: `*([0-9])`
Matches: the null string or any unsigned integer
Possible Matches: `5, 500, 6329531`
Does Not Match: `5.2, -500, +6329531`

Pattern: `care*(ful|less|ly)`
Matches: `care, careful, careless, carefully, carelessly`

Pattern: `?([+-])*([0-9]).*([0-9])`
Matches: the null string or a signed or unsigned floating-point number that contains a decimal point
Possible Matches: `+523.632, -7.2`
Does Not Match: `5.23e2, -7`

Pattern: `*(truly|very|large| |,)`
Matches: the null string, or any combination of the words `truly`, `very`, and `large`, possibly separated by commas or blank spaces
Possible Matches: `very large`
                            `truly very large`
                            `very, very, large`
Does Not Match: `Very large`
                            `large: very large`

The +(pattern1|pattern2... |patternN) Wildcard

Matches one or more of the specified patterns in any order. This pattern is identical to the pattern on the previous page except that this pattern does not match the null string.[2]

Pattern: `car+(t)`
Matches: any string beginning with `car` and followed by one or more `t`'s
Possible Matches: `cart, cartt, carttt, cartttt`
Does Not Match: `car, caret, carrot`

Pattern: `car+([ted])`
Matches: a string starting with `car` and followed by any combination of `t`'s and `e`'s
Possible Matches: `cart, care, card, carte, carted, caret, careteeted`
Does Not Match: `car, t, e, te, carets`

Pattern: `+([a-z])`
Matches: any string containing only lowercase letters
Possible Matches: `zoo, keeper, tiger`
Does Not Match: `"", 3, qb7, Kyoto`

Pattern: `care+(ful|less|ly)`
Matches: `careful, careless, carefully, carelessly`
Does Not Match: `care`

Pattern: `chapter+([0-9])`
Matches: any string beginning with `chapter` and ending with an integer
Possible Matches: `chapter5, chapter11, chapter108`
Does Not Match: `chapter, chapters, chapter2.bak, 1chapter`

Pattern: `+(*Java*&*Corba*)`
Matches: any string containing both Java and Corba, in any order
Possible Matches: "`Corba now contains a Java interface`"
Does Not Match: strings containing only Java or Corba, or strings containing neither Java nor Corba

---

2. Unless you explicitly list the null string "" as one of the patterns.

The !(subpattern1|subpattern2... |subpatternN) Wildcard

Matches anything *except* one of the specified subpatterns. Some users find this pattern hard to understand. The following equation shows one way to think about the ! pattern:

$$!(subpattern1 | subpattern2... | subpatternN) =$$
$$\text{* minus those matched by } @(subpattern1 | subpattern2... | subpatternN)$$

In general, avoid using the * wildcard just before the !.

Pattern: car!(t)
Matches: any string starting with car, except for cart
Possible Matches: car, cars, car54, carambolaS, carrot
Does Not Match: cart

Pattern: !(*.bak)
Matches: any string that does not end in .bak
Possible Matches: car, 35, QB7
Does Not Match: car.bak, 35.bak, QB7.bak

Pattern: car!(*.bak|*.bu|*_1)
Matches: any string starting with car that does not end in .bak, bu, or _1
Possible Matches: car, car54, carob
Does Not Match: car.bak, car54.bu, carob_1

Pattern: !(*.htm|*.html|*.gif)
Matches: any string not ending with .htm, .html, or .gif
Possible Matches: car, car54, carob
Does Not Match: car.bak, car54.bu, carob_1

The KornShell provides a reserved variable named **FIGNORE**, which provides a similar service to the !( ) wildcard. The **FIGNORE** variable holds a list of patterns for the KornShell to ignore whenever you use a wildcard to generate a list of filenames. For example, consider a directory that contains the following four files:

```
$ ls *
lime      lime.bak       mango    mango.bak
```

Suppose you assign the pattern *.bak to **FIGNORE** as follows:

```
$ FIGNORE="*.bak"
```

Then, when you ask for a list of files in the current directory, the KornShell skips over files whose names match the pattern *.bak:

```
$ ls *
lime      mango
```

Matching Subpatterns with \d

The wildcards we've seen so far could answer questions such as, "Are both the first and last characters in the string digits?" However, we have yet to encounter (until now) a wildcard that could answer the question, "Are the first and last characters the *same* digit?" or "Is the first word in the string also the fourth word in the string?"

Before getting to the new wildcard, we'd better nail down some terminology. Every pattern can contain multiple *subpatterns*. A subpattern consists of one of the wildcards listed in Table 5-1. For example, the following pattern consists of three subpatterns:

```
+([a-z])+([aeiou]|ay|ey)*([0-9])
```

You can think of each subpattern as matching a different substring of the whole string. The *subpattern matching wildcard* has the form:

```
\d
```

where *d* is a digit between 1 and 9 inclusive. The \d wildcard matches whatever the *d*th subpattern matched. For example, if the second subpattern matched the substring ay, then the wildcard \2 can match only the substring ay.

By the way, you can nest subpatterns.

Pattern: @([[:digit:]])*\1
Matches: any string that starts and ends with the same digit
Possible Matches: 2BE2, 898, 55, 9 to 89
Does Not Match: 2BE3, 89X, 57, 9 to 11

Pattern: @([[:digit:]])@([[:letter:]])@([[:digit:]])\2
Matches: a four-character string in which the first and third characters are digits and the second and fourth characters are the same letter
Possible Matches: 7X3X, 5Y9Y
Does Not Match: XX3X, 5YY9YY

Pattern: +([[:letter:]])+([[:space:]])*\1
Matches: any string that starts and ends with the same word
Possible Matches: boys will be boys, dog eat dog
Does Not Match: rain in sprain

Simple Commands Containing Patterns

The UNIX command ls lists the names of all the objects in the current directory.

```
$ ls
APPLES   Nancy   Nantes   apples   bananas   net.bak
```

You can specify a pattern as an argument to the ls command. For example, the following command lists the names of all objects beginning with N:

```
$ ls N*
Nancy   Nantes
```

To process the preceding command, the KornShell first expands (*globs*) the pattern into a list of filenames. Then the ls command runs, using the list of filenames as input. In other words, although you've entered ls N*, the ls command actually executes the following:

```
$ ls Nancy Nantes
```

Here are a few more ls commands containing patterns:

```
$ ls [Nn]*     # list objects beginning with N or n
Nancy   Nantes   net.bak

$ ls *n*       # list objects containing n
Nancy   Nantes   bananas   net.bak

$ ls [a-z]*    # list objects starting with a lowercase letter
apples   bananas   net.bak

$ ls +([a-z])  # list objects consisting of lowercase letters only
apples   bananas

$ ls *.bak     # list objects that end in .bak
net.bak

$ ls !(*.bak)  # list objects that do not end in .bak
APPLES   Nancy   Nantes   apples   bananas

$ ls @(apples|bananas|carambolas) # list these objects if they exist
apples   bananas
```

The ls command is not the only way to get a list of objects in the current directory. On the command line, the KornShell will expand wildcards appearing after any command. So, you can use the KornShell **print** statement and a wildcard or two to get object lists; for example:

```
$ print *  # list all (nonhidden) objects on the current directory
APPLES   Nancy   Nantes   apples   bananas   net.bak

$ print *n*  # list objects containing n
Nancy   Nantes   bananas   net.bak
```

Wildcard Summary

Table 5-3 summarizes all the KornShell wildcards.

Table 5-3. Summary of KornShell Wildcards

Wildcard	Matches	Matches null?
?	any one character	no
[*char1char2...charN*]	any one character from the specified list	no
[!*char1char2...charN*]	any one character other than one from the specified list	no
[*char1–charN*]	any character whose ASCII value is between *char1* and *charN* inclusive	no
[!*char1–charN*]	any character whose ASCII value is not between *char1* and *charN* inclusive	no
*	any character or group of characters	yes
?(*subpattern1* | *subpattern2...* | *subpatternN*)	zero or one of the specified subpatterns	yes
@(*subpattern1* | *subpattern2...* | *subpatternN*)	exactly one of the specified subpatterns (even if the matched subpattern is the null string)	no
*(*subpattern1* | *subpattern2...* | *subpatternN*)	zero, one, or more of the specified subpatterns	yes
+(*subpattern1* | *subpattern2...* | *subpatternN*)	one or more of the specified subpatterns (even if the matched subpattern is the null string)	no
!(*subpattern1* | *subpattern2...* | *subpatternN*)	any subpattern except one of the specified subpatterns	yes
d	whatever substring the dth subpattern matches (even if the matched subpattern is the null string)	no

Special Characters Inside the Square Brackets

The characters !, -, [, and] have special meaning within the square brackets wildcard. Sometimes, you will need to turn off the special meaning of these characters—for example, to search for the presence of an exclamation point in a string. Here are the rules for turning off the special meanings of these characters within the square brackets wildcard:

- Placing a \ in front of !, -,], or \ turns off their special meaning.

- Placing the dash - immediately after [, immediately before], or immediately after [! turns off the special meaning of the dash.

- Placing the closing square bracket] immediately after [or after [! turns off the special meaning of the closing square bracket.

6 Conditions

This chapter teaches you how to evaluate conditions.

If You're New to Programming . . .

A *condition* serves the same purpose in computer languages as in human languages. For example, here is a condition expressed in English:

> "If you are age 62 or older, then the movie costs $3.00; otherwise, the movie costs $6.00."

and here is the same condition expressed in the KornShell language:

```
if ((age >= 62))
then
   movie_cost='$3.00'
else
   movie_cost='$6.00'
fi
```

The only peculiar word in the KornShell syntax is **fi** (**if** spelled backwards). When speaking English, you mark the end of a declaration by lowering your tone. When writing English, you mark the end of a sentence with a period. When writing KornShell scripts, you mark the end of an **if** statement with **fi**.

The KornShell supports two different statements, **if** and **case**, for evaluating conditions. Although their syntax differs greatly, both do roughly the same kinds of evaluations. Because they serve the same purpose, how do you choose which statement to use? It's usually a matter of style. Many programmers prefer **case** when evaluating a variable that has many possible values but prefer **if** when evaluating a variable that has few possible values.

If You're an Experienced Programmer . . .

Every major computer language supports some way to evaluate conditions. The keywords and syntax may vary, but there always is some way to branch depending on the outcome of a test.

The KornShell supports two statements, **if** and **case,** for evaluating conditions. Syntactically, **if** and **case** are very similar to condition-evaluating statements found in many high-level languages, including C and Pascal. Despite these similarities in syntax, the KornShell can evaluate conditions more flexibly than either C or Pascal. That's because **if** and **case** in the KornShell can compare the value of a variable to a pattern.

In addition, you can use the **if** statement to run tests on objects in order to answer questions such as:

- Does the specified file exist?

- Do I have permission to execute the specified file?

- Is this file a symbolic link or a regular file?

Tests on Numbers and Strings

The KornShell provides six different kinds of numerical comparisons (shown in Table 6-1) and eight different kinds of string comparisons (shown in Table 6-2). The comparisons are also known as *tests*.

Place numerical tests inside a pair of double parentheses ((...)) and place string tests inside a pair of double square brackets [[...]].

A numerical test compares two numerical values. The confusing part is that a variable with the string data type *can* hold a numerical value. Therefore, if you specify $variable inside a numerical test, it isn't mandatory that *variable* be declared as an **integer** or **float**. However, it is mandatory that $variable evaluate to an integer value or a floating-point value.

A string test compares two string values.

Every test returns either true or false. For example, the following numerical test will return true if the value of **x** is equal to 6 and return false otherwise:

```
((x == 6))    # == operator inside ((...))
```

Now consider the following string comparison that returns true if **s1** and **s2** are equal, and false if they are not equal:

```
[[ $s1 = $s2 ]]    # = operator inside [[...]]
```

Let's focus on white space for a moment. Within a pair of double parentheses ((...)), you can use as much or as little white space as you desire. For example, the following numerical tests are all syntactically correct:

```
((x == 6))    # right
(( x == 6 ))  # right
(( x==6 ))    # right
```

However, inside a pair of double square brackets [[...]], you *must* specify white space between every component. For example, compare the right and wrong ways to compare strings **s1** and **s2**:

```
[[ $s1 = $s2 ]]    # right
[[$s1 = $s2]]      # wrong
[[ $s1=$s2 ]]      # wrong
```

Another syntactic point worth mentioning is that, inside ((...)), you don't need to place dollar signs in front of variable names.

Within [[...]], you generally don't need to put quotes around the string arguments. You need to do this only when the KornShell might mistakenly interpret part of a string as a wildcard.

Table 6-1. Tests on Numbers

Test	Returns true if
((*number1* == *number2*))	*number1* equals *number2*
((*number1* != *number2*))	*number1* does not equal *number2*
((*number1* < *number2*))	*number1* is less than *number2*
((*number1* > *number2*))	*number1* is greater than *number2*
((*number1* <= *number2*))	*number1* is less than or equal to *number2*
((*number1* >= *number2*))	*number1* is greater than or equal to *number2*
((! *number1*))	*number1* is equal to zero

Table 6-2. Tests on Strings

Test	Returns true if
[[*string*]]	*string* is not null; if *string* is unset or if string is null, returns false.
[[*string* = *pattern*]] or [[*string* == *pattern*]]	*string* equals *pattern*, where *pattern* is a string constant (such as "hello") or is some collection of wildcards and/or constants (such as h*). The single equal sign operator is old-fashioned, but still supported.
[[*string* != *pattern*]]	*string* does not match *pattern*, where *pattern* is a string constant (such as "hello") or is some collection of wildcards and/or constants (such as h*).
[[*string1* < *string2*]]	*string1* precedes *string2* in lexical order; for example, *string1* starts with the letter A and *string2* starts with the letter C.
[[*string1* > *string2*]]	*string1* follows *string2* in lexical order.
[[-z *string*]]	*string*'s length is zero; that is, *string* holds null value.
[[-n *string*]]	*string*'s length is nonzero; that is, *string* does not hold null value.

Comparing Numbers with if

The KornShell supports lots of different syntaxes for comparing numbers. All the syntaxes accomplish pretty much the same thing; however, some syntaxes are more equal than others. This book primarily uses the newest syntax (labeled "Syntax 1" in the following example), but we do present the other syntaxes so that if you do encounter them in older KornShell and Bourne shell scripts, they won't look completely alien to you.

```
USAGE="usage: if_num.ksh" # demonstrates if/then with numbers

 print -n "Enter two numbers: "
 read x y
 if (( x == y ))              # Syntax 1; use this one
 then
    print "You entered the same number twice."
 fi

#  if test $x -eq $y          # Syntax 2
#  then
#     print "You entered the same number twice."
#  fi
#
#  if let "$x == $y"          # Syntax 3
#  then
#     print "You entered the same number twice."
#  fi
#
#  if [ $x -eq $y ]           # Syntax 4
#  then
#     print "You entered the same number twice."
#  fi
#
#  if [[ $x -eq $y ]]         # Syntax 5
#  then
#     print "You entered the same number twice."
#  fi
#
#  if [[ $x = $y ]]           # Syntax 6
#  then
#     print "You entered the same number twice."
#  fi
```

Executing This Script

```
$ if_num.ksh # no match
Enter two numbers: 5 7
```

```
$ if_num.ksh # a match
Enter two numbers: 5 5
You entered the same number twice.
You entered the same number twice.
You entered the same number twice.
You entered the same number twice.
You entered the same number twice.
You entered the same number twice.
```

BEWARE: Common Mistakes Using if with Numbers

Beginning KornShell programmers often have a tough time mastering the syntax of numerical comparisons. We now examine a few common mistakes.

If you are accustomed to programming in the C language, the temptation to exclude the keyword **then** will be very strong. Resist that temptation; **then** is mandatory. If you omit **then,** the KornShell probably will issue the following error message when you run the script:

```
syntax error: 'fi' unexpected
```

Don't mistake the KornShell's double equal sign operator == for the single equal sign operator =. The == operator tells the KornShell to compare two numbers. The = operator tells the KornShell to assign the value on the right to the variable on the left. For example, compare these two statements:

```
if ((x = y))    # assign value of y to x
if ((x == y))   # compare value of y to value of x
```

Another common mistake is to type a single pair of parentheses around the condition instead of a double pair of parentheses; for example:

```
if ((x == y))   # right
if (x == y)     # wrong, causes the error message, "x: not found"
```

Comparing Numbers with the ? : Operator

The KornShell borrows the ? : ternary operator from the C programming language. If an operator could be said to have a cult following, this would be the one. Most programmers ignore it, though a few programmers find all sorts of elegant uses for it.

This operator takes the following syntax:

((*expression1* ? *expression2* : *expression3*))

In English, the syntax translates to "If *expression1* is true, then execute *expression2*. If *expression1* is false, then execute *expression3*."

Consider a simple mathematical expression:

(((x < 5) ? y=2 : y=3))

The preceding expression translates to, "If **x** is less than 5, then assign 2 to **y**. If **x** is 5 or greater, then assign 3 to **y**."

The preceding expression could have been written as:

```
if (( x < 5 ))
then
   y=2
else
   y=3
fi
```

Using the ? : operator reduces typing.

BEWARE: Common Mistakes in ? :

In C, the ? : operator can appear in all sorts of bizzarre places. For example, it sometimes appears as an argument to **printf**.

The ? : operator of the KornShell is not as flexible as its C counterpart. The only place where the KornShell ? : operator can be used is inside a pair of double parentheses. Furthermore, since it can appear only inside a pair of double parentheses, all the expressions must be mathematical. For example, the following code will cause a syntax error because the expression being evaluated is not mathematical:

```
(( [[ -r braile ]] ? x=7 :   y=2 ))
```

Compound Statements

If a condition is true, then the KornShell executes every line of code between **then** and **fi**. You can put multiple lines of code between **then** and **fi**. Unlike some high-level languages (such as C or Pascal), you do not mark the boundaries of such compound statements with **BEGIN** and **END** statements or with a { } pair.

By the way, you have to put at least one statement between **then** and **fi**; you can't just leave it blank. However, if you really don't want anything to happen, just place a colon between **then** and **fi**.

```
USAGE="usage: compound.ksh" # multiple commands after then
 print -n "Enter a year: "
 read year

# Associating one command with a condition:
 if (( (year % 2) == 0 ))
 then
    print "$year is even."
 fi

# Associating multiple commands with a condition:
 if (( (year % 4) == 0 ))
 then
    print "$year is divisible by four."
    print "It is probably a leap year."
 fi

# Associating "zero" commands with a condition.  Use the colon.
 if (( (year % 47) == 0 ))
 then
    :    # We'll add some commands later.
 fi
# If we had omitted the colon and just left a blank line, then the
# KornShell would have issued an error message.
```

Executing This Script

```
$ compound.ksh
Enter a year: 2004
2004 is even.
2004 is divisible by four.
It is probably a leap year.
```

By the way, the KornShell provides a statement called **true** that would have served the same purpose as the colon in the preceding script.

else **and** elif

In the previous **if/then** example, the KornShell executed statements only when the test was true. By comparison, this next script shows you how to execute one set of commands when the test is true and another set of commands when the test is false.

```
USAGE="usage: if_else.ksh"  # demonstrates else and elif

 print -n "Enter two integers: "
 read n1 n2

# This statement does only one test.
 if ((n1 < 0))          # here is the test
 then                   # the test was true
   print "The first integer is negative."
 else                   # the test was false
   print "The first integer is non-negative."
 fi

# This statement does two tests.
 if ((n2 < 0))          # here is the first test
 then                   # the first test was true
   print "The second integer is negative."
 elif ((n2 == 0))       # here is the second test
 then                   # the second test was true
   print "The second integer is zero."
 else                   # the first and second tests were both false
   print "The second integer is positive."
 fi
```

Executing This Script

```
$ if_else.ksh
Enter two integers: 5 -7
The first integer is non-negative.
The second integer is negative.

$ if_else.ksh
Enter two integers: -5 7
The first integer is negative.
The second integer is positive.
```

Comparing Strings with if

The KornShell supports three different **if** syntaxes for comparing strings. When writing new scripts, use Syntax 1 because it is more forgiving than Syntax 2 or Syntax 3. We show Syntax 2 and Syntax 3 purely for historical reasons; you may run into them in older scripts. In addition, older implementations of the KornShell do not support Syntax 1, so you may be forced to use Syntax 2 or Syntax 3 after all.

```
USAGE="usage: if_str.ksh" # using if to compare strings

print -n "Enter string1: "
read str1
print -n "Enter string2: "
read str2
print

if [[ $str1 == $str2 ]]          # Syntax 1; use this syntax
then
   print "The two strings are identical."
fi

if [[ $str1 = $str2 ]]           # Syntax 2
then
   print "The two strings are identical."
fi

if [ "$str1" = "$str2" ]         # Syntax 3
then
   print "The two strings are identical."
fi

if test "$str1" = "$str2"        # Syntax 4
then
   print "The two strings are identical."
fi
```

Executing This Script

```
$ if_str.ksh
Enter string1: The dog in the fog
Enter string2: The dog in the fog

The two strings are identical.
The two strings are identical.
The two strings are identical.
The two strings are identical.
```

Comparing Alphabetical Order with < and >

The < and > operators perform triple duty in the KornShell. If you specify < or > within ((...)), the KornShell does a numerical comparison. If you specify < or > within [[...]], the KornShell does a *lexical* comparison of two strings. (The third use of < and >, input and output redirection, is described in Chapter 12.) A string's lexical value is the ASCII value of each character in the string.

```
USAGE="usage: alphaord.ksh" # using < or > to compare strings

 print -n "Enter a string: "
 read s1
 print -n "Enter another string: "
 read s2

# Compare the lexical order of two strings. The comparison will be
# case-sensitive.
 if [[ $s1 < $s2 ]]
 then
   print "$s1 would appear before $s2 in an encyclopedia."
 elif [[ $s1 = $s2 ]]
 then
   print "$s1 and $s2 are the same string."
 else
   print "$s2 would appear before $s1 in an encyclopedia."
 fi
```

Executing This Script

```
$ alphaord.ksh
Enter a string: novas
Enter another string: supernovas
novas would appear before supernovas in an encyclopedia.

$ alphaord.ksh
Enter a string: solar system
Enter another string: astronomy
astronomy would appear before solar system in an encyclopedia.
```

Loosely speaking, if you're comparing two strings that contain only letters, then lexical order corresponds to alphabetical order. However, do read "BEWARE: Common Mistakes Comparing Strings" on page 85 for an interesting exception.

Comparing a String to a Pattern with if

The following script demonstrates how to compare a string to a pattern.

```
USAGE="usage: if_pat.ksh"   # comparing a string to a pattern

print -n "Enter a string: "
read s

if [[ $s == c* ]]     # true if $s starts with a 'c'
then
   print "$s starts with the letter 'c'."
fi

if [[ $s != *n ]]    # true if $s does not end with an 'n'
then
   print "$s does not end with the letter 'n'"
fi

# The following condition will be true if $s is one of the listed
# fruits.  See Chapter 5 If the @ pattern confuses you.
if [[ $s = @(orange|lemon|lime|grapefruit|carambola) ]]
then
   print "$s is a citrus fruit."
else
   print "$s is not a citrus fruit."
fi
```

Executing This Script

```
$ if_pat.ksh
Enter a string: carambola
carambola starts with the letter 'c'.
carambola does not end with the letter 'n'.
carambola is a citrus fruit.
```

BEWARE: Common Mistakes Comparing Strings

Use double square brackets, not double parentheses, to compare strings; for example:

```
if (( $string1 == $string2 ))  # wrong
if [[ $string1 == $string2 ]]  # right
```

Always put white space to the right of [[and to the left of]]; for example:

```
if [[ $str1 = $str2 ]] # right
if [[$str1 = $str2]]  # wrong; need white space around [[ and ]]
```

You can compare a string to a pattern, but you cannot compare a pattern to another pattern. Also, if you are comparing a string to a pattern, you must put the string on the left side of the equal sign and the pattern on the right. For example, compare these two evaluations:

```
if [[ $str = *.bak ]]  # right; string on left, pattern on right
if [[ *.bak = $str ]]  # wrong; pattern on left, string on right
```

Also, you may be comparing a string to a pattern without realizing it. This happens when the string on the right contains a wildcard. If you want the Korn-Shell to expand the wildcard into a pattern, you're fine. On the other hand, if you want the KornShell to interpret the wildcard character literally, place the string inside a pair of double quotes; for example:

```
if [[ $str = Who are you? ]] # wrong; ? treated as wildcard
if [[ $str = "Who are you?" ]] # right; ? not treated as wildcard
```

The < and > operators also impose their share of harsh justice on the unwary. The shell script called `alphaord.ksh` probably left you with the impression that the < operator was a sure-fire way to check alphabetical order. In fact, the < operator works well in comparing two uppercase strings or two lowercase strings, but may fool you when comparing an uppercase string to a lowercase string. That's because the < operator ranks all uppercase strings ahead of lowercase strings. For example, the `alphaord.ksh` script would tell you that "ZZZ" would appear before "aaa" in a dictionary. Fortunately, the KornShell provides a workaround to this problem. See Chapter 13 for a description of the **-u** and **-l** options to **typeset**.

Boolean AND, Boolean OR

Sometimes it is useful to combine tests. For example, suppose you want to specify a condition that is true only if two subconditions are true. We can combine tests with the *Boolean AND* operator **&&** and the *Boolean OR* operator **||**. By the way, another name for a Boolean AND is *logical AND*.

A Boolean AND operation takes two operands as input. If *both* operands (tests) are true, the AND operation is true; otherwise, the AND operation is false.

A Boolean OR operation also takes two operands as input. The Boolean OR is less demanding than a Boolean AND because a Boolean OR operation is true if *either* or *both* of the operands is true. A Boolean OR operation is false only if both operands are false.

```
USAGE="usage: boolean1.ksh" # demonstrates && and ||

 print -n "Enter your age -- "
 read  age

 if ((age < 6)) || ((age > 64))       # || is boolean OR
 then
   print "We give a discount to children and senior citizens."
   print "Ticket price is \$2.50"
 elif  ((age >= 13)) && ((age <= 19)) # && is boolean AND
 then
   print "You are a teenager. We charge double for teenagers."
   print "Ticket price is \$10.00"
# You can also put boolean operators within ((...)).
 elif ((age >= 40 && age <= 43))
 then
   print "These are difficult years. We won't charge you."
 else
   print "Ticket price is \$5.00"
 fi
```

Executing This Script

```
$ boolean1.ksh
Enter your age -- 15
You are a teenager. We charge double for teenagers.
Ticket price is $10.00
```

If the expression to the left of an **&&** operator evaluates to false, the KornShell does not bother evaluating the expression to the right. Similarly, if the expression to the left of an **||** operator is true, the KornShell does not bother evaluating the expression to the right. This produces slightly faster code but can sometimes lead to hard-to-detect bugs.

The case Statement

Here is a simple **case** example. Notice that you can associate any number of statements with each possible value. Just remember to put a double semicolon (; ;) after the last statement in each group.

```
USAGE="usage: case1.ksh"  # multiple statements per condition
 print -n "How do you feel? (wonderful, ok, not good): "
 read a_feeling

# Compare value of a_feeling to three possible values: "wonderful",
# "ok", and "not good". If $a_feeling matches one of these values,
# then the KornShell will execute the statements between ) and ;;
 case $a_feeling in
     "wonderful") print "I'm happy."   # if $a_feeling = "wonderful"...
                  print "Really glad." # ... then execute this statement
                  mood_quotient=10;;   # ... and this one

     "ok")        print "That's good." # if $a_feeling = "ok"...
                  mood_quotient=5;;     # ... then execute this statement

     "not good")  mood_quotient=1;;     # if $a_feeling = "not good"...
                                        # ... then execute mood_quotient=1
 esac   # esac ("case" spelled backwards) marks the end of a case
        # statement just as fi marks the end of an if statement

 print "Your mood quotient is $mood_quotient."
```

Executing This Script

```
$ case1.ksh
How do you feel? (wonderful, ok, not good): wonderful
I'm happy.
Really glad.
Your mood quotient is 10.

$ case1.ksh
How do you feel? (wonderful, ok, not good): not good
Your mood quotient is 1.
```

The problem with this script is that the user might not type in wonderful, ok, or not good; for example:

```
$ case1.ksh
How do you feel? (wonderful, ok, not good): fair
Your mood quotient is .
```

Unexpected Values in a case Statement

Sometimes, a user will enter a value that does not match the expected input. You can catch this unexpected input by specifying a simple * as the last possible value in a **case** statement. Remember that a single * matches any possible string (even the null string).

If you're an experienced C programmer, the final * may remind you of **case default** in a C **switch** statement.

```
USAGE="usage: case2.ksh"  # accounting for unexpected case values

print -n "How do you feel? (wonderful, ok, not good) -- "
read a_feeling

# if a_feeling is any value other than wonderful, ok, or not good,
# then a_feeling matches *.
case $a_feeling in
   "wonderful") print "I'm glad for you.";;
   "ok")        print "That's good.";;
   "not good")  print "I'm sorry to hear that.";;
   *)           print "I wasn't expecting that answer.";;
esac
```

Executing This Script

```
$ case2.ksh
How do you feel? (wonderful, ok, not good) -- pas mal
I wasn't expecting that answer.
```

Wildcards in a case Statement

The noble * isn't the only wildcard you can use in a **case** statement. The following script demonstrates other wildcards within a **case** statement.

```
USAGE="usage: casewild.ksh"  # demonstrates wildcards

print -n "Do you want some advice? "
read advice

case $advice in
   [Yy][Ee][Ss]) print "Plastics!";;
   [Nn][Oo])     print "Your loss.";;
   [Mm]*)        print "Be a little more decisive.";;
   +([0-9]))     print "You have a future in math.";;
   *)            print "I can't help you.";;
esac
```

Executing This Script

```
$ casewild.ksh
Do you want some advice? YES
Plastics!

$ casewild.ksh
Do you want some advice? yes
Plastics!

$ casewild.ksh
Do you want some advice?: Yes
Plastics!

$ casewild.ksh
Do you want some advice? Maybe
Be a little more decisive.

$ casewild.ksh
Do you want some advice? 542
You have a future in math.
```

Multiple Patterns in a case Statement

You can place a vertical bar | between two patterns in a **case** statement. The vertical bar means Boolean OR. Thus, a phrase such as:

    "wonderful"|"great"

matches wonderful or great.

```
USAGE="usage: case_multi_const.ksh"     # multiple constants in case
 print -n "How do you feel? "
 read a_feeling

case $a_feeling in
   "wonderful"|"great"|"excellent"|"marvelous"|"superb"|"happy")
               print "I'm glad for you."
               print "Really glad."
               mood_quotient=10;;
   "good"|"pretty good"|"ok"|"I can't complain")
               print "That's good."
               mood_quotient=5;;
   "not good"|"rotten"|"bad"|"horrible"|"I'm still living")
               mood_quotient=1;;
   *)          mood_quotient="undefined";
esac

print "Your mood quotient was $mood_quotient."
```

Executing This Script

```
$ case_multi_const.ksh
How do you feel? marvelous
I'm glad for you.
Really glad.
Your mood quotient was 10.

$ case_multi_const.ksh
How do you feel? I'm still living
Your mood quotient was 1.

$ case_multi_const.ksh
How do you feel? like sushi
Your mood quotient was undefined.
```

BEWARE: Common Mistakes in case

Here are a few things to look out for inside **case** statements.

Whenever you specify multiple constants separated by vertical bars, you must remember to enclose any constants containing white space inside single or double quotes. (See "Can I Quote You on That?" on page 21 for the difference between single and double quotes.) For example, compare the following two **case** statements:

```
case $a_feeling in
# pretty good | totally hip) mood_quotient=8;;   # wrong
 "pretty good"|"totally hip") mood_quotient=8;; # right
 esac
```

If you forget the quotes, the KornShell will probably issue a syntax error.

If your **case** statement contains wildcards, the order in which you specify the patterns may affect the behavior of your script. You must exercise care because more than one pattern in your **case** statement may match the value of the variable. If multiple patterns do match, the **case** statement picks the first match only. For example, compare the following two case statements:

```
# first
  case $a_feeling in
    "wonderful") mood_quotient=10;;
   w*)           mood_quotient=7;;
  esac

# second
  case $a_feeling in
   w*)           mood_quotient=7;;
   "wonderful") mood_quotient=10;;   # never gets here
  esac
```

Suppose that **a_feeling** contains "wonderful". The first **case** statement would assign the value 10 to **mood_quotient** and the second **case** statement would assign the value 7 to **mood_quotient**. Because order is so critical, if you do specify * as a wildcard, it must be the very last pattern in the **case** statement.

You can put a | between the constants of a **case** statement to mean Boolean OR. So, you might be tempted to put an ampersand & between constants to mean Boolean AND. In fact, the KornShell does not support this use of the &.

Tests on Files, Directories, and the Like

It has become fashionable to speak of files, directories, links, and other nouns of computer science as *objects*. The KornShell provides an easy way to determine an object's characteristics. Tables 6-3 and 6-4 list the tests that you can perform on individual objects. Place these tests inside a pair of double square brackets (and remember to leave some white space after [[and before]]); for example:

```
[[ -f $myfile ]]              # is $myfile a regular file?
[[ -x /usr/users/judyt ]]    # is /usr/users/judyt executable?
```

Each test returns either true or false. For example, the –d test returns true if the object is a directory and returns false otherwise.

If you are testing only one object and that one object does not exist, the test always returns false.

The object tests fall into three broad categories:

- Tests to determine the kind of object (regular file, directory, and so on)

- Tests to determine how an object is protected (read permission, write permission, and so on)

- Tests to determine the relative age of two objects

BEWARE: No Filename Expansion Inside [[ ]]

Within a pair of double square brackets, the KornShell does not expand wildcards into object names. For example, you might expect the following code to tell you if there is an object within the current directory whose name begins with the letter Q:

```
if [[ -a Q* ]]
then
    print "Found an object in $PWD beginning with Q"
fi
```

The KornShell does not expand Q*, but literally sees if an object named Q* exists.

What Kind of Object Is This?

There are times when it would be helpful to know what kind of object is stored at a particular pathname. Table 6-3 lists the available KornShell tests. The KornShell also provides the object tests listed in Table 6-4.

Table 6-3. Tests on Object Type

Test	Returns true if object
-a *object*	is available (same as **-e**)
-b *object*	is a block special file, which is a special kind of file that ordinarily only lives in the /dev directory
-c *object*	is a character special file, which is a special kind of file that ordinarily only lives in the /dev directory
-d *object*	is a directory
-e *object*	exists (same as **-a**)
-f *object*	is a regular file (as opposed to a directory, character special file, block special file, named pipe, or socket); note that if *object* is a symbolic link, **-f** *object* returns true
-L *object*	is a symbolic (soft) link to another object; in UNIX environments, the ln -s command creates a symbolic link
-p *object*	is a named pipe
-S *object*	is a socket; don't confuse this test with **-s** (described in Table 6-4)

Table 6-4. A Couple of Obscure Object Tests

Test	Returns true if
-k *object*	"sticky bit" is set; the sticky bit is a hint to the operating system to keep *object* resident in memory even after *object* has terminated
-s *object*	*object* has a nonzero size; if *object* contains nothing (has a length of zero bytes), this test returns false

Here's a script that uses some of the tests from Table 6-3:

```
USAGE="usage: obj_type.ksh"  # what kind of object is this?

print -n "Enter the pathname of an object: "
read pathname

# The ! operator means "not"; see next page for more details.
 if [[ ! -a $pathname ]] # Does this object not exist?
then
    print "There is no object at this pathname."
elif [[ -L $pathname ]] # Is this object a symbolic link?
then
    print "$pathname is a symbolic link."
elif [[ -f $pathname ]] # Is this object a regular file?
then
    print "$pathname is a regular file"
elif [[ -d $pathname ]] # Is this object a directory?
then
    print "$pathname is a directory"
else
# Object must be something offbeat, like a socket.
    print "$pathname is not a file, directory, or symbolic link."
fi
```

Executing This Script

One way to find out object types is to use the **ls -l** command; for example:

```
$ ls -l
-rw-r--r--    1 juggler   artistes    4742 Mar 12 10:18 apple.htm
drwxr-xr-x    8 juggler   artistes     512 Oct 24  1997 carambola.htm
lrwx------    1 juggler   artistes      34 Nov 10  1997 paint -> /u/red
```

The obj_type.ksh script provides a programmatic way of determining the type of an object:

```
$ obj_type.ksh
Enter the pathname of an object: carambola.htm
carambola.htm is a regular file.

$ obj_type.ksh
Enter the pathname of an object: paint
paint is a symbolic link.
```

Boolean NOT

Use the NOT operator ! to ask a negative question. For example, you can use **-e** to ask the KornShell if a certain object exists, or you can use ! **-e** to ask if a certain object *does not* exist.

```
USAGE="usage: bool_not.ksh"  # demonstrates the NOT operator !

# If a certain directory (/tmp/fun) does not exist, then create it.
# ~ means the HOME directory, so ~/fun means the directory named
# fun underneath your HOME directory
 if [[ ! -d /tmp/fun ]]
 then
   print "Directory /tmp/fun does not exist. Now creating it."
   mkdir /tmp/fun     # mkdir creates a directory
   print
 fi

# If the allison file exists, but the kelton file does not,
# then pause for 2 seconds.
 if [[ -f /tmp/allison && ! -f /tmp/kelton ]]
 then
   print "We must now pause for 2 seconds."
   sleep 2   # pauses script for 2 seconds
   print "Thank you."
 fi
```

Executing This Script

Before running this script, create a file at pathname /tmp/allison:

```
$ bool_not.ksh
Directory ~/fun does not exist. Now creating it.

We must now pause for 2 seconds.
Thank you.
```

Personally, I find negative tests rather confusing and try to avoid them.

How Is This Object Protected?

UNIX and Windows NT provide ways for the owner of an object to protect that object against different kinds of access. The KornShell provides tests to help you probe those permissions. These object tests are shown in Table 6-5.

Note that these object tests do not alter permissions; you'll have to rely on the chmod command for that.

Wise use of object permission tests can prevent errors before they happen. For example, suppose your script contains the following command:

```
cat tax_info
```

If you do not have permission to read file tax_info, then cat will return an error message. To avoid this error, your script can contain code like the following:

```
if [[ -r tax_info ]]
then
   cat tax_info  # only execute this command if you can read this file
fi
```

Table 6-5. Object Permission Tests

Test	Returns true if
-r *object*	the user running this script has permission to read *object*.
-w *object*	the user running this script has permission to write to (modify) *object*. If *object* is a file, then write permission means that the file can be edited. If *object* is a directory, the user may add new objects to the directory or delete objects from the directory.
-x *object*	the user running this script has permission to execute *object*. If *object* is a file, execute permission means that the file can be run as a program or script. If *object* is a directory, the user may search through the directory.
-O *object*	the user running this script is the individual who owns *object*. On UNIX, only the individual owner (or root) of *object* can change *object*'s protections.
-G *object*	the user running this script belongs to the group that owns *object*.
-u *object*	*object*'s set-user-id bit is set, meaning that the operating system will run *object* using the permissions of *object*'s owner rather than the permissions of the person who invoked *object*.
-g *object*	*object*'s set-group-id bit is set, meaning that the operating system will run *object* using the permissions of *object*'s group owner rather than the permissions of the group to which the person invoking the *object* belongs.

The following script uses several object permission tests to probe the permissions of one object:

```
USAGE="usage: obj_perm.ksh"     # check object permissions

print -n "Enter the pathname of a file: "
read pathname

if [[ -r $pathname ]]   # -r checks for read permission
then
  print "You can read it"
else
  print "You cannot read it."
fi

if [[ -w $pathname ]]      # -w checks for write permission
then
  print "You can write to it."
else
  print "You cannot write to it."
fi

if [[ -x $pathname ]]      # -x checks for execute permission
then
  print "You can execute it."
else
  print "You cannot execute it."
fi
```

Executing This Script

```
$ obj_perm.ksh
Enter the pathname of a file: /usr/users/my_plans
You can read it.
You cannot write to it.
You cannot execute it.
```

Comparing the Time of Last Modification

The tests in Table 6-6 compare two objects. For example, the **-ot** test returns true if a particular object is "older than" another object. An object's age, in this context anyway, refers to the last time the file was modified. So, a file last modified in April is older than a file last modified in May.

Table 6-6. Comparing Two Objects

Test	Returns true if
object1 **-nt** *object2*	*object1* is newer than *object2*
object1 **-ot** *object2*	*object1* is older than *object2*
object1 **-ef** *object2*	*object1* is another name for *object2*; **-ef** stands for equivalent file or equivalent stream.

Here are the rules if one or both of those objects don't exist:

- If neither *object1* nor *object2* exists, the test is automatically false.

- If one of the objects does not exist but the other does, the KornShell considers the existing object to be newer than the nonexistent one.

```
USAGE="usage: file_age.ksh"  # demonstrates -ot test
# Suppose program.c is a C program and that a.out is the executable
# version of program.c. This script compiles program.c only if it
# has been modified some time after a.out was modified.
 if [[ a.out -ot program.c ]]
 then    # a.out is older than program.c, or a.out does not exist
   print "Must compile program.c"
   cc -c program.c  # you might need a different compile command
 else    # a.out is not older than program.c
   print "No need to compile program.c; a.out is up-to-date."
 fi
```

This script is overly simplistic. It might be necessary to compile program.c even if a.out were younger. For example, program.c might contain some **#include** files that changed after compilation.

Executing This Script

Suppose that a.out was last modified on May 1 and program.c was last modified on April 1:

```
$ file_age.ksh
No need to compile program.c; a.out is up-to-date.
```

Mixing Tests

You can use Boolean operators to combine several simple tests into a more complex test. To ensure that the Boolean operations happen in the desired order, use pairs of braces to group the operations.

```
USAGE="usage: mixtests.ksh"     # combining a variety of tests
 print -n "Enter your age: ";   read age
 print -n "Are you mature (yes or no): "; read mature

# Perform four tests. Notice that this complex condition spans four lines.
 if { (( age >= 18)) ||
     { ((age >= 16)) && [[ $mature = [Yy]* ]] }  &&
        [[ -r lawrence.txt ]]
    }
 then
    print "You may read this classic."
    print
    cat lawrence.txt
 else
    print "I'm sorry, but you may not read this classic."
 fi
```

Executing This Script

Before running this script, use a text editor to create a short text file named lawrence.txt, and then put some text into the file. Here's what happened when I ran the script:

```
$ mixtests.ksh
Enter your age: 17
Are you mature (yes or no): no
I'm sorry, but you may not read this classic.

$ mixtests.ksh
Enter your age: 16
Are you mature (yes or no): yes
You may read this classic.

            Lady Chatterley's Louvers

    Young Lady Chatterley was torn between her tempestuous desire to
find quality vinyl replacement windows and her overwhelming passion
to stay within the ancestral family budget.
```

if — *Execute one or more commands if a condition is true.*

Syntax

if/then statement	**if/then/else** statement	**if/then/elif/else** statement

if *condition*
then
  command1
  ...
  [commandN]
fi
	if *condition*
	then
	  command1
	  ...
	  [commandN]
	else
	  command1
	  ...
	  [commandN]
	fi
		if *condition1*
		then
		  command1
		  ...
		  [commandN]
		elif *condition2*
		then
		  command1
		  ...
		  [commandN]
		else
		  command1
		  ...
		  [commandN]
		fi

where:

condition   usually is a numerical comparison, string comparison, or object test; however, *condition* also can be the name of any user program, operating system command, KornShell script, or KornShell statement (except for **then**, **elif**, or **else**). In short, *condition* can be anything that evaluates to true or false. Every program, operating system command, and KornShell statement returns an exit status. The error status is a number symbolizing the success or failure of the command. An error status of zero symbolizes success (or true), and a nonzero exit status symbolizes failure (or false).

command   is the name of any user program, operating system command, KornShell script, or KornShell statement (except for **fi**). For example, a *command* could be a user-written program such as **a.out,** a UNIX utility such as **sort,** or a KornShell **print** statement. In fact, a *command* could be anything that is legal outside of an **if** statement. In addition, *command* can also be a colon **:** by itself, indicating that no commands will be executed.

Quick Summary

The **if** statement evaluates a *condition*. If the *condition* is true, something happens; if the *condition* is false, something else happens. You can choose among several formats of the **if** statement depending on how many conditions you wish to evaluate.

In the simplest format (the **if/then** syntax), if the *condition* is true, the KornShell executes the *commands* between **then** and **fi**. If the *condition* is false, the KornShell ignores all the *commands* between **then** and **fi**.

In the **if/then/else** syntax, if the *condition* is true, the KornShell executes the *commands* between **then** and **else**. If the *condition* is false, the KornShell executes the *commands* between **else** and **fi**.

The **if/then/elif/else** syntax supports multiple conditions. The KornShell evaluates *condition1* first, then *condition2,* and so on. (There is no practical limit to the number of **elif** statements in an **if**.) As soon as the KornShell finds a true *condition,* it executes the associated *commands* and then ignores all remaining conditions. In other words, although several *conditions* may be true, only the first true *condition* matters. If none of the *conditions* is true, the KornShell executes the commands between **else** and **fi**.

case — *Execute commands associated with a matching pattern.*

Syntax

case *value* **in**
      *pattern1***)** *command1*
            . . .
            *commandN***;;**
      *pattern2***)** *command1*
            . . .
            *commandN***;;**
    . . .
      *patternN***)** *command1*
            . . .
            *commandN***;;**
  esac

where:

value   is any value. Typically, you specify the value of a variable.

pattern   is any constant, pattern, or group of patterns. A *constant* could be any integer (such as 18) or string value (such as "`marvelous`"). A *pattern* could be any pattern described in Chapter 5. You are allowed to specify multiple patterns; separate each pattern with a | symbol.

command is the name of any program, shell script, or KornShell statement (except for **esac**). For example, a "command" could be a user-written program such as `a.out`, a UNIX command such as `sort`, or a KornShell statement such as **print**. You can specify any number of *commands* or no commands at all. Just remember to place two semicolons (**;;**) after the last command.

Quick Summary

In a **case** statement, you specify a *value* and one or more *patterns*. The KornShell first compares *value* to *pattern1*. If *value* matches *pattern1*, the KornShell executes the commands associated with *pattern1* and skips over the remainder of the **case** statement. If *value* does not match *pattern1*, the KornShell ignores the commands associated with *pattern1* and compares *value* to *pattern2*. If *value* matches *pattern2*, the KornShell executes the commands associated with *pattern2* and skips the rest of the **case** statement. If *value* does not match *pattern2*, the KornShell ignores the commands and compares *value* to *patttern3*, and so on through *patternN*. It is possible that *value* will not match any *patterns*. **esac** terminates a **case** statement.

7 Loops

This chapter teaches you how to create loops.

If You're New to Programming . . .

A *loop* executes the same group of commands or KornShell statements many times. By creating a loop, you can reduce the length of your KornShell script. If you're new to programmmg, you may well ask why you'd want to execute the same group of commands over and over again. The answer is that although the commands themselves remain constant, input to the commands can change on every loop iteration.

For example, suppose you create a group of commands that counts the number of vowels in a word. Further suppose that you intend to count the number of vowels in four input words. If you don't create a loop, the structure of your script will be something like the following:

```
input word #1
count number of vowels in word #1

input word #2
count number of vowels in word #2

input word #3
count number of vowels in word #3

input word #4
count number of vowels in word #4
```

By writing the same script as a loop, you simplify the code to:

```
loop 4 times
   input a word
   count number of vowels in word
end loop
```

The KornShell supports three statements for looping: **while, until,** and **for.**

The **while** loop continues looping while a specified condition is true. That is, when you specify a **while** loop, you also specify a condition. The loop continues as long as that condition stays true. When the condition becomes false, the script stops looping. For example, the condition might be something like ((x != 5)). Therefore, the loop continues as long as **x** doesn't equal 5. The loop could conceivably run for thousands or even millions of iterations before **x** becomes 5. On the other hand, if **x** equals 5 before the loop begins, the loop won't execute even once.

The `until` loop is the reverse of a `while` loop. The `until` loop continues looping while a specified condition is false. You will probably find `while` loops easier to use than `until` loops. Unlike a `while` loop, an `until` loop always executes at least once.

When you write a **for** statement, you usually specify a list of values. The list could be a bunch of numbers, a bunch of strings, a bunch of filenames, or any combination of these things. For example, the list might be a simple shopping list: `apples`, `rice`, `corn`. During the first **for** loop iteration, the KornShell assigns the first element in the list (`apples`) to a specified variable. During the second iteration, the KornShell assigns the second element in the list (`rice`) to the specified variable. During the third iteration, the KornShell assigns the third element in the list (`corn`) to the specified variable. After the third iteration, the list ends, so the loop ends. You can use a wildcard to generate a list.

If You're an Experienced Programmer . . .

The KornShell supports three statements for looping:

- `while`

- `until`

- `for`

The `while` loop of KornShell bears a lot of similarity to the while loop of the C language. The `until` loop of KornShell is similar to a `do/while` loop in C.

Many languages support **for** loops; however, the KornShell **for** loop is rather unusual. In the KornShell, you use the **for** loop to establish a list of values for a variable. Each time through the loop, the KornShell will assign a new value from the list to the variable. For example, if the list is ten items long, the loop will execute ten times, each time assigning a new value to the specified variable.

In addition to **for, while,** and **until,** the KornShell also supports two statements that have meaning only within a loop—**break** and `continue`. Use **break** to jump out of a loop; use `continue` to skip to the next iteration of the loop. If you're used to the C language, you should recognize that the **break** and `continue` of the KornShell work as in C.

Simple while, until, and for Loops

On these two pages, we compare the three looping statements of the KornShell. Each of these example scripts produces the same output, which is:

```
1
2
3
4
```

The following script demonstrates a **while** loop. Each time through the loop, the Script prints the value of a loop counter. The loop executes as long as the value of **n** is less than or equal to 4.

```
USAGE="usage: while_ex.ksh" # demonstrates while loop

 integer n=1 # declare n as an integer; initialize it to 1

# Loop while condition is true.
 while ((n <= 4))
 do
     print "$n"
     ((n = n + 1))  # increment the loop counter
 done
# This loop executes four times.
```

The next script uses an **until** loop instead of a **while** loop. The **until** loop iterates until the condition becomes false.

```
USAGE="usage: until_ex.ksh"  # a simple until loop

 integer n=1  # declare n as an integer and initialize loop counter

# Loop until condition becomes false.
 until ((n > 4))
 do
     print "$n"
     ((n = n + 1))
 done
# This loop executes four times.
```

The **for** loop features two completely different syntaxes. The syntax that better lends itself to the current problem looks remarkably similar to the **for** loop syntax of the C programming language. Here's a solution based on C-style **for** loop syntax:

```
USAGE="usage: for_loop_c_style.ksh"

# Loop while n is less than or equal to 4
 for (( n=1; n<=4; n++ ))
 do
    print "$n"
 done
```

The other **for** loop syntax starts off like this:

> **for** *variable* **in** *list*

where *list* is one or more values. The first time through the loop, the **for** statement assigns the value of the first element in *list* to *variable*. The next time through the *list*, the **for** statement assigns the value of the second element in *list* to *variable*, and so on.

For example, in the following **for** loop, the variable is **n** and the list consists of four elements: 1, 2, 3, and 4. Because there are four elements in *list*, the **for** loop will iterate four times. In the first iteration, the **for** statement assigns the value 1 to variable **n.** The second time through the loop, the **for** statement assigns the value 2 to variable **n**, and so on.

```
USAGE="usage: for_ex.ksh"        # for loop

# Loop as long as there is another element in the list. By the way,
# the word "in" is a keyword that separates the name of the variable
# from the list of elements.
 for n in 1 2 3 4    # a list with four elements
 do
    print "$n"
 done
# This loop executes four times.
```

Using while to Average Five Floats

The following script uses a **while** loop to average exactly five input floating-point values.

```
USAGE="usage: average_while.ksh"     # averaging five float values

# Declare two float variables, initializing the first to 0.
 float running_total=0
 float test_score

# The loop will iterate as long as loop_counter is less than 5
 integer loop_counter=0
 while ((loop_counter < 5))
 do
   print -n "Enter a test score: "
   read test_score
   ((running_total += test_score))  # keep a running total of test scores
   ((loop_counter++))    # increment loop_counter by 1
 done

# Get an average by dividing the running_total by five.
 ((average = running_total / 5))

 print "\nThe average is $average"
```

Executing This Script

```
$ average_while.ksh
Enter a test score: 4.2
Enter a test score: 7.3
Enter a test score: 5.95
Enter a test score: 6.25
Enter a test score: 7.8
The average is 6.3
```

BEWARE: while Loop Not Guaranteed to Iterate

If the opening condition of a **while** loop is false, the **while** loop won't iterate even a single time. In other words, don't assume that the body of the **while** loop will always be executed.

An **until** loop is guaranteed to execute at least once.

Using a C-Style for Loop to Average Five Floats

In the C-style **for** loop, you typically specify three expressions inside a pair of double parentheses:

- The first expression typically initializes a variable.

- The second expression is the loop continuation condition. The loop will continue to iterate as long as the second expression is true.

- The third expression typically increments or decrements the variable you initialized in the first expression.

The following example is almost identical to the one on the previous page. The sole difference is that the following example uses a C-style **for** loop instead of a **while** loop:

```
USAGE="usage: average_for.ksh"  # averaging five float values

# Initialize two float variables, initializing the first to 0
 float running_total=0
 float test_score

# Initialize loop_counter to 0 and increment it by 1 on each trip through
# the loop. Iterate as long as loop_counter is less than 5.
 for (( loop_counter=0; loop_counter < 5; loop_counter++ ))
 do
    print -n "Enter a test score: "
    read test_score
    ((running_total += test_score))  # keep a running total of test scores
 done

# Get an average by dividing the running_total by five.
 ((average = running_total / 5))

 print "\nThe average is $average"
```

Executing This Script

```
$ average_for.ksh
Enter a test score: 4.2
Enter a test score: 7.3
Enter a test score: 5.95
Enter a test score: 6.25
Enter a test score: 7.8
The average is 6.3
```

Using break to Leave a Loop

This script finds the average of up to four integers. Ordinarily, you establish the loop termination condition at the beginning of a loop. Use a **break** statement to establish a loop termination condition in the middle of a loop.

```
USAGE="usage: break1.ksh"  # demonstrates break
 integer loop_counter=0
 integer running_total=0
 while ((loop_counter < 4)) # a loop termination condition
 do
   print -n "Enter a test score (or -99 if finished): "
   read test_score
   if ((test_score == -99)) # a second loop termination condition
   then
     break     # stop looping
   fi
   ((running_total = running_total + test_score)) # sum input values
   ((loop_counter = loop_counter + 1))            # count input values
 done

# The break statement skips over remainder of loop, so that script
# next executes the following line:
 if ((loop_counter != 0))
 then   # calculate the average
   print "The average is $((running_total / loop_counter))"
 else
   print "No data to average."       # avoid dividing by zero
 fi
```

Executing This Script

```
$ break1.ksh
Enter a test score (or -99 if finished): 4
Enter a test score (or -99 if finished): 7
Enter a test score (or -99 if finished): 2
Enter a test score (or -99 if finished): 5
The average is 4

$ break1.ksh
Enter a test score (or -99 if finished): 4
Enter a test score (or -99 if finished): 8
Enter a test score (or -99 if finished): -99
The average is 6
```

Using continue to Skip Part of One Loop Iteration

Use **continue** to skip a portion of one loop iteration. In essence, **continue** tells the KornShell to ignore the remainder of the loop and return to the beginning of the loop. The following script finds the average of five test scores but ignores "suspicious" scores.

```
USAGE="usage: cont1.ksh"  # demonstrates continue statement

integer loop_counter=0
integer running_total=0
while ((loop_counter < 5)) # loop termination condition
do
  print -n "Enter a test score: "
  read test_score

# Ignore input values less than 0 or greater than 100.
  if (( (test_score < 0) || (test_score > 100) ))
  then
    print "This value looks suspicious; ignoring it."
    continue  # skip the rest of this loop iteration
  fi
  (( running_total += test_score ))
  (( loop_counter++ ))
done

print "The average is $((running_total / loop_counter))"
```

Executing This Script

```
$ cont1.ksh
Enter a test score: 90
Enter a test score: 87
Enter a test score: 94
Enter a test score: 130
This value looks suspicious; ignoring it.
Enter a test score: 93
Enter a test score: -5
This value looks suspicious; ignoring it.
Enter a test score: 88
The average is 90
```

Using : to Create an Always True Loop

Starting a **while** loop like this:

```
while true
```

or like this:[1]

```
while :
```

establishes a potentially infinite loop. Since it is unlikely that you would desire an infinite loop, you must provide some loop termination condition inside the body of the loop—that is, somewhere between **do** and **done.** Then, when the termination condition becomes true, you can issue a **break** statement (to leave the loop) or an **exit** statement (to leave the script altogether).

Incidentally, the while true KornShell statement serves the same purpose as the while (1) statement in C.

```
USAGE="usage: trueloop.ksh"  # using the colon to mean "always true"

integer grand_total=0   # initialize grand_total
integer number

# This while loop sums any number of input integers.
 while true     # potentially infinite loop
 do
   print -n "Enter an integer, or enter -99 to quit: "
   read number
   if ((number == -99))  # loop termination condition
   then
     break   # jump out of the loop
   else
     ((grand_total += number))
   fi
done
print "The sum of all input values is $grand_total"
```

Executing This Script

```
$ trueloop.ksh
Enter an integer, or enter -99 to quit: 25
Enter an integer, or enter -99 to quit: 100
Enter an integer, or enter -99 to quit: -99
The sum of all input values is 125
```

---

1. Actually, the colon : is the null statement. The error status of the null statement is always 0. Because 0 corresponds to "true," the null statement always evaluates to a true condition.

BEWARE: The Nature of Truth

C language programmers should be aware that the KornShell and the C programming language view truth differently. In C, zero means false, and any non-zero number means true. In the KornShell, zero means true, and any nonzero number means false.

In C, there are rather complicated rules as to how a statement (and each expression within a statement) evaluates to true or false. In KornShell, the only thing that matters is the exit status of the statement. So, if the exit status is 0, then the statement is true and if the exit status is nonzero, then the statement is false.

Because of these philosophical differences, some care must be taken in translating C to KornShell or KornShell to C. Nevertheless, code such as the following, which should look familiar to C programmers, will, in fact, work fine on the KornShell:

```
USAGE="usage: ala_c.ksh"  # what is truth?
 integer n=3
 while ((n))  # loop as long as the condition is true
 do
   print $n
   (( n-- ))
 done
```

Executing This Script

```
$ ala_c.ksh
3
2
1
```

How in the world did the preceding script work? After all, the KornShell interprets a nonzero value as false. Since **n** equals 3 (false) at the start of the loop, why did the loop execute at all? The answer is that the KornShell views the following statement

```
((n))
```

as:

```
((n != 0))
```

Since **n** has a starting value of 3, the statement has an exit status of 0 (true). When **n** eventually becomes 0, the statement will have an exit status of 1 (false) and the loop finally will terminate.

Lists in for Loops

So far, we have concentrated on the C-style **for** loop syntax. In fact, the other **for** loop syntax—the one involving lists—is more popular. In the other **for** loop syntax, you specify a variable and a list of items. The loop will iterate one time for every item in the list. For example, a list of six items creates a **for** loop that will iterate six times. On each iteration, the KornShell assigns the next item to the specified variable.

```
USAGE="usage: for_list.ksh"  # lists in for loops

for city in Boston Kyoto Copenhagen     # a list of three strings
do
   print -n "$city\t"      # print a city then a tab
done
print; print

integer number
integer square
for number in 1 50 100                  # a list of three integers
do
   ((square = number * number))
print "The square of $number is $square"
done
print

# If a list entry contains white space (spaces or tabs), enclose the
# entry inside a pair of single quotes or double quotes.
for mixture in Miami 7 "San Fran" 9     # a list of integers and strings
do
   print $mixture
done
```

Executing This Script

```
$ for_list.ksh
Boston    Kyoto    Copenhagen

The square of 1 is 1
The square of 50 is 2500
The square of 100 is 10000

Miami
7
San Fran
9
```

A List of Filenames in a for Loop

In the following **for** loop, the list consists of three explicit pathnames. Thus, the loop will iterate three times.

```
USAGE="usage: for_cnst.ksh"  # list of filenames in a for loop

# Generate a list of three explicit object names:
 for object in tiger.c /usr/users/lion.c panther
 do
   if [[ ! -a $object ]]
   then
     print "$object does not exist."
   elif [[ -f $object ]]
   then
     print "$object exists and is a regular file."
     print "$object contains the following text:\n"
     cat $object # cat is the UNIX command to display a file's contents
     print
   else
     print "$object exists but is not a regular file."
   fi
 done
```

Executing This Script

Before running this script, create a file named `tiger.c` and a directory named `panther`. Put some text into `tiger.c`; any text will do. Here's what happened when I ran the script:

```
$ for_cnst.ksh
tiger.c exists and is a regular file.
tiger.c contains the following text:

main() /* main routine of tiger */
{
    printf("Tiger, tiger, burning bright. \n");
}

/usr/users/lion.c does not exist.
panther exists but is not a regular file.
```

The previous script contains a flaw. The script will execute `cat` on *all* regular files, even those containing binary code. For example, if `$object` points to an executable binary file (such as `a.out`), the script will display all sorts of gibberish.

The KornShell does not provide a test to determine if a file is a binary file. However, many operating systems come with a command named `file` (yep, a very confusing name) that can determine whether a file is a binary file.

Patterns in a for Loop

The previous example contained an explicit list of object names, but what do you do if you want to create a list of all the object names in the current directory? The answer is simple: use wildcards. For example, the following **for** loop generates a list of all the objects in the current directory:

```
for x in *
```

You might be thinking, "What if I don't want every object in the current directory? What if I only want regular files?" Well, as the following script shows, you should still use the * wildcard to generate a list of all objects, but then use object tests (like **-f** or **-d**) within the body of the loop.

```
USAGE="usage: for_pat.ksh"   # patterns in a for loop list

print "Here is a list of every object in the current directory:"
for object in *
do
  print "\t$object"
done

print "\nHere is a list of every regular file"
print "in the current directory:"
for object in *     # generate list of every object
do
  if [[ -f $object ]]    # only print regular files
  then
    print "\t$object"
  fi
done

print "\nHere is a list of every modifiable C and assembly language"
print "source file in the current directory:"
for object in *.c *s
do
  if { [[ -f $object ]] && [[ -w $object ]] }
  then
    print "\t$object"
  fi
done
```

Executing This Script

Before running the script, we'll issue an `ls -l` command to find out what's in the current directory:

```
$ ls -l  # UNIX command to display contents of current directory
total 11
-rw-rw-rw-    1 rosenber    1300 Feb 5    09:39 a.out
-rw-rw-rw-    1 rosenber     413 Feb 5    09:42 debbie.s
-rw-rw-rw-    1 rosenber      78 Feb 5    09:41 ev.c
-rw-rw-rw-    1 rosenber     623 Feb 5    09:39 ev.o
-rw-rw-rw-    1 rosenber     608 Feb 5    09:42 for_pat
drwxrwxrwx    1 rosenber    1024 Feb 5    09:43 libraries
-rw-rw-rw-    1 rosenber     732 Feb 5    09:41 lou.c
-rw-rw-rw-    1 rosenber     623 Feb 5    09:39 lou.o
-rw-rw-rw-    1 rosenber      17 Feb 5    09:42 sarah.s
drwxrwxrwx    1 rosenber    1024 Feb 5    09:43 under
```

Now run the script:

```
$ for_pat.ksh
Here is a list of every object in the current directory:
        a.out
        debbie.s
        ev.c
        ev.o
        for_pat
        libraries
        lou.c
        lou.o
        sarah.s
        under

Here is a list of every regular file
in the current directory:
        a.out
        debbie.s
        ev.c
        ev.o
        for_pat
        lou.c
        lou.o
        sarah.s

Here is a list of every modifiable C and assembly language
source file in the current directory:
        ev.c
        lou.c
        debbie.s
        sarah.s
```

Searching for Objects in Subdirectories

Often, you will want to search not only the current directory, but its subdirectories as well. The * pattern matches all objects in the current directory, */* matches all objects one level underneath the current directory, */*/* matches all objects two levels underneath the current directory, and so on.

If you want to match *all* the objects underneath a certain directory (as opposed to matching directories down to a certain depth), you can:

- Use the UNIX command find

- Use the UNIX command ls -R

- Write a recursive KornShell function (see the section "Recursive Functions" on page 183)

```
USAGE="usage: dive.ksh" # scanning a directory and its subdirectories

print "Here is a list of all the objects in the current directory,"
print "its subdirectories, and its subdirectories' subdirectories."
for object in * */* */*/*
do
  print "\t$object"
done

print
print "Here is a list of directory names only: "
for object in * */*
do
  if [[ -d $object ]]
  then
    print "\t$object"
  fi
done
```

Executing This Script

```
$ dive.ksh # assume that current directory is /tmp/fruit
Here is a list of all the objects in the current directory,
its subdirectories, and its subdirectories' subdirectories.
          apple
          banana
          grapefruit
          apple/green
          apple/red
          grapefruit/pink
          grapefruit/yellow
          apple/green/granny
          apple/red/cortland
          apple/red/mac
          grapefruit/pink/fairchild

Here is a list of directory names only:
          apple
          banana
          grapefruit
          apple/green
          apple/red
          grapefruit/pink
          grapefruit/yellow
```

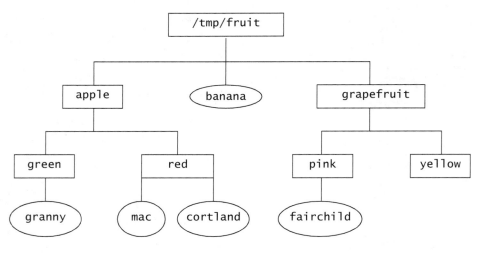

Figure 7-1. Organization of Directory /tmp/fruit

BEWARE: Nonexistent Patterns

Suppose that no filename matches the pattern in a **for** loop. For example, consider the following loop:

```
for file in st*
do
  wc -1 $file    # UNIX command that counts lines in a file
done
```

If no file matches the pattern st*, does the KornShell issue an error? Yes and no. Let's examine this situation carefully.

The KornShell attempts to expand the pattern st*; however, no filename matches this pattern. Since st* cannot be expanded, the KornShell sets the loop list to the literal value st*. In other words, the list will consist of only one value, st*. So far, none of the preceding activity causes the KornShell to issue an error. However, the command wc -1 will attempt to count the lines in a file named st*. Since no file by that name exists, the wc -1 command will issue an error such as the following:

```
st*: No such file or directory
```

Here is a better way to write the same loop:

```
for file in st*
do
  if [[ -f $file ]]
  then
    wc -1 $file
  fi
done
```

A Loop Within a Loop

The KornShell permits you to create *nested loops*; in other words, you may put a loop inside another loop. For example, in the following script, we put a **for** loop inside a **while** loop. The script tests each integer from 11 to 99 to determine whether it is prime or composite.

```
USAGE="usage: nested.ksh"  # demonstrates nested loops

# The outer loop generates integers from 11 to 99
integer n=11
 while ((n <= 99))     # here's the start of the outer loop
 do
   answer=prime
  # The inner loop tests each value of n to determine whether n is
  # prime or composite. The values of d (2, 3, 5, and 7) are the prime
  # factors of integers less than 100.
   for d in 2 3 5 7   # here's the start of the inner loop
   do
     ((remainder = n % d))
    # If a number is evenly divisible by a prime factor,
    # then it is composite.
    if ((remainder == 0))
    then
       answer=composite
       break
    fi
   done  # end of inner loop

   print "$n is $answer"
   ((n = n + 1))
 done  # end of outer loop
```

Executing This Script

```
$ nested.ksh
11 is prime
12 is composite
13 is prime
  .
  . omitting the next 83 lines of output
  .
97 is prime
98 is composite
99 is composite
```

The break **Statement Within a Nested Loop**

The following script demonstrates a **break** statement within a nested loop. You can optionally specify an integer argument, **n**, to **break.** If you do, the KornShell will jump out of the **n** loops enclosing **break.**

```
USAGE="usage: break2.ksh"  # using break within a nested loop
print "Here are pairs of numbers whose products are less than 50:"
for x in 1 2 3
do
  for y in 10 20 30
  do
    if (( (x * y) >= 50 ))
    then
       break     # use break to jump out of inner loop
    fi
    print -n "$x x $y,\t"
  done
  print
done

print "\nAll done."
```

Executing This Script

```
$ break2.ksh
Here are pairs of numbers whose products are less than 50:
1 x 10,     1 x 20,      1 x 30,
2 x 10,     2 x 20,
3 x 10,
All done.
```

Now make a small change to the program. Change the break statement to break 2. Now, the KornShell will break out of the current loop *and* the loop enclosing it.

```
$ break2.ksh # run it again, this time with break 2
Here are pairs of numbers whose products are less than 50:
1 x 10,     1 x 20,     1 x 30,
2 x 10,     2 x 20,
All done.
```

while — *Loop as long as the specified condition is true.*

until — *Loop as long as the specified condition is false.*

Syntax

while *condition*	**until** *condition*
do	**do**
command1	*command1*
...	*...*
commandN	*commandN*
done	**done**

where:

condition   is usually a numerical comparison, string comparison, or object test; however, *condition* also could be the name of any user program, operating system command, KornShell script, or KornShell statement (except for **do** or **done).** In short, *condition* can be anything that evaluates to true or false. Every program, operating system command, and KornShell statement returns an error status. The error status is a number symbolizing the success or failure of the command. An error status of zero symbolizes true, and a nonzero error status symbolizes false. See "BEWARE: The Nature of Truth" on page 112.

conmmand   is the name of any user program, operating system command, KornShell script, or KornShell statement. For example, a *command* could be a user-written program such as `a.out`, a UNIX utility such as `sort`, or a Korn-Shell statement such as **print**. In fact, a command could be anything that is legal outside of a **while** statement. If *command* is a colon (**:**) by itself, no commands will be executed between **do** and **done**.

Quick Summary

The **while** statement establishes a loop. The loop consists of all the commands between **do** and **done.** The KornShell executes the loop as long as the condition is true.

The **until** statement is identical to **while** except that **until** executes the loop as long as the condition is false. In other words, as soon as the condition becomes true, the **until** loop stops executing.

for (C-Style) — *for loop based on C for loop syntax.*

Syntax

```
for (( [expr1]; [expr2]; [expr3] ))
do
  command1
  ...
  commandN
done
```

where:

expr1   is any statement that can be issued within a pair of double parentheses. You typically use *expr1* to initialize the value of a variable that will count trips through the loop, although other uses for *expr1* are possible. Note that *expr1* is optional; there is no default behavior.

expr2   is any statement that can be issued within a pair of double parentheses. Typically, *expr2* is an expression that compares two mathematical values. When *expr2* is true (zero), the loop iterates. When *expr2* is false (nonzero), the loop ends and control resumes at the first executable statement after **done**. Note that *expr2* is optional. Omitting *expr2* causes the loop to iterate indefinitely.

expr3   is any statement that can be issued within a pair of double parentheses. You typically use *expr3* to increment or decrement the value of the counter variable that was initialized in *expr1*, although other uses for *expr3* are possible. Note that *expr3* is optional; there is no default behavior.

command   is the name of any user program, operating system command, KornShell script, or KornShell statement. For example, a *command* could be a user-written program such as `a.out`, a UNIX utility such as `sort`, or a Korn-Shell statement such as **print**. If *command* is a colon (`:`) by itself, no commands will be executed between **do** and **done**.

Quick Summary

The C-style **for** statement establishes a loop. The loop consists of all the commands between **do** and **done.** The KornShell executes the loop while *expr2* is true.

for — *Loop through all elements of a list.*

Syntax

for loop (syntax A)	for loop (syntax B)

```
for variable in list          for variable
do                            do
  command1                      command1
  ...                           ...
  commandN                      commandN
done                          done
```

where:

variable   is the name of a variable, typically, a user-defined variable and not a KornShell reserved variable.

list   is a list of strings or numbers. (Remember that the KornShell regards just about everything as a string.) If the list contains any KornShell wild-cards, the KornShell expands the wildcards into filenames before beginning the loop.

command   is the name of any user program, operating system command, KornShell script, or KornShell statement. For example, *command* could be a user-written program such as `a.out`, a UNIX utility such as `sort`, or a Korn-Shell statement such as **print**. If *command* is a colon (**:**) by itself, no commands will be executed between **do** and **done**.

Quick Summary

The **for** statement establishes a loop. The body of the loop consists of all the *commands* between **do** and **done.** The KornShell executes the body of the loop one time for every element in *list*. During the first iteration of the loop, the KornShell assigns the first element in *list* to *identifer*. During the second iteration, the Korn-Shell assigns the second element in *list* to *identifier,* and so on.

If you specify **for** *variable* without specifying **in** *list* (syntax B), the list of elements consists of the entire set of positional parameters. See Chapter 9 for details on positional parameters.

break — *Jump out of the current loop(s).*

continue — *Skip to the next iteration of the current loop(s).*

Syntax

break *number*   **continue** *number*

where:

number   is an optional integer corresponding to the number of levels of nesting to
jump out of (**break**) or to skip iterations of (**continue**). The default
value of *number* is 1.

Quick Summary

Use a **break** statement to stop execution of the current loop and resume execution immediately after the end of the loop. In other words, use a **break** statement
to jump out of a loop.

Use a **continue** statement to stop execution of the current loop iteration and
resume execution at the top of the loop. In other words, use a **continue** statement
to skip part of the loop for one cycle.

The optional *number* only has meaning when the current loop is enclosed
(nested) inside another loop. In that case, you can specify the *number* of enclosing
loops to which the **break** or **continue** applies. For example, suppose that the current loop is enclosed by two other loops. A **break** (or **break** 1) statement will cause
a jump out of the current loop only; a **break** 2 statement will exit from the current
loop and the loop enclosing it; a **break** 3 statement will exit from the current loop
and both loops enclosing it.

Incidentally, you may specify a *number* greater than the number of enclosing
loops. That is, if you are inside a single loop, specifying **continue** 9 (or **break** 9)
will not cause a KornShell error. Instead, the KornShell will apply the **continue** or
break to all enclosing loops.

Beginning programmers often confuse **exit, break,** and **continue.** All three
change the flow of control, but let's see how their use differs:

- Use **exit** to leave a KornShell script altogether.

- Use **break** to leave a loop but continue the KornShell script.

- Use **continue** to leave the current iteration of the loop but continue the loop.

Yet another related statement, **return**, will be discussed later in the book.

8   Creating Menus

Restaurant menus display food and beverage choices. In KornShell scripts, menus display choices of actions the user can take. After the user selects an entry from the menu, the script has to process the choice just as a chef has to prepare the dish that the restaurant patron selects.

To create menus, you can:

- Let a browser (such as Netscape Navigator) display menus and then have your KornShell script (a CGI script) analyze the user's choice. See Chapter 17 for details.

- Use the Desktop KornShell (`dtksh`) to generate very spiffy menus and to take appropriate actions depending on the user's choice. We'll briefly describe the `dtksh` in this chapter.

- Use the KornShell **select** command to display menus and to respond to the user's choice.

Of the three options, the KornShell **select** command is the least sophisticated. Nevertheless, it still is the best "KornShell-only" way to make menus.

In many Chinese restaurants in America, each entry on the menu is prefaced with a number. Thus, patrons can be spared the embarrassment of mispronouncing "Swan Lo Chow Shen" by simply asking for "a number 17 appetizer, please," or "What looks good in a prime number?" Similarly, the **select** statement lets users make selections by typing a number instead of typing out a more complex action. For example, instead of forcing the user to type, "I want to do the full install," the user can simply type the number 1. Laugh if you want at their quaint, old-fashioned ways, but **select** menus are much easier to code than any other menu mechanism and provide menus that users have no trouble understanding.

I like to use **select** to insulate users from the brutalities of UNIX command syntax. For example, can you remember the options that accompany the UNIX ps command? I can't. That's why I like to place the options inside a **select** loop and give myself useful prompts.

A Simple `select` Example

The following script generates a two-entry menu. After displaying the two entries, the script prompts the user for input. The prompt is stored inside a variable named **PS3**. No matter what the user enters, the script responds with a polite "Thank you." In other words, the script makes no attempt to process the user's choice.

```
USAGE="usage:select1.ksh"    # a simple select statement

print "To stop the script, type the character(s) that signify "
print "end-of-file for your operating system. If you are using "
print "the UNIX operating system, end-of-file is usually <CONTROL>d."

PS3="Enter your choice: "    # PS3 is the prompt

select menu_list in English Francais   # list consists of two entries
do
   print "Thank you. \n"    # a case statement usually goes here
done
```

Executing This Script

```
$ select1.ksh
To stop the script, type the character(s) that signify
end-of-file for your operating system. If you are using
the UNIX operating system, end-of-file is usually <CONTROL>d.
1) English
2) Francais
Enter your choice: 1
Thank you.
Enter your choice: 2
Thank you.
Enter your choice: <CONTROL>d *** EOF***
```

(My system happens to print ***EOF*** when I type the end-of-file character; your system might not.)

A select with a case

This script is similar to the previous one except that this one contains a **case** statement to process user input. In this script, the **case** statement takes an action that depends on the user's input.

```
USAGE="usage: select2.ksh" # select statement containing case

 print "To stop the script, type the character(s) that signify "
 print "end-of-file for your operating system. If you are using the "
 print "UNIX operating system, end-of-file is usually <CONTROL>d."

 PS3="Enter your choice: "       # PS3 is the prompt

 select menu_list in English francais   # list consists of two entries
 do
   case $menu_list in
     English) print "Thank you";;
     francais) print "Merci.";;
   esac
 done
```

Executing This Script

```
$ select2.ksh
To stop the script, type the character(s) that signify
end-of-file for your operating system. If you are using the
UNIX operating system, end-of-file is usually <CONTROL>d.
1) English
2) francais
Enter your choice: 1
Thank you
Enter your choice: 2
Merci.
Enter your choice: <CONTROL>d *** EOF ***
```

Unexpected User Input

Even though you're spoon-feeding the user, the user still might blow it. What happens if the user doesn't enter one of the menu choices?

```
USAGE="usage: select3.ksh"  # unexpected user input
 print "To stop the script, type the character(s) that signify "
 print "end-of-file for your operating system. If you are using the "
 print "UNIX operating system, end-of-file is usually <CONTROL>d."

 PS3="Enter your choice: "      # PS3 is the prompt

select menu_list in English francais   # list consists of two entries
do
   case $menu_list in
     English) print "Thank you.";;
     francais) print "Merci.";;
# Use a * pattern to catch any input values other than 1 or 2.
       *) print "You can only enter 1 or 2.";;
  esac
done
```

Executing This Script

```
$ select3.ksh
To stop the script, type the character(s) that signify
end-of-file for your operating system. If you are using the
UNIX operating system, end-of-file is usually <CONTROL>d.
1) English
2) francais
Enter your choice: 1
Thank you.
Enter your choice: 5
You can only enter 1 or 2.
Enter your choice: <CONTROL>d *** EOF ***
```

Gracefully Exiting from Menus

The following script demonstrates how to exit gracefully from a **select** statement. In this one, the user won't have to type an end-of-file character to end the menu selection; instead, he or she simply selects a particular menu entry (number 3). When the user selects menu entry 3, the KornShell invokes a **break** statement. In this context, **break** causes the **select** statement to terminate; control then resumes at the statement immediately following **done**.

```
USAGE="usage: select4.ksh"  # leaving a select statement

 PS3="Enter your choice: "      # PS3 is the prompt

# This menu contains three entries.
# If the user picks "I've had enough", the script ends.
 select menu_list in English francais "I've had enough"
 do
   case $menu_list in
     English) print "Thank you.";;
     francais) print "Merci.";;
     "I've had enough") break;;
     *) print "You can only enter 1, 2, or 3.";;
   esac
done

print "So long!"
```

Executing This Script

```
$ select4.ksh
1) English
2) francais
3) I've had enough
Enter your choice: 2
Merci.
Enter your choice: 3
So long!
```

Repeating the Menu Selections

The previous script lists the menu choices only once. The following script (which is almost identical to the previous script) allows the user to see the menu choices any time he or she wants. In fact, the only difference between this script and the last is in the value of **PS3**. This script tells the user to press **<RETURN>** to repeat the menu choices. In fact, whenever the user enters a blank line, the script will repeat the menu choices. The reason this works has to do with a bizarre variable named **REPLY**. I say "bizarre" because if you look at the script you won't see it. Nevertheless, it's there. (Trust me on this one.) The KornShell automatically assigns to **REPLY** whatever the user types in as a response to **PS3**. The **select** statement always looks at the value of **REPLY**. If the value of **REPLY** is the null string (a blank line), **select** redisplays the menu choices.

```
USAGE="usage: select5.ksh" # repeating menu entries

 PS3="Enter your choice (or press <RETURN> to repeat): "

# Create a potentially infinite loop.
 select menu_list in English francais "I've had enough"
 do
     case $menu_list in
         English) print "Thank you.";;
         francais) print "Merci.";;
         "I've had enough") break;;      # break ends the loop
         *) print "You can only enter 1, 2, or 3.";;
     esac
 done
```

Executing This Script

```
$ select5.ksh
1) English
2) francais
3) I've had enough
Enter your choice (or press <RETURN> to repeat): 2
Merci.
Enter your choice (or press <RETURN> to repeat): <RETURN>
1) English
2) francais
3) I've had enough
Enter your choice (or press <RETURN> to repeat): 3
```

Wildcards in Menu Entries

The **select** statement (like the **for** statement) allows you to use wildcards to generate a list of menu entries. Like **for,** the KornShell will expand any wildcards in a **select** statement to all appropriate object names. For example, the following **select** statement contains the pattern chapter? So, if there are six files that match this pattern, the menu will contain six entries (plus the "stop script" entry).

```
USAGE="usage: select6.ksh"  # wildcards in menus

 PS3="Status of which chapter: "    # PS3 is the prompt

 select menu_list in chapter? "stop script"
 do
   case $menu_list in
      chapter1)  print "Half completed.";;
      chapter2)  print "Nearing completion.";;
      chapter3)  print "Nearing completion.";;
      chapter4)  print "Completed.";;
      chapter5)  print "Nearing completion.";;
      chapter6)  print "Half completed.";;
      "stop script") exit 2;;
      *)         print "Improper choice.";;
   esac
 done
```

Executing This Script

Before running this script, create six files. It makes no difference what you put inside the six files; in fact, each of the files could be empty. Name the files chapter1, chapter2, chapter3, chapter4, chapter5, and chapter6.

```
$ select6.ksh
1) chapter1
2) chapter2
3) chapter3
4) chapter4
5) chapter5
6) chapter6
7) stop script
Status of which chapter: 4
Completed.
Status of which chapter: 1
Half completed.
Status of which chapter: 7
```

Wildcards in case Statements

The preceding script was useful, but the following script goes it one better by using wildcards within the **case** patterns.

```
USAGE="usage: select7.ksh"  # more wildcards in menus

 PS3="Status of which chapter: " # PS3 is the prompt

 select menu_list in chapter* "stop script"
 do
   case $menu_list in
       chapter[16])  print "Half completed.";;
       chapter[235]) print "Nearing Completion.";;
       chapter[4])   print "Completed.";;
       "stop script") exit;;
       *)            print "Improper choice.";;
   esac
 done
```

Executing This Script

If you created six files in order to run the select6.ksh example, you're ready to run select7.ksh. If you didn't create those files, you had better do so now. (Read the description on page 133.)

```
$ select7.ksh
1) chapter1
2) chapter2
3) chapter3
4) chapter4
5) chapter5
6) chapter6
7) stop script
Status of which chapter: 4
Completed.
Status of which chapter: 1
Half completed.
Status of which chapter: 7
```

A Practical select Example

This script shows a practical use of **select.** This script hides the syntax of UNIX commands from the user. The user can select the kind of operation he or she wants to perform without knowing the name of the UNIX command that gets it done.

```
USAGE="usage: select8.ksh"        # using OS commands in menus
 PS3="Please enter a number: "  # here is the prompt
 select cmd in "list files" "delete a file" "copy file" "quit menu"
 do
   case $cmd in
     "list files")
        ls;;    # UNIX command to list contents of directory
     "delete a file")
        print "which file do you want to delete?"
        read doomed file
        rm $doomed_file;;  # UNIX command to delete files
     "copy file")
        print "what existing file do you want to copy?"
        read file_to_copy
        print "what do you want to call the copy?"
        read file_to_create
        cp $file_to_copy $file_to_create;;# UNIX command to copy files
     "quit menu")  # if user enters 4, leave the script
        exit;;
     *)  # if user enters an unexpected number, print error message
        print "You did not enter a number between 1 and 4.";;
   esac
done
```

Executing This Script

```
$ select8.ksh
1) list files
2) delete a file
3) copy file
4) quit menu
Please enter a number: 1
a           chapter3       repeat_selections
ch.doc      chapter4       select_case
Please enter a number: 2
which file do you want to delete?
chapter3
Please enter a number: 4
```

Menus Inside of Menus (Submenus)

The following script shows you how to create a submenu, which is a menu within another menu. That is, one of the menus leads to a second menu.

In case you aren't familiar with UNIX commands, the ls command lists the names of all objects in a directory, and ls -l lists detailed information about every object.

```
USAGE="usage: select9.ksh"   # menus within other menus

main_menu_prompt="Main Menu: enter 1, 2, or 3 (or <RETURN>): "
submenu_prompt="Submenu: please enter 1 or 2: "

   PS3="$main_menu_prompt"  # assign main menu prompt to PS3
   select cmd in "list files" "delete a file" "quit menu"
   do
      case $cmd in
         "list files")
            # If user selects "list files", a submenu will appear.
            PS3="$submenu_prompt"   # assign submenu prompt to PS3
            select option in "quick list" "detailed list"
            do
                case $option in
                  "quick list") ls
                                 break;;      # leave submenu
                  "detailed list") ls -l
                                 break;;  # leave submenu
                  *) print "You must enter 1 or 2."
                       break;;
                esac
            done
            PS3=$main_menu_prompt;;  # change prompt back again

         "delete a file")
            print "which file do you want to delete?"
            read doomed file
            rm "$doomed_file";;   # UNIX command to delete files

         "quit menu")   # if user enters 3, leave the script
            exit;;

         *)      # if user enters a bad number, print an error message
            print "You did not enter a number between 1 and 3."
      esac
done   # end of outer select
```

Executing This Script

   $ **select9.ksh**

```
1) list files
2) delete a file
3) quit menu
Main Menu: enter 1, 2, or 3 (or <RETURN>): 1
1) quick list
2) detailed list
Submenu: please enter 1 or 2: 2
total 115
drwxrwxrwx  1 rosenberg     1024 Dec  2 10:24 a
-rw-rw-rw-  1 rosenberg    20492 Dec 11 10:35 ch.doc
-rw-rw-rw-  1 rosenberg    20219 Dec 11 10:32 ch.doc.bak
-rw-rw-rw-  1 rosenberg    20492 Dec 11 11:14 ch.doc.bu
-rw-rw-rw-  1 rosenberg     7939 Dec 11 10:31 ch.mm
-rw-rw-rw-  1 rosenberg     7275 Nov 20 09:23 ch.mm.bak
1) list files
2) delete a file
3) quit menu
Main Menu: enter 1, 2, or 3: 3
```

Notice how select9.ksh sets the value of **PS3** and then resets it later in the script. If the script had failed to reset the value of **PS3**, the user would have seen a misleading prompt at certain points.

The Desktop KornShell (dtksh)

The Desktop KornShell is a fascinating technology that, unfortunately, is destined for the sidebars of computer history rather than its crisp white pages.

The Desktop KornShell is essentially KornShell 93 plus Motif. For those unfamiliar with Motif, it is the dominant graphical user interface for the UNIX world. Motif is to UNIX what Windows 3.1 was to DOS. Back in the early 1990s, Motif was the fair-haired boy of the UNIX world. Nowadays, though, the boy is getting its butt kicked by the much slicker Windows 95/98/NT user interface.

In Motif programming, the programmer creates menus by laying out a set of objects known as *widgets*. For example, one kind of widget—the **Label**—displays text or a bitmap. By laying out four **Label** widgets in a row or column, you create a menu with four choices. When the user clicks on the desired widget, a *callback routine* runs. A callback routine is a function that executes when that menu entry is activated. For instance, consider a **Label** widget that displays the text Save. When this widget is activated, the associated callback routine probably would write unsaved data to the disk.

Motif programming is tricky. It is filled with slimy pitfalls and manuals that go from here to eternity. Motif programs usually are written in the C programming language. Writing programs with the Desktop KornShell won't make the pitfalls any less slimy, but because of the coding advantages of the Desktop KornShell, at least you'll be able to get the wrong GUI much quicker than with C.

Desktop KornShell programs do run slightly slower than those written in C. So, you might want to create a prototype in Desktop KornShell and then convert the production code to C. Or you could write most of the program in Desktop KornShell and then recode some of the sluggish parts in C.

The Desktop KornShell is available only through a package called the Common Desktop Environment (CDE). This package is distributed by several UNIX vendors. However, as of this writing, there is no CDE or Desktop KornShell available for any of the Windows operating systems.

For complete details on the Desktop KornShell, see Stephen Pendergrast's *Desktop KornShell Graphical Programming*.

REFERENCE

select — *Generate a menu.*

Syntax

select *variable* **in** *list*   **select** *variable*
do   **do**
   command1   *command1*
   ...   *...*
   commandN   *commandN*
done   **done**

where:

variable   is the name of a variable. The KornShell will set the value of *variable* to the item chosen by the user.

list   is a list of strings, numbers, or filenames. If the list contains any Korn-Shell wildcards, the KornShell expands the wildcards into filenames before beginning the loop.

command   is the name of any user program, operating system command, KornShell script, or KornShell statement. However, *command* is typically a **case** statement.

Quick Summary

The **select** and **for** statements share the same syntax. Both statements create loops; however, the primary purpose of the **select** statement is to create a looping menu. The elements of *list* form the menu's entries. So, if *list* consists of six elements, the menu will contain each of those six entries. The **select** statement places a number in front of each of the menu entries.

After displaying the menu entries, the KornShell automatically prompts the user to enter a menu entry. You control the text of the prompt by assigning a string to variable **PS3.** In other words, whatever text you assign to **PS3** will be the prompt that the user sees. The user then selects a menu entry by typing a number.

If you specify **select** *variable* without specifying **in** list, the list of elements consists of the entire set of positional parameters. See Chapter 9 for details on this syntax.

9 Command Line Arguments and Positional Parameters

This chapter describes command line arguments and positional parameters.

If You're New to Programming . . .

How do KornShell scripts get input data from users? So far, the scripts we've seen have prompted the user for information and then used the **read** statement to record the user's input. So, typical script invocation, prompts, and input might go something like this:

```
$ juggler.ksh    # invoke the script
Enter the juggler's name: Ignatov
Enter the number of rings this juggler can do: 11
```

Another way of gathering data is to have the user specify it when invoking the script, something like this:

```
$ juggler.ksh Ignatov 11   # invoke the script and pass it data
```

The user types the name of the script followed by one or more values. These values are called *command line arguments* because they are passed on the script command line. You need to know how to analyze command line arguments. Fortunately, such analysis is neither mysterious nor particularly difficult because the KornShell provides quite a few programming constructs to help you.

Command line arguments are one way of setting *positional parameters*. The set of positional parameters is a collection of values, each stored in a different cell and each accessible by number. That definition should remind you of arrays. In fact, the set of positional parameters is akin to an array of strings without a name.

The KornShell automatically assigns a special name to each positional parameter. For example, the KornShell gives the name **$1** to the command line argument immediately following the script name. See Table 9-2 on page 159 for a complete list of positional parameter names. The KornShell does support a powerful, if complicated, statement called **getopts** to help you analyze single-letter arguments known as *switches* or *options*. However, its purpose and syntax may be too convoluted for beginners.

If You're an Experienced Programmer . . .

Picking arguments off the command line can be a nuisance in many high-level programming languages. I've certainly thrown my hands in the air and screamed "argv!" on occasion. For this reason and others, many programmers use KornShell scripts as "front-ends" to their compiled programs. That is, they use the KornShell to swallow the command line whole and then feed a predigested version of it to the compiled program.

Broadly speaking, a user can specify three classes of information on the Korn-Shell command line:

- Simple arguments (such as numbers, strings, and pathnames)

- Single-letter options preceded by a minus sign (-**x**) or a plus sign (+**x**)

- I/O redirection operators (such as > or <)

This chapter describes simple arguments and single-letter options; the next chapter will describe I/O redirection operators.

Command line arguments are one form of *positional parameters*. The positional parameters have names like **$1**, **$2**, and **$9**. Command line arguments are just one way of setting the positional parameters. Another way is with the **set** statement. A third way is by calling functions (described in Chapter 10).

Command Line Arguments

This script demonstrates how to invoke a KornShell script and pass it arguments on the command line. The KornShell automatically assigns the first command line argument to positional parameter **$1,** the second command line argument to positional parameter **$2,** and the third command line argument to positional parameter **$3.** In addition, the KornShell will assign the complete list of positional parameters to **$*.**

```
USAGE="usage: param1.ksh arg1 arg2 arg3" # assigning $1, $2, and $3

print "The name of the shell script is $0"
print "The first argument after the shell script name is $1"
print "The second argument after the shell script name is $2"
print "The third argument after the shell script name is $3"
print

print "Here are all the arguments:"
print $*
```

Executing This Script

The **USAGE** line of this script tells us that in order to invoke this script properly, you need to specify the name of the script (param1.ksh) followed by three arguments. The usage line does not tell us what kind of arguments must be specified, so any three arguments ought to be just fine.

```
$ param1.ksh dog fish 352.5
The name of the shell script is param1.ksh
The first argument after the shell script name is dog
The second argument after the shell script name is fish
The third argument after the shell script name is 352.5

Here are all the arguments:
dog fish 352.5

$ param1.ksh spaghetti gnocchi "angel hair"
The name of the shell script is param1.ksh
The first argument after the shell script name is spaghetti
The second argument after the shell script name is gnocchi
The third argument after the shell script name is angel hair

Here are all the arguments:
spaghetti gnocchi angel hair
```

Notice that by enclosing angel hair in a pair of quotes, the KornShell interprets it as a single argument. Had the quotes been omitted, the KornShell would have assigned angel to **$3** and hair to **$4.**

Counting the Number of Command Line Arguments

The KornShell assigns the total number of command line arguments to the special positional parameter $#. Your script then can examine $# to determine how many command line arguments the user passed. For example, the following script requires the user to pass exactly one command line argument. By checking the value of $#, the script can determine whether the user really did enter exactly one argument.

Notice that the usage line in the following script contains $0 instead of the actual script filename. Remember that $0 stands for the name of the script file itself. Using $0 instead of an explicit filename ensures that the usage line will always match the actual filename, even if you rename the file containing the script.

```
USAGE="usage: $0 arg1"      # counting command line arguments
# This script expects the user to pass exactly one command line argument.
# If the user does not, the script reports the proper usage.

# The symbol $# equals the number of arguments.
 if (($# > 1))
 then
   print "You passed too many command line arguments."
   print "$USAGE"
 elif (($# == 1))
 then
   print "You invoked $0 correctly."
 else
   print "You forgot to pass a command line argument."
   print "$USAGE"
 fi
```

Executing This Script

Assume that the preceding script is stored in a file named param2.ksh.

```
$ param2.ksh # invoke script with zero arguments
You forgot to pass a command line argument.
usage: /users/barry/param2.ksh arg1

$ param2.ksh apricot  # invoke script with one argument
You invoked /users/barry/param2.ksh correctly.

$ param2.ksh apricot banana # invoke script with two arguments
You passed too many command line arguments.
usage: /users/barry/param2.ksh arg1
```

Giving the User a Choice of How to Enter Arguments

The following script is very forgiving. The user is supposed to pass an argument on the command line. However, if the user forgets, the script will prompt for a value and then use a **read** statement to gather the user's input. In other words, there is no wrong way to call this script.

```
USAGE="usage: param3.ksh [dir_pathname]"  # command line or run time

 if (($# > 0))
 then  # user has entered one or more command line arguments
    dir_name=$1
   # If user enters multiple arguments, the script ignores all
   # but the first argument.
 else # user has entered zero command line arguments
    print -n "Enter the name of one directory: "
    read dir_name
 fi

 print "You specified the following directory: $dir_name"
 if [[ !-d $dir_name ]]
 then
    print "Gee, I'm sorry, but $dir_name isn't a directory."
 fi
```

Executing This Script

```
$ param3.ksh # zero directories on command line
Enter the name of one directory: /home/jan
You specified the following directory: /home/jan

$ param3.ksh /home/jan # one directory on command line
You specified the following directory: /home/jan

$ param3.ksh /home/jan /home/jan/songs # two dirs. on command line
You specified the following directory: /home/jan
```

BEWARE: Can't Put Positional Parameters to Left of =

You can use the assignment operator (=) to assign the value of a positional parameter to other values but you cannot use = to assign a value to a positional parameter; for example:

```
x=$1      # right
$1="hi"   # wrong, positional parameter cannot be on left side
1="hi"    # wrong
```

Default Values of Positional Parameters

The following script is a subtle variant of the preceding one. In the following script, the user can optionally specify a command line argument. If the user does specify a command line argument, that argument will be used. However, if the user does not specify an argument on the command line, the script automatically assigns a *default* argument (/home/eddie).

The following syntax establishes a default value for a positional parameter:

result=${*positional_parameter*:-*default_value*}

So, if a *positional_parameter* (like **$1** or **$2**) is set, the KornShell will assign the value of that positional parameter to *result*. However, if the positional parameter is not set, the KornShell will assign the *default_value* to *result*.

```
USAGE="usage: param4.ksh [pathname_of_directory]"  # default values

# If user specifies at least one command line argument, then the value
# of dir_name will be $1. If user specifies zero command line
# arguments, then the value of dir_name will be /home/eddie.

 dir_name=${1:-/home/eddie}

print "checking the following directory: $dir_name"
if [[ !-d $dir_name ]]
then
   print "Gee, I'm sorry, but $dir_name isn't a directory."
fi
```

Executing This Script

```
$ param4.ksh  # don't specify a dir. on the command line
Checking the following directory: /home/eddie

$ param4.ksh /home/lena # specify a directory on the command line
Checking the following directory: /home/lena
Gee, I'm sorry, but /home/lena isn't a directory
```

The ${*positional_parameter*:-*default_value*} expression belongs to a class of expressions called *parameter expansion modifiers* explained on page 277.

Processing Positional Parameters with shift

The **shift** statement eliminates the leftmost argument(s). That is, **shift** slides all the positional parameters to the left by one or more positions. Incidentally, shifting too far causes a KornShell error. For example, if there are only four positional parameters, the statement shift 5 will cause an error.

```
USAGE="usage: shift_ex.ksh arg1 arg2 arg3 arg4 arg5" # shift statement

print "You specified $# arguments."
print "The first argument is $1."

print
shift 1
print "Following a shift, there are only $# arguments."
print "The first argument is now $1."

print
shift 2
print "Following a shift 2, there are only $# arguments."
print "The first argument is now $1."
```

Executing This Script

```
$ shift_ex.ksh apricot banana carambola daikon eggplant
You specified 5 arguments.
The first argument is apricot.

Following a shift, there are only 4 arguments.
The first argument is now banana.

Following a shift 2, there are only 2 arguments.
The first argument is now daikon.
```

Table 9-1 illustrates what happens.

Table 9-1. The Influence of shift on Positional Parameters

	$1	$2	$3	$4	$5
Original	apricot	banana	carambola	daikon	eggplant
After first shift	banana	carambola	daikon	eggplant	\<unset\>
After second shift	daikon	eggplant	\<unset\>	\<unset\>	\<unset\>

Processing Positional Parameters with $* and $@

The KornShell expands the expressions **$*** or **$@** to mean the value of all the positional parameters. The expressions **$*** and **$@** are interchangeable, though as we'll see on the next page, **"$*"** and **"$@"** have different meanings.

The following script averages all the integers specified on the command line.

```
USAGE="usage: average2.ksh int1 [int2 ... intN)"  # using $*

 integer running_total=0
 integer average

 if (($# == 0))  # if user didn't specify any arguments, stop script
 then
   print $USAGE
   exit 1
 fi

# Each time through the loop, the KornShell will assign the value of
# the next integer on the command line to variable number.
 for number in $*
 do
   ((running_total += number))
 done

# Divide running_total by number of arguments.
   ((average = running_total / $#))
   print "The average is $average"
```

Executing This Script

```
$ average2.ksh 6 4  # average two integers
The average is 5

$ average2.ksh 221 178 153 195 201  # average five integers
The average is 189
```

"$*" Versus "$@" Part 1

The KornShell expands "$@" into $# separate elements, where each element is enclosed in a pair of double quotes. For example, if there are three positional parameters, the KornShell expands "$@" into "$1" "$2" "$3".

The KornShell expands "$*" into a single element, where the entire set of positional parameters is encased in a pair of double quotes. For example, if there are three positional parameters, the KornShell expands "$*" into "$1 $2 $3".

As the following script shows, the difference between "$@" and "$*" has a significant influence on **for** loops:

```
USAGE="usage: expand1.ksh arg1 ... [argN]"  # demonstrates "$*" vs "$@"

# The KornShell expands "$@" into multiple elements
 print '"$@"' "creates a loop that iterates $# times:"
 for element in "$@"
 do
   print "\t$element"
 done

# The KornShell expands "$*" into one long element: "$1 $2 $3".
 print '"$*"' "creates a loop that iterates once:"
 for element in "$*"
 do
   print "\t$element"
 done
```

Executing This Script

```
$ expand1.ksh a b c d
"$@" creates a loop that iterates 4 times:
        a
        b
        c
        d
"$*" creates a loop that iterates once:
        a b c d
```

"$*" Versus "$@" Part 2

Another difference between "$*" and "$@" is that:

- The KornShell separates elements of "$*" with the first character of **IFS.**

- The KornShell always places blank spaces between elements of "$@".

IFS is a KornShell reserved variable. Chapter 12 provides details on this important variable. For now, assume that **IFS** is a string variable to which you can assign one or more characters.

```
USAGE="usage: expand2.ksh arg1 ... [argN]"  # influence of IFS

# By default, the first character of IFS is a blank space.
# Therefore, printing "$*" and "$@" will produce the same output
 print "First character of IFS is a blank space: "
 print '"$*":' "$*"
 print '"$@":' "$@"


 IFS=';:.'  # assign a semicolon as the first character of IFS.
# Now the difference between "$*" and "$@" will become apparent.  The
# KornShell will place a semicolon between each expanded element of "$*"
# and will still place white space between each expanded element of "$@".
 print "\nFirst character of IFS is a semicolon: "
 print '"$*":' "$*"
 print '"$@":' "$@"
```

Executing This Script

```
$ expand2.ksh apple "banana bread" "carambola cookies"
First character of IFS is a blank space:
"$*": apple banana bread carambola cookies
"$@": apple banana bread carambola cookies

First character of IFS is a semicolon:
"$*": apple;banana bread;carambola cookies
"$@": apple banana bread carambola cookies
```

The first character assigned to **IFS** influences the printing of an entire array. For example, suppose we assign three values to an array named **flowers:**

```
set -A flowers rose "bird of paradise" gardenia
```

Setting the first character of **IFS** to a semicolon influences ${flowers[*]} though not ${flowers[@]}:

```
IFS=';'
print "${flowers[*]}"    # Output: rose;bird of paradise;gardenia
print "${flowers[@]}"    # Output: rose bird of paradise gardenia
```

Using the set Statement to Assign Positional Parameters

Command line arguments are not the only way to assign positional parameters. Another way is with the ubiquitous **set** statement.

```
USAGE="usage: set1.ksh"    # the set statement

# Use set to assign positional parameters.
 set Ignatov Brunn Gatto Rastelli
# $1 now contains Ignatov; $2 contains Brunn;
# $3 contains Gatto; $4 contains Rastelli

 print "Here is a list of $# great jugglers: "
 for jugglers in "$@"
 do
    print "\t$jugglers"
 done

 set -s     # sort all the positional parameters in lexical order
 print "\nHere is the same list, sorted lexically: "
 for jugglers in "$@"
 do
    print "\t$jugglers"
 done

 set --      # this statement unsets all positional parameters
 print "\nWhere have all the jugglers gone? Long time passing: "
 for jugglers in "$@"
 do
    print "\t$jugglers"
 done
```

Executing This Script

```
$ set1.ksh
Here is a list of 4 great jugglers:
        Ignatov
        Brunn
        Gatto
        Rastelli
Here is the same list, sorted lexically:
        Brunn
        Gatto
        Ignatov
        Rastelli
Where have all the jugglers gone? Long time passing:
        # empty list
```

Processing Simple Switches with getopts

A *switch* (also called an *option*) is a command line argument that starts with a - or +
and is followed by one character. One-letter switches are all the rage in the UNIX
operating system. Use the **getopts** statement to analyze switches. Typically, you
specify the **getopts** statement as part of a **while** loop. The body of the **while** loop
usually contains a **case** statement. It is really the combination of all three KornShell
statements—**getopts, while,** and **case**—that provides a way to analyze switches.

```
USAGE="usage: getopts1.ksh [-x] [-y]"  # a simple getopts example

# This while loop executes as long as there are switches to evaluate.
 while getopts xy arguments
 do
   case $arguments in
      x) print "You entered -x as an option.";;
      y) print "You entered -y as an option.";;
   esac
 done
```

Executing This Script

The **USAGE** line in this script says that the user may optionally specify **-x** or **-y** when
invoking the script. If both options are specified, the order in which they are specified is irrelevant.

```
$ getopts1.ksh -x
You entered -x as an option.

$ getopts1.ksh -y
You entered -y as an option.

$ getopts1.ksh -x -y
You entered -x as an option.
You entered -y as an option.

$ getopts1.ksh -xy
You entered -x as an option.
You entered -y as an option.

$ getopts1.ksh -t -y  # enter an option other than -x or -y
getopts1.ksh[4]: getopts: t bad option(s)
You entered -y as an option.

$ getopts1.ksh +x        # nothing happens; user must specify -x
```

What If the User Enters an Invalid Switch?

The previous example (`getopts1.ksh`) did not handle undefined switches very gracefully. For example, when the user entered an undefined switch (such as **-t**), the script issued an error message. The following script reports undefined switches to the user but does not end the script.

Notice the colon (**:**) at the beginning of `:xy`. This leading colon tells **getopts** to:

- Set the value of **arguments** to **?** if the user specifies any option other than **x** or **y.**

- Set the value of a KornShell reserved variable named **OPTARG** to the name of the undefined switch.

In the **case** statement, you have to precede the **?** with the escape character \ or else the KornShell will interpret the **?** as a wildcard.

```
USAGE="usage: getopts2.ksh [-x] [-y]"  # handling undefined switches

while getopts :xy arguments  # note the leading colon
do
  case $arguments in
     x) print "You entered -x as a switch.";;
     y) print "You entered -y as a switch.";;
     \?) print "$OPTARG is not a valid switch."
         print "$USAGE";;
  esac
done
```

Executing This Script

```
$ getopts2.ksh -k -x
k is not a valid switch.
usage: getopts2.ksh [-x] [-y]
You entered -x as a switch.

$ getopts2.ksh -x -k
You entered -x as a switch.
k is not a valid switch.
usage: getopts2.ksh [-x] [-y]
```

On and Off Switches

By convention, a minus sign (-) preceding a switch means turn something on, and a plus sign + means turn something off. For example, in the following script, a -d switch sets variable **compile** to "on" and a +d switch sets **compile** to "off."

```
USAGE="usage: getopts3.ksh [+-d] [+-q]" # + and - switches

while getopts :+dq arguments
do
  case $arguments in
    d) compile=on;;    # don't precede d with a minus sign
   +d) compile=off;;
    q) verbose=on;;    # don't precede q with a minus sign
   +q) verbose=off;;
   \?) print "$OPTARG is not a valid switch"
       print "$USAGE";;
  esac
done

print "compile = $compile; verbose = $verbose"
```

Executing This Script

```
$ getopts3.ksh -d +q
compile = on; verbose = off

$ getopts3.ksh +d -q
compile = off; verbose = on
```

Processing Switch Arguments

The following script demonstrates how to analyze *switch arguments*. A switch argument is a word or number that follows a switch. For example, perhaps the switch -x requires a switch argument that specifies the number of x-coordinate pixels on the screen.

The user can enter a switch argument so that it fits snugly against the switch (for example, -x1024) or the user can specify any number of spaces or tabs between the switch and the argument (for example, -x 1024). Regardless, the **getopts** statement still can analyze the switch argument. In fact, this is one reason why **getopts** can be such a pleasure to use.

To tell **getopts** that a switch requires a switch argument, place a colon (:) after the argument name. Then, when you run the script, the KornShell will assign the switch argument to a reserved variable named **OPTARG**.

```
USAGE="usage: getopts4.ksh [-x number] [-y number]"  # switch arguments
# The colons after the x and the y tell getopts that -x and -y each
# require a switch argument.
 while getopts :x:y: arguments
 do
   case $arguments in
     x) print "You entered -x as a switch."
        argument_to_x=$OPTARG # getopts sets OPTARG to switch argument
        print "You entered $argument_to_x as an argument to x.";;
     y) print "You entered -y as a switch."
        argument_to_y=$OPTARG # getopts sets OPTARG to switch argument
        print "You entered $argument_to_y as an argument to y.";;
     \?) print "$OPTARG is not a valid switch."
         print "$USAGE";;
   esac
 done
```

Executing This Script

```
$ getopts4.ksh -x 1024 -y 800
You entered -x as a switch.
You entered 1024 as an argument to x.
You entered -y as a switch.
You entered 800 as an argument to y.

$ getopts4.ksh -x1024 -y800 # okay if arg. is flush against switch
You entered -x as a switch.
You entered 1024 as an argument to x.
You entered -y as a switch.
You entered 800 as an argument to y.
```

Processing Missing Switch Arguments

There is always a chance that the user will forget to enter a required switch argument. The following script notices the mistake and gives appropriate feedback. As you've already seen, a leading colon in the list of options helps you find invalid switches. In addition, the leading colon in the following script tells **getopts** to:

- Set the value of **arguments** to a colon (:) if the user forgets to specify a switch argument to -y.

- Set the value of **OPTARG** to the name of the switch with the missing argument.

```
USAGE="usage: getopts5.ksh [-x number] [-y number]" # missing args

while getopts :y: arguments
do
   case $arguments in
     y) height=$OPTARG;;
# If the user forgets to specify a switch argument to x or y,
# then the KornShell assigns a colon : to arguments.
     :) print "You forgot to enter an argument to $OPTARG";;
    \?) print "$OPTARG is not a valid switch."
        print "$USAGE";;
   esac
done
```

Executing This Script

```
$ getopts5.ksh -y 800   # user remembers to enter a switch argument

$ getopts5.ksh -y       # user forgets to enter a switch argument
You forgot to enter an argument to y
```

A Command Line Containing More Than Just Switches

The following script demonstrates how to analyze a command line that contains switches, switch arguments, and arguments unassociated with switches. Consider the following command line.

```
$ getopts6.ksh -x 1024 -y 800 red green blue # right
```

The preceding command line contains two switches (-x and -y) and two switch arguments (1024 and 800). The command line also contains three extra values (red, green, and blue) unassociated with any switches. On a mixed command line such as this, the user must specify switches and switch arguments at the beginning of the command line; that is, just after the name of the script. So, for example, **getopts** would not be able to find any switches on the following command line:

```
$ getopts6.ksh red -x 1024 -y 800 green blue # wrong
```

The KornShell reserved variable **OPTIND** stores the OPTion INDex of the command line argument that **getopts** is currently evaluating. That is, when **getopts** is evaluating the first command line argument (assuming it's a switch), the KornShell sets the value of **OPTIND** to 1.

```
USAGE="usage: getopts6.ksh [-x width] [-y height] [color1 ... ColorN]"
while getopts :x:y: arguments
do
    case $arguments in
      x) width=$OPTARG;;   # assign switch argument to variable width
      y) height=$OPTARG;;  # assign switch argument to variable height
      \?)  print "$OPTARG is not a valid switch."
           print "$USAGE";;
    esac
done


# OPTIND now contains a number representing the identity of the first
# nonswitch argument on the command line. For example, if the first
# nonswitch argument on the command line is positional parameter $5,
# OPTIND holds the number 5.
 ((positions_occupied_by_switches = OPTIND - 1))
# Use a shift statement to eliminate all switches and switch arguments
# from the set of positional parameters.
 shift $positions_occupied_by_switches
# After the shift, the set of positional parameters contains all
# remaining nonswitch arguments.

print "Screen width: $width"
print "Screen height: $height"
print "Screen colors: $*"
```

Executing This Script

```
$ getopts6.ksh -x 1024 -y 800 red green
Screen width: 1024
Screen height: 800
Screen colors: red green

$ getopts6.ksh -y2048 yellow cyan silver
Screen width:
Screen height: 2048
Screen colors: yellow cyan silver
```

BEWARE: The Colon of getopts

The colon (:) causes no end of confusion. You can place colons anywhere within the list of options. Unfortunately, the colon's purpose varies depending on where within the list you place it. A colon at the very beginning of the option list tells **getopts** how to handle undefined switches or switches that need an argument. A colon anywhere else in the option list tells **getopts** that a particular switch requires an argument.

For example, the colon in the following statement causes **getopts** to set the value of **thingy** to a question mark (?) when it encounters an undefined switch on the command line:

```
getopts :xyz thingy
```

On the other hand, the next use of the colon tells **getopts** to expect an argument right after the -y switch:

```
getopts xy:z thingy
```

You can specify multiple colons. For example, the following statement tells **getopts** to expect arguments with -x and -z, and to handle undefined switches by setting **thingy** to a question mark.

```
getopts :x:yz: thingy
```

The colon also helps scripts process missing switch arguments as shown on page 156.

Positional Parameters Syntax Overview

Whenever you invoke a script, issue certain **set** statements, or make a function call, the KornShell automatically assigns values to the positional parameters. Table 9-2 lists all the positional parameters and ways to access them.

Table 9-2. Syntactic Summary of Positional Parameters

Syntax	Meaning
$0	If command line argument, name of script; if function call, name of function; if **set** statement, pathname of the KornShell itself.
$1	First argument to script, function, or **set**.
$2 . . . $9	Second argument to script, function, or **set**. ... Ninth argument to script, function, or **set**.
${$N$}	N^{th} argument to script, function, or **set**; when N is greater than 9, N must be enclosed in the pair of braces.
$#	Number of currently set positional parameters.
$*	$1 $2 ... $N; that is, all positional parameters, each separated from the next by a blank character.
"$*"	"1c$$2$c...$N"; that is, all positional parameters; the entire set enclosed in a single pair of double quotes, and each parameter separated from the next by the first character (c) in **IFS**. For example, if the first character assigned to IFS is a comma, a comma will separate each positional parameter.
${*:$X$}	$X...$last; that is, all positional parameters from $X to the last positional parameter.
"${*:$X$}"	"Xc...$c$last"; that is, all positional parameters from $X to the last positional parameter; the entire set enclosed in a pair of double quotes and each parameter separated from the next by the first character (c) in **IFS**.
${*:$X$:quantity$}	$X ... ${$X$+($quantity$-1)$}; that is, $quantity$ positional parameters beginning with the Xth, each separated from the next by a blank character.
"${*:$X$:quantity$}"	"Xc...c{X+(quantity-1)}"; that is, $quantity$ positional parameters beginning with the Xth; the entire set enclosed in a single pair of double quotes and each parameter separated from the next by the first character (c) in **IFS**.
$@	$1 $2 ... $N; that is, all positional parameters, each separated from the next by a blank character.

Table 9-2. (Continued)

Syntax	Meaning
"$@"	"$1" "$2" ... "$N"; that is, all positional parameters, each enclosed in its own pair of double quotes and each pair of double quotes separated by white space.
${@:X}	$X ${X+1}... $last; that is, all positional parameters from $X to the last positional parameter, each separated from the next by a blank character.
"${@:X}"	"$X" "${X+1}" ... "$last"; that is, all positional parameters from the Xth to the last positional parameter; each enclosed in its own pair of double quotes and each pair of double quotes separated by white space.
${@:X:quantity}	$X ... ${X+(quantity-1)}; that is, quantity positional parameters beginning with the Xth, each separated from the next by a blank character.
"${@:X:quantity}"	"$X" "${X+1}" ... "${X+(quantity-1)}"; that is, quantity positional parameters beginning with the Xth; each enclosed in its own pair of double quotes and each pair of double quotes separated by white space.

Special Notes About Positional Parameters

Positional parameters greater than **$9** must be enclosed in braces; for example:

```
print ${11} # right
print $11   # wrong, means $1 followed by the digit 1
```

The KornShell imposes no limit on the number of positional parameters.
Positional parameters $* and $@ are identical; however, "$*" and "$@" are not identical. In brief, the differences are:

- "$*" expands to "$1c$2c...$n", where c is the first character assigned to the **IFS** variable.

- "$@" expands to "$1" "$2" ...   "$n".

REFERENCE

getopts — *Parse command line switches.*

Syntax

getopts *possible_switches var_name [data1... dataN]*

where:

possible_switches	is a list of legal one-character switch names, possibly including one or more colons. (See the previous page for a lengthy discussion of the colon.)
var_name	is any variable name.
[data1 ... dataN]	is one or more strings separated by white space. If you do not specify data, **getopts** will analyze the current set of positional parameters (usually the positional parameters passed on the command line). If you do specify data, **getopts** will evaluate data instead of the positional parameters. Generally speaking, you won't specify data as part of the **getopts** statement; however, specifying it this way may be helpful when debugging your script.

Quick Summary

The primary purpose of **getopts** is to analyze command line switches and their (optional) arguments. Switches begin with a + or - and are followed by a character. A switch can be optionally followed by a switch argument.

10 Functions

This chapter covers functions, which are named sections of code.

If You're New to Programming . . .

Picture yourself in Hawaii, pen in one hand, pineapple juice in the other, writing a short postcard to a jealous friend. Presumably, given the short length and inane content of the postcard, you won't need to worry much about organizing your thoughts.

Now picture yourself on a January's eve in Michigan, cranking out the definitive treatise on "Our Friend the Wolverine." Since your grand project weighs in at over 600 pages, you'll find it necessary to organize your book into chapters.

In the same vein, you won't have to give a lot of thought to organizing a five-line KornShell script. However, when writing a long script, you'll probably want to organize your script into *functions*. A function is essentially a chapter of your script.

Each chapter of your wolverine book will describe a discrete aspect of wolverines; for example, "Chapter 19: Wolverine Diet." Once the chapter has a name, you can refer to it as many times as you want from anywhere in the book. For example, in Chapter 2 you might write, "... and then the wolverine ordered take out. See Chapter 19 for details."

Similarly, each function in a script will perform a discrete aspect of the script and each function will have a unique name; for example—count_words_in_paragraph. Now that the function has a name, you can *call* the function whenever you need to count the number of words in a paragraph. You can call this function as many times as you like; perhaps you'll call it once for every paragraph that the script analyzes.

Lest we carry the analogy too far, please note that KornShell functions can do things that chapters cannot. In particular, when you call a function, you can optionally *pass* one or more values to it. For example, suppose you define a function named find_area_of_rectangle. When calling this function, you pass two values to it: the length of the rectangle and the width of the rectangle. In the KornShell language, the call will look something like this:

```
find_area_of_rectangle $length $width
```

When you pass grain through a mill, the mill's output is flour. Similarly, when you pass the length and width of the rectangle through the function, the function's output is the area of the rectangle. A KornShell function can optionally *return* one value to the part of the script that called it. For example, perhaps the function find_area_of_rectangle returns the actual area of the rectangle.

If You're an Experienced Programmer . . .

The KornShell, like most high-level languages, supports *functions*. (You may be more familiar with terms such as procedure, subprocedure, or subprogram, instead of function.) As with most other programming languages, you can use functions to organize a large script into smaller, more manageable units.

The caller can pass arguments to a KornShell function and can receive return values back from the KornShell function. Unlike many high-level languages, however, the KornShell does not provide function prototyping.

The code inside a KornShell function is executed only when called by some other portion of the script. However, the KornShell does check the function for syntax errors when you invoke the script, even if the function never gets called.

As with most high-level languages, the KornShell allows you to declare variables having function scope. That is, the values of such local variables can be accessed only from within the function in which they were declared.

BEWARE: Two Kinds of Functions

The KornShell supports two different styles of functions:

- *POSIX-style functions*, which start with the syntax *name*( )

- *KornShell-style functions*, which start with the syntax **function** *name*

POSIX-style functions have serious limitations; for example, there is no way to declare local variables inside them. Because of the limitations of POSIX-style functions, this book focuses exclusively on KornShell-style functions.

A Disorganized Script Without Functions

Here's a messy script, the kind of script you really shouldn't write. It contains a lot of redundant code.

```
USAGE="usage: funkless.ksh"  # a script that ought to have function
 print -n "What file contains the ingredients: "
 read object
 if [[ ! -f $object ]]
 then
   print "$object is not a file."
 elif [[ ! -r $object ]]
 then
   print "You don't have permission to read $object."
 else
   print "$object contains: "
   cat $object
 fi

 print -n "\nWhat file contains the data: "
 read object
 if [[ ! -f $object ]]
 then
   print "$object is not a file."
 elif [[ ! -r $object ]]
 then
   print "You don't have permission to read $object."
 else
   print "$object contains: "
   cat $object
 fi
```

Executing This Script

```
$ funkless.ksh
What file contains the ingredients: gamma
gamma is not a file.

What file contains the data: alpha
alpha contains:
78
49
```

The Same Script Organized into Functions

Here's a better script. It's better because now it's organized into functions.

```
USAGE="usage: funky.ksh"        # a script containing a function

# This function, named examine_the_file_if_possible, won't execute
# until it is called by some other portion of the script.
function examine_the_file_if_possible
{
   if [[ ! -f $object ]]
   then
      print "$object is not a file."
   elif [[ ! -r $object ]]
   then
      print "You don't have permission to read $object."
   else
      print "$object contains: "
      cat $object
   fi
} # The function ends here.

##################################################################
# The script will begin execution at the next line:
 print -n "What file contains the ingredients: "
 read object
 examine_the_file_if_possible  # call the function

 print -n "\nwhat file contains the data: "
 read object
 examine_the_file_if_possible  # call the function again
```

Executing This Script

```
$ funky.ksh
What file contains the ingredients: gamma
gamma is not a file.

What file contains the data: alpha
alpha contains:
78
49
```

Simple Function with One Argument

In this script, the caller passes a numeric value to a function named sqr. Within the confines of function sqr, the KornShell assigns the integer value to positional parameter **$1**. The function sqr takes the value (**$1**) squares it, and prints it. After the function finishes, the KornShell returns control to the statement immediately following the function call.

```
USAGE="usage: one_arg.ksh"        # passing a value to a function

####################################################################
# This is a function named sqr.  This function will be executed only
# if some other portion of the script calls it.
 function sqr
 {
# In this context, $1 is not a command line argument, but is the
# value of the argument passed by the caller.
   ((s = $1 * $1))
   print "The square of $1 is $s"
 }


####################################################################
# The shell script begins execution at the next line
 print -n "Enter a number: "
 read a_number

# Call function sqr and pass it the value of a_number as an argument.
 sqr $a_number  # call function sqr and pass $a_number to it
 print "Done."  # after function completes, control returns to this line
```

Executing This Script

```
$ one_arg.ksh
Enter a number: 7.3
The square of 7.3 is 53.29
Done.
```

BEWARE: When $1 Isn't the First Command Line Argument

By now, you may have noticed that function arguments look just like command line arguments. In fact, specifying arguments on the command line and specifying arguments to a function are two different ways of setting positional parameters. Because of the similarity, some programmers mistakenly assume that command line arguments automatically become function arguments. For example, consider the following script:

```
USAGE="usage: confused.ksh number"  # confused function call
function sqr  # a function to square a number
{
  ((s = $1 * $1)) # $1 is undefined because caller didn't set it
  print $s
}

sqr    # call function sqr, but don't pass any arguments to it
```

Inside the preceding sqr function, **$1** does not mean the first command line argument. Instead, within sqr, **$1** means the first function argument. Because the caller does not pass any function arguments to sqr, **$1** is undefined and problems ensue:

```
$ confused.ksh 7
sqr: line 2: s = * : arithmetic syntax error
```

If you want the first command line argument to ultimately become **$1** within function sqr, then write the script as follows:

```
USAGE="usage: clearer.ksh number"  # less confused function call
function sqr  # a function to square a number
{
  ((s = $1 * $1))
  print $s
}

sqr $1  # call function sqr and pass one argument to it, namely
        # the value of the first command line argument
```

The first command line argument to clearer.ksh will become the first function argument to sqr and happier results will appear:

```
$ clearer.ksh 7
49
```

A Function with Multiple Arguments

You can pass a function any number of arguments. The arguments don't all have to be the same data type. In the following example, function sqr expects to receive two arguments in which the first argument is a number and the second argument is a string.

```
USAGE="usage: multiple_args.ksh" # passing multiple values to a function

###################################################################
# This is a function named "sqr". It takes two arguments.
 function sqr
 {
   ((s = $1 * $1))
   print "$2: the square of $1 is $s"
 }

###################################################################
# The shell script begins execution at the next line.
 integer an_integer
  print -n "Enter an integer: "
  read an_integer
  print -n "Enter your name: "
  read your_name

# Call function sqr and pass it the values of an_integer and your_name.
# Enclose all string arguments inside a pair of double quotes,
 sqr $an_integer "$your_name"
 print "Done."
```

Executing This Script

```
$ multiple_args.ksh
Enter an integer: 20
Enter your name: Fox in Socks
Fox in Socks: the square of 20 is 400
Done.
```

The KornShell does not provide function prototyping. So, the preceding sqr function would not detect a problem if the caller passed only one argument or more than two arguments. To ensure that the user calls sqr correctly, a more rigorous version of the sqr function might begin as follows:

```
function sqr
{
  if (( $# != 2 ))
  then
    ... # code to handle error
```

A Script That Calls Another Script

One of the central dogmas of UNIX religion is that programmers should write every program, command, or script in such a way that it can be easily called by any other program, command, or script. In the following example, the script named call_another_script.ksh calls another script (square.ksh). Calling a separate script is pretty much the same thing as calling a function. Note that a script cannot access a variable defined in another script.

```
USAGE="usage: call_another_script.ksh" # this script calls another script

 print -n "Enter an integer: "
 read an_integer

# Call the script named "square.ksh" and pass the value of an_integer
# as an argument to it.
 square.ksh $an_integer
```

Here's the script that gets called. Its name is square.ksh:

```
USAGE="usage: square.ksh"

# Pass one input argument to this script when you call it.

 ((s = $1 * $1))
 print "The square of $1 is $s"
```

Executing This Script

```
$ call_another_script.ksh
Enter an integer: 6
The square of 6 is 36
```

Two Ways to Return Values

The called function or script is termed the *callee*. We've seen how the caller can send arguments to the callee. It is only natural to wonder how data can flow in the reverse direction—that is, from the callee back to the caller.

If you've programmed in high-level languages, you probably expect the callee to return values to the caller in a certain way. In fact, the KornShell's methods are rather unusual. Experienced programmers should momentarily suspend their experience and keep an open mind while reading this passage.

The KornShell provides two independent ways for the called function or script to send information back to the callee:

- The callee can send one integer value back to the caller by using the **return** statement. The **return** statement assigns an integer value to the predefined variable **$?**. The caller then can use or ignore the value of **$?**. On most operating systems, the integer returned by **$?** must be in the range 0 to 255. As such, the **return** statement is useful for returning error codes and other small numbers, but little more than that.

- The callee can send any kind of data back to the caller, if the caller uses the command output return parameter **$(...)**.

These two methods are independent of each other. The callee can return an integer value with **return**, and also return string data back to the caller if the caller uses **$(...)**. We explore both methods in the next few scripts.

Beyond the **return** statement and the **$(...)** syntax, one could argue that there are two additional ways for a function to communicate with its caller:

- The function could write information into a global variable and the caller could read that value. However, programming purists usually frown on this method.

- The function could write information into a file and the caller read data out of the file. Chapter 12 details file input and output.

Returning a Value from a Function with `return`

In the following script, the callee uses **return** to send an error status back to the caller. The returned integer must be between 0 and 255, but is usually 0, 1, or 2, where 0 symbolizes success and 1 or 2 symbolize different kinds of failure. So, the number returned by a function is analogous to the exit status returned by a script. The KornShell automatically assigns the returned value to variable **$?**.

```
USAGE="usage: return_integer.ksh"

function file_status
{
 # Return 0 if $1 is an existent readable regular file.
 # Return 1 if $1 is an existent, but unreadable, regular file.
 # Return 2 if $1 is not an existent regular file.
 file_to_test=$1

  if [[ ! -f $file_to_test ]]
  then
     return 2
  elif [[ ! -r $file_to_test ]]
  then
     return 1
  else
     return 0
  fi
}
#######################################################
# The script begins at execution at the next line.
 for potential_file in $*
 do
    file_status $potential_file
    returned_value=$?
    if (( $returned_value == 0 ))
    then
       print "Here are the contents of $potential_file:"
       cat $potential_file
    fi
 done
```

Executing This Script

Suppose that file mo.txt is a readable regular file but that oh.txt does not exist.

```
$ return_integer.ksh mo.txt oh.txt
Here are the contents of mo:
We've got the mighty mo.
```

BEWARE: $? Doesn't Stick Around Long

If you intend to use the value of **$?** returned by the **return** statement, you had better use it right away because it won't last past the next command. In fact, every KornShell statement, KornShell script, operating system command, and user program modifies the value of **$?**. So, for example, if you mistakenly add a **print** statement after the function call, the exit status of the **print** statement will overwrite the value returned by function get_age:

```
get_age             # call a function named get_age
print "anything"    # this statement overwrites the returned value
returned_age=$?     # assign exit status of print to returned_value
```

Using $(...) to Return Values from a Function

In the following script, the function sqr returns a string to the caller. To fetch this string, the caller must use the $(...) syntax to call sqr. The string returned by function sqr will be automatically assigned to variable **returned_value**.

```
USAGE="usage:return_string.ksh"      # returning values from functions

function sqr # square the input argument
{
  ((s = $1 * $1))
  print "Input -> $1; Output -> $s"
}

###################################################################
# The shell script begins execution at the next line.
 print -n "Enter an integer: "
 read an_integer

# Call function "sqr" and pass the value of an_integer as an
# argument to the function. Assign all the output of function
# sqr to the returned_value variable.
 returned_value=$(sqr $an_integer)
# By surrounding the function call in a pair of parentheses, we've
# effectively "bottled" all the output from function sqr and stored
# it in the variable "returned_value".

 print "Function sqr returned this value: $returned_value"
```

Executing This Script

```
$ return_string.ksh
Enter an integer: 6
Function sqr returned this value: Input -> 6; Output -> 36
```

By the way, there is nothing magic about the name **returned_value**; this name is not reserved. I could have just as easily named the variable **x** or **y** or **fred**.

Local Variables Versus Global Variables

By default, all KornShell variables are *global.* You can access or modify the value of a global variable from anywhere in the script.

If you declare a variable (with **typeset**, **integer**, **float**, or **readonly**) within the body of a function, that variable is *local* to that function. You can access or modify the value of a local variable only within the function in which it is defined. If you try to access or modify the value of a local variable from another function or from an area outside a function, the KornShell will not know the value of that local variable.

If you do not explicitly declare a variable, the variable is automatically global.

In the following script, variables **ocean, sky,** and **earth** are global. Variable **ocean** is global because it is explicitly declared at the top of the script, outside of any function. Variables **sky** and **earth** are global because they are never explicitly declared.

Variable **rain** is local to function think and variable **cloud** is local to function act. These two variables are local because they are explicitly declared within their respective functions.

```
USAGE="usage: local_global.ksh"  # comparing local and global variables

integer ocean=10  # ocean is global
######################################################################
function think
{
 integer rain=5  # rain is local to function think
 print "Within function think, rain = $rain"
 ((ocean *= 5))
 print "ocean = $ocean"
}
######################################################################
function act
{
 typeset cloud  # cloud is a string variable local to function act
 cloud="cirrus"          # okay to modify cloud
 print "cloud = $cloud"
 sky="blue"              # sky is global because it isn't declared
}
######################################################################
# The script begins execution at the next line:
 think                   # call function think
 act                     # call function act
 print "sky = $sky"      # access global variable sky
 print "Outside of function think, rain = $rain"    # cannot access rain
 print "ocean = $ocean"  # access global variable ocean
 earth="mother"          # create a global variable named "earth"
```

Executing This Script

```
$ local_global.ksh
Within function think, rain = 50
ocean = 50
cloud = cirrus
sky = blue
Outside of function think, rain =
ocean = 50
```

BEWARE: Global and Local Variables with the Same Name

It is legal, though not advisable, to declare a local variable and a global variable with the same name. For example, the following script contains two variables named **x**, one of them global and the other local to function **foo**. Note that these are two distinct variables, each having a distinct value. Assigning a new value to one of the variables has no effect on the value of the other variable.

```
USAGE="usage: samename.ksh" # confusing local and global variables
  integer x    # this is global variable x

function foo
{
  integer x    # this is local variable x
  x=3  # this statement doesn't change value of global variable x
  print "Within foo, the value of local x is $x"
}
##################################################################
# Script starts execution at next line.
 x=10
 print "The current value of global x is $x"
 foo
 print "The current value of global x remains $x"
```

Executing This Script

```
$ samename.ksh
The current value of global x is 10
Within foo, the value of local x is 3
The current value of global x remains 10
```

The moral—try not to confuse global and local variables having the same name.

By the way, you can declare two local variables in two separate functions, each having the same name. For example, two functions might each declare a local variable named **counter**. Although the two **counter** variables have the same name, they are distinct variables because they are local to two different functions. Changing the value of one variable has no effect on the value of the other variable.

Passing Arrays as Function Arguments: Call-by-Reference

You can pass arguments to a function using either of the following two mechanisms:

- Pass a value (typically, the value of a variable) as an argument. This is often termed call-by-value or pass-by-value.

- Pass the name of a variable (not its value) as an argument. This is often termed call-by-reference or pass-by-reference. The called function must create a **nameref** variable that will serve as a stand-in for the passed variable name. Whatever happens to the **nameref** variable will automatically happen to the passed variable.

Call-by-value is the more commonly used mechanism. So far in this chapter, all the example scripts that passed arguments to functions have used call-by-value. It is easier to implement. However, when passing a variable that represents a whole bunch of data—for example, when passing an array or a compound variable—call-by-reference is better.

```
USAGE="call_by_reference.ksh"  # passing arrays by reference

function double_each_value  # doubles each value in the input array
{
 # Create a nameref variable named ar. Associate ar with the
 # variable passed as the first function argument.  Whatever
 # happens to ar will happen to my_array
  nameref ar=$1

  integer elements_in_array=${#ar[*]}
  for (( c=0; c < $elements_in_array; c++ ))
  do
    (( ar[$c] *= 2 ))  # double each value
  done
}
###################################################################
# The script begins execution at the next line.
 for (( t=0; t<5; t++ ))
 do
   (( my_array[t] = t * t ))  # initialize an array with squares
 done

 double_each_value my_array   # call-by-reference
 print ${my_array[*]} # After function completes, my_array is altered.
```

Executing This Script

```
$ call_by_reference.ksh
0 2 8 18 32
```

Sorting Arrays Using Call-by-Value

Never say never. Sometimes, passing an array by value has its advantages.

For example, suppose you need to sort an array. Because the KornShell does not provide a built-in sort statement, you might be tempted to write your own sort routine. And what a fabulous way to spend your hours, puzzling your way through the intricacies of the shell sort or the recursive quicksort.

An alternative to writing your own sort routine is to use a little trick. Notice that the KornShell *does* provide a way to sort positional parameters. So, if you can just convert the array values into positional parameters, you'll be all set. The trick is to use call-by-value to pass the entire array to a function. By using call-by-value, the called function will automatically view the array elements as positional parameters. Then, simply have the called function sort the positional parameters.

```
USAGE="usage: sort_array.ksh"   # sorting an array

# This function sorts the input array.

function sort_input_array
{
 # The first element of the input array becomes $1, the second element
 # of the input array becomes $2, and so on.

 # Sort all the positional parameters in lexical order, from lowest
 # to highest.
   set -s

 # Print the sorted array.
   print   # blank line
   print "$*"
}
##################################################################
# The script begins execution at the next line.
# Store values in array as three-digit integers. If an input value takes
# up less than three digits, pad with leading zeros.
 typeset -Z3 array
 for (( count = 0; count < 5; count++ ))
 do
    print -n "Enter an integer: "
    read array[$count]
 done

# Call function, passing the entire array as an argument.
 sort_input_array ${array[*]}    # pass by value
```

Executing This Script

```
$ sort_array.ksh
Enter an integer: 187
Enter an integer: 93
Enter an integer: 462
Enter an integer: 853
Enter an integer: 8

008 093 187 462 853
```

Why was it necessary to declare **array** as follows?

```
typeset -Z3 array
```

The answer is complicated, but before getting into the whys and wherefores, I'd like you to try a little experiment. Delete `typeset -Z3 array` from the script and then re-execute the script with the same data. When you do, the sorted data will come out as:

```
187 462 8 853 93
```

Aha, the wrong answer, but why? The problem is that `set -s` sorts positional parameters based on their ASCII values rather than on their numerical values. Because the digit 4 in 462 has a lower ASCII value than the digit 8, `set -s` sorts 462 before 8.

By declaring **array** as `typeset -Z3`, you are telling the KornShell to pad integers that have less than three digits with leading zeroes so that the resulting integers will end up having three digits. When all the data has exactly three integers, a sort based on ASCII values will end up sorting the data numerically.

Discipline Functions Overview

Discipline functions are peculiar functions that you define but do not call. Instead, the KornShell automatically calls them for you when certain conditions are true.

When creating a discipline function, be sure to pick an appropriate name. All discipline functions must have two-part names in which:

- The first part must be the name of a variable, probably a variable used elsewhere in the script.

- The second part must be **get**, **set**, or **unset**.[1]

The two parts of a discipline function's name are separated by a dot. Thus, `meters.get`, `meters.set`, and `meters.unset` are legal names of discipline functions for variable **meters**.

The KornShell automatically calls:

- `meters.get`, whenever the script accesses **meters**.

- `meters.set`, whenever the script assigns a value to **meters**.

- `meters.unset`, whenever the script unsets **meters**.

All three of the discipline functions are optional. You can create one discipline function without creating the other two.

C++ programmers will recognize the `.get` discipline function as a pseudoaccessor method, the `.set` discipline function as a pseudoassignor method, and the `.unset` discipline function as a pseudodestructor.

Within a discipline function, you can use some or all of the following special KornShell-reserved variables:

- `.sh.name`, which holds the name of the variable you are examining

- `.sh.value`, which holds the current value of the variable you are examining

- `.sh.subscript`, which holds the name of the subscript (if you are examining an array variable)

---

1. If you extend the KornShell by writing your own **builtin** functions (see the section "Extending the KornShell by Writing C Functions" on page 187), your **builtin** functions can supply additional discipline function names. However, for the standard KornShell, **get**, **set**, and **unset** are the only three possible names.

Using a .set Discipline Function to Monitor a Variable

The KornShell automatically calls a .set discipline function whenever your script assigns a value to the corresponding variable. For example, the KornShell will automatically call discipline function distance.set whenever you assign a value to variable **distance**.

One of the simplest uses for this kind of discipline function is in debugging an errant script. If you have a variable that you suspect of causing problems, you can create a .set discipline function for it. Such a discipline function can tell you how the value of this variable changes and may help you determine when things start going wrong.

```
USAGE="usage: tracer.ksh"  # using discipline functions to monitor

# The following discipline function would not be in the final
# version of your code.  Use it as a debugging tool.
function xj.set
{
  print "TRACE: ${.sh.name} = ${.sh.value}"
}

integer xj=35     # xj.set will be called
(( r = xj * 2 ))     # xj.set will not be called
print "r = $r"

print -n "Enter a number: "
read xj   # xj.set will be called because rj is being assigned
```

Executing This Script

```
$ tracer.ksh
TRACE: xj = 35
r = 70
Enter a number: 22
TRACE: xj = 22
```

BEWARE: Data Type Declarations and Discipline Functions

In a sense, the discipline function *is* the data type of the variable. If you declare another data type for the variable—say **integer** or **float**—the discipline function won't get called. Depending on where in the script you specify a data type for the variable, the discipline function may or may not be called, or might be called for only part of the script.

So, kids, the moral here is to avoid specifying a data type on variables that rely on discipline functions.

Using a `.set` Discipline Function to Constrain a Value

The `.set` discipline function can be more than just a dull-witted reporter of variable values. You also can use it to constrain a variable's value. For example, the following discipline function ensures that if an input value is outside a certain range, this input value is not included in the set of stored data.

```
USAGE="usage: constrainer.ksh"  # using .set to constrain a variable
function pH.set
{
 # The legal range of pH values is 0 to 14, exclusive.
   if (( .sh.value >= 14.0 )) || (( .sh.value <= 0.0 ))
   then    # this value is illegal
      subscript=${.sh.subscript}
      bad_value=${.sh.value}
      print "Element $subscript contains illegal value: $bad_value"
      unset .sh.value   # remove that bad element
   fi
}

# Gather four input values, some of which may be bad.
for (( count = 1; count <= 4; count++ ))
do
    read pH[$count]
done

# What actually got stored
print "\nThe legal values were: "
print "${pH[*]}"
```

Executing This Script

```
$ constrainer.ksh
5.4
7.2
19.8
Element 3 contains illegal value: 19.8
2.5

The legal values were:
5.4 7.2 2.5
```

Recursive Functions

A *recursive function* is a function that calls itself. Many programmers find recursion daunting, although programmers who cut their teeth on Lisp actually embrace recursion. I don't use recursion much in KornShell programming, but I do find it useful when descending an entire directory tree. As such it is an alternative to the UNIX find command.

```
USAGE="usage: recursive_tree_traversal.ksh [directory]"  # recursion

######################################################################
# This function recursively descends a directory tree.
function expand_a_directory
{
 typeset object # object is a local string variable
 cd "$*"         # change directory
 for object in "$PWD"/*
 do
   # When the object is a directory, make a recursive call.
    if [[ -d "$object" ]]
      then
         expand_a_directory "$object"

   # Print the names of all regular files.
    elif [[ -f "$object" ]]
      then
         print "$object"
    fi

   # Ignore all objects except regular files and directories
 done
}
######################################################################
# If the user does not enter a directory name on the command line,
# default to the $HOME tree.
 expand_a_directory ${1:-$HOME}
```

Notice the frequent use of double quotes to enclose the names of directories. The double quotes keep us out of harm's way when directory names contain white space.

Executing This Script

Figure 10-1 on page 184 shows the organization of the /tmp/movies10000 directory tree.

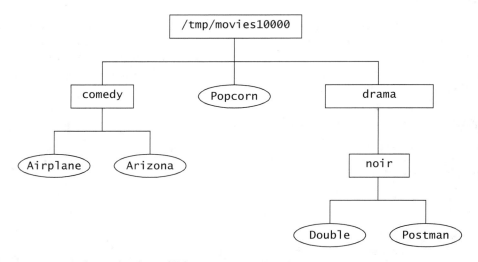

Figure 10-1. Organization of Directory /tmp/movies10000

```
$ recursive_tree_traversal.ksh /tmp/movies10000
/tmp/movies10000/comedy/Airplane
/tmp/movies10000/comedy/Arizona
/tmp/movies10000/drama/noir/Double
/tmp/movies10000/drama/noir/Postman
/tmp/movies10000/Popcorn
```

Autoloaded Functions

(Inexperienced programmers probably should skip this section.)

All the functions we have seen so far have been located in the same file as the caller. The KornShell also supports special *autoloaded functions* that live in a different file than the caller. You can create any number of files containing autoloaded functions.

A directory containing multiple autoloaded functions is analogous to a Dynamic Linked Library (DLL) on Windows or a shared library on UNIX. As in a DLL or shared library, autoloaded functions only get loaded if they are called. For example, suppose you create a directory containing ten autoloaded functions. If you write a script that requests two of those ten, the KornShell only loads those two. It does not waste time loading the other eight.

You can create directories of autoloaded functions to hold code that might be useful in more than one script. Making this directory accessible to others will allow multiple programmers to share the same code. Why reinvent the wheel?

Now let's turn our attention to a working example. First, create a new directory to hold your autoloaded functions; for example:

```
$ mkdir $HOME/my_funcs
```

Next, using a text editor, type the following autoloaded function into a file. You must name the file $HOME/my_funcs/sqr. If you give it some other name, this demonstration won't work.

```
function sqr      # an autoload function
{
   ((s = $1 * $1))
   print "The square of $1 is $s"
}
```

Next, type the following script into a file named `callauto.ksh`. The directory in which you place `callauto.ksh` is irrelevant.

```
USAGE="usage: callauto.ksh"  # calling an autoloaded function

# Tell the KornShell that sqr is defined outside this file:
 autoload sqr

 print -n "Enter an integer: "
 read an_integer

# Call function sqr and pass it the value of an_integer.
 sqr $an_integer
```

In the preceding script, the following statement tells the KornShell that function sqr is to be autoloaded:

```
autoload sqr
```

Executing This Script

Before running the script, you have to assign at least one directory to the reserved variable **FPATH**. This variable holds the names (separated by colons) of all the directories containing autoloaded functions. There is no default value for **FPATH**. Since sqr is in your $HOME/my_funcs directory, you need to make sure the $HOME/my_funcs is one of the directories assigned to **FPATH**. You can assign directories to **FPATH** on the KornShell command line, inside a start-up script (see Chapter 11), or inside callauto.ksh. The following statement assigns two directories to **FPATH**:

```
FPATH=$HOME/my_funcs:/usr/local/ksh_functions
```

When callauto.ksh runs, the KornShell will look for sqr inside directory $HOME/my_funcs. If sqr isn't there, the KornShell will search for it inside directory /usr/local/ksh_functions. If sqr isn't there either, the KornShell will issue the error message:

```
sqr: not found
```

We are finally ready to run callauto.ksh:

```
$ callauto.ksh
Enter an integer: 7
The square of 7 is 49
```

BEWARE: Tricky Loading Rules

If you assign the same directory to both **PATH** and **FPATH**, the KornShell automatically loads all the functions in that directory when the KornShell starts up. This is desirable if you will need those functions during the KornShell session.

You can put multiple autoloaded functions in the same file. If you do, you must create links to the file containing the code. For example, suppose a file named mymath contains functions named fibonacci and magic. In this case, you would create the links:

```
$ ln mymath fibonacci
$ ln mymath magicsquare
```

If you put multiple autoloaded functions in the same file, the KornShell will automatically load *all* the functions in the file when any one of those functions is accessed. For example, if a script accesses fibonacci, the KornShell autoloads fibonacci and magicsquare.

Extending the KornShell by Writing C Functions

Autoloaded functions provide one way of extending the KornShell; *KornShell extension functions* written in C provide another. To create a KornShell extension function, you must:

1. Write a KornShell extension function in the C programming language.

2. Build this function (and, possibly, other functions) into a shared library.

3. Register the KornShell extension function with the KornShell.

4. Test the new KornShell extension function.

Step 1: Write Code in C

Here's a KornShell extension function to get you started. Take out a text editor and enter the following code into a file named `hello.c`:

```
int
b_hello(int argc, char *argv[])
{
  /* How many arguments did user pass to hello? */
  if (argc != 1) {
    fprintf(stderr, "You must pass exactly one argument to hello.\n");
    return 1; /* error */
  }

  fprintf(stdout, "The argument you passed to hello was %s\n", argv[0]);
  return 0; /* success */
}
```

Let's dissect this simple code:

- Every KornShell extension function takes the same function prototype, which is the one shown for `b_hello`. It is the same function prototype that the `main` function has in traditional C programming.

- The name you specify for the function must begin with `b_`. Thus, `b_hello` and `b_hi` would be legal names, but `hello`, `hi`, and `main` would not be.

- A user can pass arguments to a KornShell extension function. The Korn-Shell automatically assigns these arguments to `argv` and writes a count of the number of arguments into **argc**. Yep, your KornShell extension function uses the same parameter passing protocols as the `main` function does in traditional C.

- Your KornShell extension function should return 0 if the function was successful and a nonzero integer if the function was not.

Step 2: Build This Function into a Shared Library

The mechanism you use to build C source code into a shared library varies from system to system. Please refer to the documentation that accompanies your C development environment.

Let's use the Solaris operating system as an example development environment. On Solaris, to build the KornShell extension function in hello.c into a shared library named libhello.so, you would type:

```
$ cc -K PIC -G -o ./libhello.so hello.c  # Solaris only
```

I chose to put the shared library in the current directory; you'll probably want to put all your shared libraries into a common directory that others can access.

By the way, you don't have to make a separate shared library for each function; that is, you can put multiple KornShell extension functions into the same library.

Step 3: Registering the KornShell Extension Function

The KornShell does not automatically scan certain directories looking for shared libraries of KornShell extension functions. Instead, you must explicitly tell the Korn-Shell about each new extension function by invoking the **builtin** statement. For example, to introduce an extension function named hello stored in shared library libhello.so, enter:

```
$ builtin -f ./libhello.so hello  # right
```

The preceding **builtin** statement specified the directory containing the shared library. If you don't specify the directory, the KornShell searches for the shared library in the directories of the **LD_LIBRARY_PATH** environment variable. Note that unless the current directory is assigned to **LD_LIBRARY_PATH**, the following command will fail:

```
$ builtin -f libhello.so hello  # might fail
```

You usually invoke **builtin** statements from one of the start-up scripts described in Chapter 11.

Step 4: Testing the KornShell Extension Function

To invoke the hello function, just type hello followed by an argument; for example:

```
$ hello world  # invoke the function correctly
The argument you passed to hello was world.
```

Invoking hello with the wrong number of arguments should generate an error:

```
$ hello planet earth  # invoke the function with too many arguments
You must pass exactly one argument to hello.
$ print $?  # what was exit status?
1
```

Limitations of KornShell Extension Functions

One of the best features of the KornShell is portability; the KornShell script you write on your system should run, without modification, on another system. However, once you start adding KornShell extension functions, that whole portability advantage disappears. However, if you're really willing to go that extra mile and develop shared libraries for all the platforms on which your KornShell script runs, your KornShell script should become portable once again.

The Desktop KornShell (dtksh) provides several functions to make Korn-Shell extension functions easier to write. For example, dtksh provides a **getenv** function that allows a KornShell extension function to obtain the value of any variable in the calling function.

The AT&T distribution of U/WIN also provides a wealth of helper functions for those programmers who want to write KornShell extension functions. A header file named shell.h contains prototypes for these helper functions.

Unfortunately, as these helper functions are not standardized, you can't count on them being available on all platforms that run KornShell. You can, however, always count on the ANSI C **getenv** function to get the value of an environment variable.

The calling conventions for KornShell extension functions have essentially the same limitations as the calling conventions for arguments passed to main in regular C programs. One of the biggest problems is that you cannot pass a value by reference to a KornShell extension function. For example, you cannot pass an entire array by reference to a KornShell extension function.

Ever Faster

Once you get a KornShell script working, you probably will become obsessed with making it run faster. This page suggests a few ways to turn a Kornsnail into a Kornschnell.

Wherever possible, try to use KornShell statements instead of outside programs. By outside programs, I mean any executable binary files, including operating system commands and user programs. When you invoke an outside program, the operating system must load the program from disk to main memory before it can be run. The loading takes a comparatively long time. Using KornShell statements instead of system commands or user programs generally saves time. That's because (among other reasons) KornShell statements usually are already loaded into main memory.

Math is relatively slow in the KornShell. To speed things along, declare your operands as integers or floats whenever possible. If you don't, the KornShell has to convert the operands from strings into floats, do the math, and then convert the operands back to strings.

Avoid creating extra processes.

A general rule of programming: Try to write the script in as few lines as possible. That is not to say that a shorter script is always going to outperform the longer version. For example, using a recursive algorithm often reduces code but makes scripts run slower.

Use the KornShell **time** statement to measure how long it takes your script to run. The **time** statement is a sort of software stopwatch. For example, to time a script named turtle.ksh, you'd issue the following command:

```
$ time turtle.ksh
real 0m0.50s
user 0m0.05s
sys  0m0.15s
```

The preceding **time** statement indicates that the script took a total of 0.50 seconds to run. During that 0.50 seconds, turtle.ksh itself used up 0.05 seconds. The turtle.ksh script required 0.15 seconds of kernel time. Presumably, the missing 0.30 seconds was used up by another process on the system. With these baselevel times recorded, you can experiment with turtle.ksh—changing this, removing that—and then retime turtle.ksh to see if it runs any faster.

By the way, if you specify **time** followed by a pipeline; for example:

```
$ time ls -l | grep 'rwx'
real 0m6.43s
user 0m0.23s
sys  0m0.46s
```

time measures the amount of time it takes to run *all* the commands in the pipeline, not just the first one.

Practical Example: The Game of moo

The game of moo hones a player's logic skills. This game is available on many UNIX systems as an executable C program. Here, we show a KornShell version of the game.

The game generates a random four-digit number, which the user attempts to guess in as few tries as possible. The script gives clues in the format "*m* bulls; *n* cows," where *m* indicates the number of correct digits in the correct position and *n* indicates the number of correct digits in incorrect positions. So, for example, if the clue is "2 bulls; 1 cows," you know that 2 digits in your guess are in precisely the correct position, 1 digit is in the wrong position, and 1 digit of your guess isn't part of the answer at all.

The script contains two functions:

- generate_random_digits, which generates the four-digit number that the user will try to guess

- give_the_user_a_clue, which counts the number of bulls and cows

The code not inside a function prompts the user to make a guess and then calls the other two functions as needed.

```
USAGE="usage: moo.ksh"        # a game of logic

# The following are global variables.
integer number_to_guess       # this is an array of integers
integer cows=0
integer bulls=0
integer mystery
###################################################################
# Start by generating a random four-digit number in which each digit
# is unique; for example, 0392 is an appropriate number, but
# 2393 is not appropriate because the digit 3 appears twice.
function generate_random_digits
{
 for (( c=1; c<=4; c++ ))
 do
    (( mystery[c] = RANDOM % 10 ))
 done

 # If the array contain any repeats, generate a fresh set of four.
  if (( mystery[1] == mystery[2] )) || (( mystery[1] == mystery[3] )) ||
     (( mystery[1] == mystery[4] )) || (( mystery[2] == mystery[3] )) ||
     (( mystery[2] == mystery[4] )) || (( mystery[3] == mystery[4] ))
  then
     generate_random_digits
  fi
}
```

```
#############################################################
# Figure out the number of cows and bulls in the user's guess.
function give_the_user_a_clue
{
# Count the number of bulls
 bulls=0
 for pos in 1 2 3 4
 do
    if (( mystery[pos] == guess[pos] ))
    then
      (( bulls++ ))
    fi
 done

# Count the number of cows
 cows=0
 for npos in 1 2 3 4
 do
    for upos in 1 2 3 4
    do
      if (( mystery[npos] == guess[upos] ))
      then
        (( cows++ ))
      fi
    done
 done
 (( cows -= bulls ))

 print "$bulls bulls; $cows cows\n"
}
```

```
# The shell script begins execution at the next line.
 integer number_of_guesses=0

generate_random_digits  # call function to generate a number

while  (( bulls != 4 ))  # user keeps guessing until correct
do
   print -n "Enter your guess: "
   read guess_as_a_string

  # Is the users guess a four-digit number?
   if [[ $guess_as_a_string == [0-9][0-9][0-9][0-9] ]]
   then  # yes, the guess has the correct format
     (( number_of_guesses++ ))
   else  # no, this guess is improper
     print "You entered an improper guess."
     continue
   fi

# The user's guess is a four-digit string; convert this string into
# four separate digits, assigning each digit to array user_guess.
   for pos in 0 1 2 3
   do
      (( position = pos + 1 ))
      guess[$position]=${guess_as_a_string:$pos:1}
   done

   give_the_user_a_clue
done  # end of while loop

print "\nYou figured out the answer in $number_of_guesses tries."
```

Executing This Script

```
$ moo.ksh
Enter your guess: 1234
1 bulls; 2 cows

Enter your guess: 5678
0 bulls; 0 cows

Enter your guess: 9123
1 bulls; 1 cows

Enter your guess: 0124
1 bulls; 2 cows

Enter your guess: 0134
2 bulls; 2 cows

Enter your guess: 4130
4 bulls; 0 cows

You figured out the answer in 6 tries.
```

function — *A callable named section of code*

Syntax

```
function name
{
  [variable_decl]

  [code]
}
```

where:

name   is the name of the function. Function names follow the same rules as variable names. See Chapter 2 for details on variable names.

variable_decl zero or more variable declarations (see Chapter 3). Any explicitly declared variables will have a value and scope local to function *name*. That is, if you explicitly declare a variable (with **typeset** or one of its aliases), that variable has meaning only within the function. By the way, you can explicitly declare a local string variable with the syntax:

> **typeset** *string_variable_name.*

code   zero or more KornShell statements. For example, *code* could be a Korn-Shell statement, an operating system command, or a call to another function or script. In fact, *code* could even be another **function**. However, if you embed a function inside another function, the outer function cannot access the inner function's local variables. Furthermore, the inner function cannot access the outer function's local variables.

Quick Summary

A function is a named section of your script. To invoke a function, the caller must specify the function's name optionally followed by one or more arguments. The optional arguments become positional parameters within the called function.

You cannot call a function unless it appears earlier in the script. In other words, you cannot make a "forward reference" to a function.

Note that *variable_decl* and *code* are both optional; however, every function must contain at least one of them. For example, the following function is illegal:

```
function badness  # illegal, because there's nothing between { and }
{
}
```

exit — *Halt execution of the current script and return to the caller.*

return — *Halt execution of the current function and return to the caller.*

Syntax

exit *[number]*   **return** *[number]*

where:

number   (optional) is any integer value representing the error status of the script
(**exit**) or the function (**return**). The default value of *number* is the current value of variable **$?**. In other words, if you do not specify *number*,
the exit status of the previous command is the value returned.

Quick Summary

A KornShell script finishes running and returns to its caller when any of the following happens:

- The KornShell executes the last line of the script.

- Your script receives a signal (such as **<CONTROL>C**) that tells it to stop running.

- Your script issues an **exit** statement.

If you do not supply an **exit** statement, the KornShell returns the current
value of variable **$?** to the caller.

A KornShell function finishes running and returns to the caller when any of
the following happens:

- The KornShell executes the last line of the function.

- Your script issues a **return** statement.

If you do not supply a **return** statement, the KornShell returns the current
value of variable **$?** to the caller.

When a KornShell script or function returns to the caller, the KornShell
assigns the value of *number* to **$?** in the caller.

11   Start-Up Scripts and Environments

This chapter explains start-up scripts, environment inheritance, dot scripts, and aliases.

Start-Up Scripts

The first thing that many programs do when they start running is to invoke their *start-up scripts*. Generally speaking, the purpose of a start-up script is to ensure that certain things happen to a program whenever it is invoked. For example, the start-up script for a certain graphics program might tell the program what size terminal the program is running on.

The KornShell supports three start-up scripts. The first two are *login scripts*, which are executed when you log in. A third start-up script runs whenever you create a KornShell or run a KornShell script by typing **ksh** followed by the name of the script.

When you log in, the system has to know which kind of shell to log you into. (After all, most UNIX systems support several different kinds of shells.) Typically, the system administrator at a UNIX site stores the identity of your login shell inside the `/etc/passwd` file. If your login shell is a KornShell, the system automatically executes the following two login scripts immediately after starting the KornShell:

```
/etc/proflle
$HOME/.profile
```

The `/etc/profile` script runs first. Every KornShell user on the system will share this script; therefore, it is a good place for the system administrator to store information that every user should have.

The `$HOME/.profile` (that is, `.profile` in every user's login directory) script runs second. Because this script is inside each user's **HOME** directory, each user can customize the script to his or her needs.

The third start-up script is called the *environment script*. The KornShell invokes the environment script when any of the following happens:

* You start up a KornShell.

- You invoke a script whose first line contains #! followed by the pathname of the KornShell, for example, #!/bin/ksh.

- You invoke a script by specifying **ksh** followed by its name (for example, **ksh bambi.ksh**) as opposed to just specifying its name (for example, **bambi.ksh**).

The KornShell variable **ENV** holds the pathname of the environment script. For example, if the value of **ENV** is $HOME/.kshrc, the system will automatically invoke the script located at $HOME/.kshrc under the conditions just listed.

Figure 11-1 summarizes KornShell start-up scripts. The end of this chapter contains a sample $HOME/.profile script and a sample environment script.

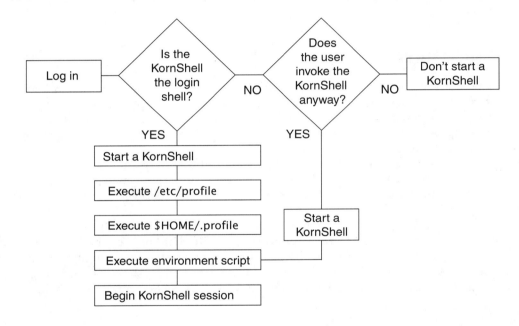

Figure 11-1. Sequence of KornShell Start-Up Scripts

Environments

A boy was arrested and dragged before the judge. Before passing sentence, the judge asked the boy if he had anything to say. "Please have mercy, Your Honor," the child begged. "I'm the product of a bad environment."

The preceding bit of melodrama has a certain relevance to KornShell users. When bad things happen to good shell scripts, the environment may be to blame. Sometimes even a well-meaning parent will fail to provide the proper environment for a child. But I'm getting ahead of myself. What's a child? What's a parent? What's an environment?

Suppose you are in the KornShell and you invoke a script by typing its pathname, for example:

```
$ myscript.ksh
```

The running script, `myscript.ksh`, is the *child* of the KornShell. The KornShell is the *parent* of the script. Other parent–child relationships exist on the system, but for the following discussion assume that the parent is the KornShell itself and the child is a KornShell script.

Every process has an *environment*. This environment is essentially a collection of traits, privileges, and resources held by the process.

Table 11-1. Environmental Characteristics a Child Inherits from Its Parent

Environmental characteristic	Does child inherit this from parent?
The parent's ability to read, write, or execute objects; that is, the parent's access rights to files, directories, and so on.	yes
The streams that the parent has opened.	yes
The parent's resource limits; you can use the **ulimit** statement to set or display these limits (see page 399). An example of a resource limit is the amount of main memory that a process can use.	yes
The parent's response to signals (see Chapter 15).	yes
Aliases defined by the parent.	no
Functions defined by the parent.	yes, if function is exported; otherwise, no
Variables defined by the parent, whether programmer defined or reserved (like **SECONDS** and **PATH**), but excluding the **IFS** variable.	yes, if variable is exported; otherwise, no
The value of the **IFS** variable in the parent (see Chapter 14).	no, even if exported.
The parent's option settings; to get a list of these settings, enter the command: `set -o`.	no

A parent cannot inherit any characteristics of its child's environment. However, as Table 11-1 illustrates, a child does inherit certain characteristics of its parent's environment.

Consider the KornShell variable **PWD**, which holds the current directory. This variable is part of an environment. If a child modifies the value of **PWD**, does the parent's version of **PWD** change? Let's find out with a simple experiment. Consider the following script:

```
USAGE="usage: talky_cd.ksh"     # child can't change parent

cd $1       # change current directory (which also changes PWD)
print $PWD
```

Before running the script, determine what the parent's version of **PWD** holds:

```
$ print $PWD # what is current directory before running the script?
/usr/kalonymus
```

Now, run the `talky_cd.ksh` script. This script alters its value of **PWD**.

```
$ talky_cd.ksh /usr/jessica    # run the script
/usr/jessica      # the value of PWD within the child
```

Now that the script is finished, did the script change the value of **PWD** in the parent's environment?

```
$ print $PWD
/usr/kalonymus    # same as before the script ran
```

No, the child does not faze the parent. Thus, an errant child cannot damage the environment of its parent.

Now let's look at the flip side of the parent–child relationship. What does a parent pass to its child?

By default, a parent passes its rights and privileges to its children. For example, if the parent has permission to read a particular file, so do its children. However, by default, the parent does not pass variables, aliases, or functions to the child. For example, suppose you declare a variable named **st** on the KornShell command line as follows:

```
$ st="world enough and time"
```

If you try to access **st** inside a KornShell script, the script won't have any idea what **st**'s value is. In other words, the KornShell script can't see **st**. For a child to see a variable or function of the parent, the parent must *export* it (as illustrated in Figure 11-2 on page 201) to the child.

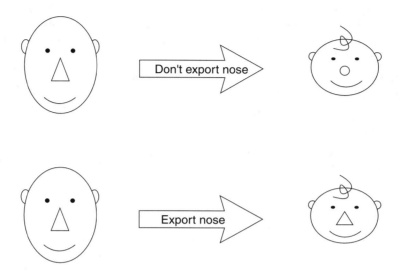

Figure 11-2. Children Inherit All Variables Explicitly Exported by Their Parents

For example, suppose that you issue the following statements in the KornShell itself:

```
$ st="world enough and time"      # declare variable st
$ export st                       # export st to children
```

Here's a script that accesses **st**:

```
USAGE="usage: marvel.ksh"          # experiment with export

print "st = $st"         # access the exported variable named st
st="would be no crime."  # change its value within the script
print "st = $st"         # print its new value
export st # will not cause new value of st to be accessible to parent
```

Remembering that the KornShell is the parent and the script is the child, here's what happens when we run the script:

```
$ marvel.ksh
st = world enough and time
st = would be no crime.
```

Notice that the child was able to see the value of the variable (**st**) that its parent exported. However, even though the child gamely issued an **export** statement, the child cannot pass the value of **st** up to its parent. So, if after running marvel.ksh, we ask what is the value of **st**, well, the value of **st** is exactly as the parent had left it:

```
$ print $st              # what's in st now?
world enough and time
```

By the way, you can use the following statements to get a list of all exported objects available to the current environment:

```
$ typeset -x             # list all exported variables
$ typeset -fx            # list all exported functions
```

Aliases, which we'll explain shortly, cannot truly be exported.

Dot Scripts

It is pretty easy to get frustrated by the parent–child rules. For example, the rule about a child not being able to change its parent can be a nuisance sometimes. Fortunately, the KornShell provides an interesting workaround to this problem called the *dot script.*

A dot script is a script that runs in the parent's environment. In other words, unlike a regular script, a dot script is *not* a child of the caller. The dot script inherits all of the caller's environment, including variables that haven't been exported.

A dot script can contain any code that a regular script can contain. In fact, the only difference between regular scripts and dot scripts is in how you invoke them. To invoke a regular script, usually you type its name; for example:

```
$ ficus.ksh   # run this script as a child
```

To invoke a dot script, you type a dot, then white space, then the name of the script; for example:

```
$ . ficus.ksh  # run this script as a dot script
```

Let's go back to the `talky_cd.ksh` script introduced earlier in this chapter. Here it is again:

```
USAGE="usage: talky_cd.ksh"     # child can't change parent

cd $1       # change current directory (which also changes PWD)
print $PWD
```

Running `talky_cd.ksh` as a regular script cannot actually change the working directory of the KornShell; however, running `talky_cd.ksh` as a dot script can; for example:

```
$ print $PWD # where are we?
/usr/kalonymus
$ . talky_cd.ksh /usr/jessica  # run talky_cd.ksh as a dot script...
/usr/jessica
$ print $PWD # which changes the current directory of the KornShell
/usr/jessica
```

You might be surprised to find that the environment script (**ENV**) is itself a dot script. That is, whenever you create a KornShell or run a KornShell script, the system automatically runs the environment script as a dot script. By the way, if you make any changes to the **ENV** file, you can test these changes by running the environment script explicitly as a dot script; for example:

```
$ . $ENV
```

Invoking a script as a dot script in the KornShell is like "sourcing" a script in the C shell.

Aliases

An *alias* is a nickname for a KornShell statement, KornShell script, user program, or operating system command.

One popular reason for creating aliases is to reduce typing. For example, I used to type the UNIX command ls -l all the time. Since I was forever typing ls -l, I decided to create an alias named g as a nickname for ls -l. I created this alias by placing the following command in my environment file:

```
alias g='ls -l'
```

With this alias in place, I now can issue the simple command:

```
$ g
```

instead of the longer ls -l. Since the KornShell expands g to ls -l, the following commands are synonymous:

```
$ g $HOME
$ ls -l $HOME
```

Another good reason to create aliases is to give commands new names that are easier for you to remember. For example, perhaps you're one of the many people who have trouble remembering the name of the pattern matching utility, grep. For this reason, you might place the following alias definition in your environment file:

```
alias pattern='grep'
```

Now that pattern and grep are equivalent, a user can use either one to search for a pattern; for example, the following two commands are equivalent:

```
$ grep 'poodle' canines
$ pattern 'poodle' canines
```

Aliases also can keep you out of harm's way. For example, consider the UNIX command rm, which deletes objects off the disk. By default, the rm command does not ask users for confirmation before blasting it to bits. To get a confirmation prompt ("Do you really want to delete this file?"), you have to use the -i option to rm. If you're a paranoid user who always wants to get confirmation, you might consider setting up the following alias in an environment script:

```
alias rm='rm -i'  # when you specify rm, KornShell substitutes rm -i
```

The KornShell comes with a few predefined aliases of its own. For example, the KornShell predefines **history** as an alias for hist -l because the word **history** is easier to remember than hist -l. If you want to see a list of all aliases, including those defined by the KornShell itself, just type:

```
$ alias
```

If an alias should become tiresome, you can use the **unalias** statement to remove it. For example, here's how to delete the alias g:

```
$ unalias g
```

You can put KornShell variables inside alias definitions. For example, the following alias definition prints the values of all the positional parameters:

```
alias pp='print $*' # if you type pp, KornShell substitutes print $*
```

Before you go wild with aliases, I'd better warn you that they are not as powerful as functions or scripts. For example, you can pass arguments to scripts or functions; the KornShell will convert the arguments into positional parameters. By contrast, if you try to pass arguments to an alias, the KornShell won't convert them into positional parameters. Instead, the KornShell will simply append the arguments to the end of whatever the alias expands into. For example, consider the following alias declaration:

```
alias pm='print "Try to pass $1 as an argument to this alias."'
```

The KornShell will expand the **$1** in the alias definition into the value of the first positional parameter, not the first argument to the alias. Let's experiment:

```
$ set apple banana  # assign "apple" to $1 and "banana" to $2

$ pm      # call pm without any arguments
Try to pass apple as an argument to this alias.

$ pm MYARG  # append MYARG to the end of the expanded alias
Try to pass apple as an argument to this alias. MYARG
```

Example of a $HOME/.profile **Start-Up Script**

The $HOME/.profile script is a very good place to specify the values of KornShell reserved variables and variables required by other programs. (See Chapter 14 for details on KornShell reserved variables.) Although you can put function definitions inside this script, it would be better to put them into one of your **FPATH** directories. (See Chapter 10 for details on **FPATH**.)

```
# The set -o allexport statement tells the KornShell to export all
# subsequently declared variables.
 set -o allexport

 PATH=.:/bin:/usr/bin:$HOME/bin:/usr/ucb  # define command search path
 CDPATH=.:$HOME:$HOME/games   # define search path for cd
 FPATH=$HOME/mathlib:/usr/common/funcs     # define path for autoload
 PS1='! $PWD>'                 # define primary prompt
 PS2='Line continues here>'   # define secondary prompt
 HISTSIZE=25                   # define "size" of history file
 HISTEDIT=/usr/ucb/vi          # use vi when editing hist commands
 ENV=$HOME/.kshrc              # pathname of environment script
 TMOUT=0                       # KornShell won't be timed out
 VISUAL=vi                     # make vi the command line editor

 set +o allexport          # turn off allexport feature
```

Example of an Environment (ENV) Script

The environment script is a very good place to put aliases. You also can put function definitions inside the environment script, but putting them inside an autoload function directory (see Chapter 10) usually is more efficient.

```
# Example environment script. Store this file at the pathname
# assigned to the ENV variable.

# If you want an alias to be accessible to a KornShell script, you
# must specify alias -x. The -x option does not truly export the
# alias definition to children, but does make it accessible to
# KornShell scripts.
 alias -x pattern='grep'
 alias -x disk='du'
 alias -x copy='cp'
 alias -x rm='rm -i'
 alias -x g='ls -al'
```

12 Input and Output

This chapter details input and output in the KornShell.

If You're New to Programming . . .

Even people whose experience with computers is limited to reading science fiction novels seem to have a pretty good idea what input and output mean. The term *input* refers to information that the computer gathers from the outside world. The term *output* refers to data that the computer presents to the outside world. Collectively, they are known as I/O.

Your body acquires all sorts of sensory input (for example, the things that you hear), processes it, and presents output (for example, the things you say) to the outside world. Similarly, KornShell scripts can acquire input, process it, and present output. For example, a KornShell script can gather 500 numbers (acquire input), find their average (process it), and write the average to a computer monitor (present output).

A wide variety of devices (for example, a mouse, a trackball, a light pen) can gather input for modern computers, but the KornShell typically is interested in input from only two sources:

- Input typed on a keyboard

- Input read from a file

You use the **read** statement to gather both kinds of input. Similarly, you can use the **print** statement to generate two kinds of output:

- Output written to the screen (that is, the monitor or the CRT)

- Output written to a file

(By the way, to a UNIX guru, keyboards and monitors *are* files.)

A third I/O statement, **exec,** allows KornShell programmers to explicitly open files before reading from or writing to them. Some beginners may find the **exec** statement rather complicated and may wish to skip over it.

If You're an Experienced Programmer . . .

I/O in the KornShell looks deceptively simple-minded. After all, the total arsenal of KornShell I/O consists of the following:

- A **read** statement for doing input

- The **print** and **printf** statements for doing output

- An **exec** statement for opening and closing streams

- Several operators (for example, |, <, and >) for redirecting input and output

However, after a little experimentation, you will discover the true power of these simple statements, particularly **read.**

The **read** statement gathers a line of input and then parses the line into tokens. This statement should remind C programmers of the **scanf** function. The KornShell **read** statement is more versatile, however, because it permits you to define token delimiters. For example, you might specify that commas and periods are token delimiters, but white space is not. To define a token, assign a set of token delimiters to the **IFS** variable.

To output, you can use the now-familiar **print** statement or the spiffy new **printf** statement. The **printf** of KornShell is a superset of the **printf** function of the standard C library.

The KornShell automatically opens three default streams: standard input, standard output, and standard error. You can get plenty of work done with these three streams. However, the KornShell also provides the **exec** statement so that you can create and manipulate additional streams. The **exec** statement is like the **OPEN** procedure of many Pascal implementations or the **fopen** function of the C library.

Using the **exec** statement, you can open sockets (see page 365 for details).

read, REPLY, **and Prompts**

The following script demonstrates the humble **read** statement. Since the book already contains lots of other **read** statements, the following script shows off a few new twists. In particular, this script shows how to combine a prompt and input into one statement. It also demonstrates one use of the KornShell reserved variable called **REPLY**.

```
USAGE="usage: read1.ksh" # fancy footwork with simple read statements

# You can prompt with a print statement then gather input with a read
# statement:
 print -n "Enter any string: "
 read st     # variable st is a string
 print "st = $st"

# Or, you can prompt and gather input in the same statement:
 print
 read name?"Enter a name: "
 print "$name"

# If you do not specify an argument to the read statement, the KornShell
# automatically assigns the input to a special KornShell variable
# named REPLY.
 print
 print -n "Enter a country: "
 read        #
 print "The value of variable REPLY is $REPLY"
 place=$REPLY
 print "The value of variable place is $place"
```

Executing This Script

```
$ read1.ksh
Enter any string: The Rain in Spain
st = The Rain in Spain

Enter a name: Don Quixote
Don Quixote

Enter a country: Portugal
The value of variable REPLY is Portugal
The value of variable place is Portugal
```

Reading Three Values

The following script illustrates a **read** statement that assigns values to three variables. The **read** statement divides up user input into tokens. In the following script, a token is any consecutive group of characters (letters, numbers, or punctuation marks). The first character in the group marks the start of the token and any white space character marks the end of the token. The KornShell assigns the first input token to variable **first,** the second to variable **middle,** and all remaining input to variable **last.**

```
USAGE="usage: read_multiple_tokens.ksh" # read three tokens

print -n "Enter your full name (first middle last): "
read first middle last
print "First Name: $first"
print "Middle Name: $middle"
print "Last Name: $last"
```

Executing This Script

If the user enters only two words, the KornShell assigns the null value to the variable named **last:**

```
$ read_multiple_tokens.ksh  # user enters only two words
Enter your full name (first middle last): Rachel Rosenberg
First Name: Rachel
Middle Name: Rosenberg
Last Name:

$ read_multiple_tokens.ksh # user enters exactly three words
Enter your full name (first middle last): Rachel Elisa Rosenberg
First Name: Rachel
Middle Name: Elisa
Last Name: Rosenberg

$ read_multiple_tokens.ksh # what happens if user enters four words?
Enter your full name (first middle last): Mar Joyce Tucker Rosenberg
First Name: Mar
Middle Name: Joyce
Last Name: Tucker Rosenberg
```

Ignoring Extraneous Input

The following script shows how to ignore extraneous input. For example, in the following script, the **read** statement expects to receive exactly three input tokens. If the user enters more than three tokens, all input after the third token will be assigned to a variable called **ignore_others.**

```
USAGE="usage: read3.ksh"  # ignoring extra input

print -n "Enter the three top finishers in the race: "
read win place show ignore_others

print "Winner: $win"
print "Second Place: $place"
print "Third Place: $show"
```

Executing This Script

```
$ read3.ksh  # user enters exactly three tokens
Enter the three top finishers in the race: Carl Michael Jessie
Winner: Carl
Second Place: Michael
Third Place: Jessie

$ read3.ksh # user enters more than three tokens
Enter the three top finishers in the race: Pat Henry Kelton Ben
Winner: Pat
Second Place: Henry
Third Place: Kelton
```

Reading Values Having Different Data Types

The variable arguments of a **read** statement don't all have to be of the same data type. For example, in the following script, variables **month, day,** and **year** are all arguments to the same read statement even though **month** is a string, and **day** and **year** are integers.

```
USAGE="usage: read_different_types.ksh"  # input of various data types

 integer day
 integer year

# Read in one line containing three tokens. The first token is a
# string, but the last two are integers.
 print -n "Enter today's date as Month Day Year: "
 read month day year   # month is a string; day and year are integers
 print "The current year is $year."
```

Executing This Script

```
$ read_different_types.ksh # user enters exactly three words
Enter today's date as Month Day Year: February 20 1998
The current year is 1998.
```

If the user mistakenly enters a noninteger value for **year**, the KornShell will assign the value 0 to year; for instance:

```
$ read_different_types.ksh # user enters exactly three words
Enter today's date as Month Day Year: February 20 NinetyEight
The current year is 0.
```

Rushing Users to Supply Input

Most interactive scripts are mellow. *("Take all the time you need to remember your name, man.")* However, some interactive scripts need to hurry along the user. *("Hey pal, I don't have all day. While you're trying to remember your name, I'm locking out other users.")* To get pushy, specify the **-t** option to **read**.

```
USAGE="usage: hurry_up.ksh"  # getting the user to respond quickly

 integer count=0

# The condition [[ ! $name ]] will be true as long as the user doesn't
# supply a name.
 while [[ ! $name ]] && (( count < 2 ))
 do
   print -n "Enter your name and be snappy about it: "
   read -t 10 name   # give user 10 seconds to type their name
   print
   (( count++ ))
 done

 if [[ $name ]]    # will be true if user supplied a name
 then
    print "Welcome to the system, $name"
 else
    print "Better study up next time!"
    exit 2
 fi
```

Executing This Script

```
$ hurry_up.ksh
Enter your name and be snappy about it:
Enter your name and be snappy about it:

Better study up next time!

$ hurry_up.ksh
Enter your name and be snappy about it: Milhouse

Welcome to the system, Milhouse.
```

The IFS Variable

By default, the **IFS** variable equals *white space.* That is, white space marks the end of one token, and any non-white-space character marks the beginning of the next token. The KornShell defines *white space* as the following three characters: space, tab, and newline in that order. (You usually generate a newline character when you press **<ENTER>** and you generate a space character when you press the space bar at the bottom of your keyboard.)

You can specify a different value of **IFS.** For example, the following script parses input into sentences by specifying a value of **IFS** equal to any character that ends a sentence (.!?).

```
USAGE="usage: read_IFS.ksh" # the IFS variable

# We haven't redefined IFS, so IFS is white space.
 print -n "Enter three words: "
 read word1 word2 word3
 print "First word: $word1"
 print "Second word: $word2"
 print "Third word: $word3"

IFS=".!?" # redefine IFS; IFS is now the three characters: . ! ?
# (The newline still marks the end of input.)
 print -n "\nEnter three sentences: "
 read sent1 sent2 sent3 junk
 print "First sentence: $sent1"
 print "Second sentence: $sent2"
 print "Third sentence: $sent3"
```

Executing This Script

```
$ read_1FS.ksh
Enter three words: red green blue
First word: red
Second word: green
Third word: blue

Enter three sentences: The cat. A fog? Silent shores of sand!
First sentence: The cat
Second sentence:  A fog
Third sentence:  Silent shores of sand
```

Notice that **sent1, sent2,** and **sent3** do not contain any periods, question marks, or exclamation points. Also, notice that the KornShell does not strip white space. Both of these effects are due to the redefinition of **IFS.**

By the way, if you want to read lines of text from a file verbatim, you should set:

```
IFS=''  # special definition to ensure verbatim reads
```

Input Longer Than One Line

Sometimes you may want a single **read** statement to gather more than one line. If the last character in an input line is a backslash (\), **read** assumes that the input continues on the next line. If this next line ends in a backslash, **read** assumes that the input line continues on the third line, and so on.

In some cases, you don't want the terminating \ to mean line continuation. That is, you might want to read in only one line at a time but the input line might just happen to end on a \. For that reason, the KornShell provides **read -r**. The **-r** tells the KornShell to treat a terminating \ as just another character of input.

```
USAGE="usage: read_r.ksh" # reading input longer than one line

print "Enter a paragraph. End each line (except the final one)"
print "with a backslash:"
read paragraph
print "$paragraph"

print
# Try it again; this time with read -r:
print "Enter a line that ends with a backslash:"
read -r paragraph  # ignore special meaning of closing backslash
print "$paragraph"
```

Executing This Script

```
$ read_r.ksh
Enter a paragraph. End each line (except the final)
with a backslash:
The cat. \
A fog? \
Silent shores of sand!
The cat. A fog? Silent shores of sand!

Enter a line that ends with a backslash:
The cat. \
The cat. \
```

BEWARE: Put Nothing After the Backslash

Nothing, not even white space, can follow the backslash. If any character does follow the token, the backslash won't mean line continuation. Putting white space after the backslash is a frustrating, hard-to-detect, very common cause of errors.

Using a Loop to Process Input

As noted back in Chapter 7, a **while** loop runs as long as its condition is true, but what is truth?

All UNIX commands and all KornShell statements return an error status (or exit status) upon completion. This error status is 0 if the command ran successfully and some integer other than 0 (usually 1 or 2) if it did not. The value 0 corresponds to a true condition, and any value other than 0 corresponds to a false condition.

In the following loop, the **read** statement returns the error status 0 when it can successfully gather input. Since the value 0 corresponds to a true condition, the **while** loop will continue running. When the **read** statement reaches the end of a file, the **read** statement returns 1 as an error status. Because the value 1 corresponds to a false condition, the **while** loop stops running.

```
USAGE="usage: readloop.ksh"      # reading data until end of input

 integer running_total=0
 integer a_number

 print "Enter integer values, one per line. When you are finished,"
 print "enter an end-of-file mark (usually <CONTROL>d or <CONTROL>z)"

# This loop will execute until the read statement reaches an
# end_of_file mark.
 while read a_number  # read until end of input
 do
   ((running_total += a_number)) # sum input integers
 done
 print "\nTotal = $running_total"
```

Executing This Script

```
$ readloop.ksh
Enter integer values, one per line. When you are finished,
enter an end-of-file mark (usually <CONTROL>d or <CONTROL>z)
10
15
11
<CONTROL>d*** EOF ***

Total = 36
```

Reading Text out of a File with <

This script is almost identical to the previous script. However, in the previous script, you provided input by typing data on the keyboard. By contrast, the following script takes input data from a file. The difference in the two scripts is the way you invoke them.

Before running this script, create a separate file named scores containing only integers (one integer per line). You can create this separate file with a text editor.

Use the < symbol to redirect standard input. If you don't specify the < symbol, the **read** statement will take its input from the keyboard. The < symbol tells the **read** statement to take its input from the specified file.

```
USAGE="usage: redirect_input1.ksh < datafile" # redirecting stdin

integer a_number
integer running_total=0

# This loop sums all the integers in datafile.
while read a_number   # read until end-of-file
do
   ((running_total += a_number))
done

print "Total = $running_total"
```

Executing This Script

Before running this script, use a text editor to place some numbers into a file named scores.txt. I placed three numbers into this file.

```
$ cat scores.txt # display the contents of file scores.txt
10
15
11

$ redirect_input1.ksh < scores.txt # read data from file scores.txt
Total = 36
```

With only 3 input integers, the advantages of input redirection might not be very obvious. However, with 3,000 input integers the advantages become clearer. Typing those 3,000 integers every time you run the script would be an awful job. Putting them into a file such as scores.txt once and then having your script read from the file is a far simpler solution.

Putting < Within a Statement

The following script is similar to the previous script. However, unlike the previous script (in which we redirected standard input for the entire script), the following script redirects input within one loop only. So, within the loop, the script reads from a file named `scores`, and outside the loop the script reads from standard input, which probably is the keyboard. In other words, this script has two different sources of input.

```
USAGE="usage: redirect_input2.ksh" # getting input from two sources
 integer a_number
 integer running_total=0

# This loop sums all the integers stored in file scores.  Note that
# this loop will read from scores even if the user redirects standard
# input on the command line.
 while read a_number
 do
    ((running_total += a_number))
 done < scores.txt      # redirect input within this while loop

# Since the while loop has finished, we can now get input
# from the keyboard.
 print -n "Enter one more integer: "
 read a_number
 print "Total = $((running_total + a_number))"
```

Executing This Script

Before running this script, use a text editor to place some numbers into a file named `scores.txt`.

```
$ cat scores.txt # display the contents of file scores.txt
10
15
11
```

Now run the script.

```
$ redirect_input2.ksh
Enter one more integer: 20
Total = 56
```

BEWARE: Common Input Mistakes

The **read** statement is a feast to the trained KornShell script writer, but beginners should be wary of the following sources of indigestion:

- If you want to redirect input within a loop, remember to place the <
  operator right after the keyword **done.** Do not put the < operator on the
  line that contains the **read** statement. Doing so probably will create an
  infinite loop. For example, the following statement causes the **read**
  statement to gather input from the same line (the first line of `file`) on
  each iteration of the loop:

  ```
  while read < file  # this will create an infinite loop
  ```

- Make sure that the file you are trying to read from is a regular file and
  is readable. To do so, use the object tests **-f** and **-r** before reading from
  the file.

- Extraneous input information can ruin your script unless you remember to supply an additional variable argument to every **read** statement
  (as in the `read3.ksh` example on page 213).

Many experienced KornShell scripters are in the habit of using **read -r**
instead of **read.** The **read -r** tends to keep you out of trouble more often than
just plain **read**.

Up Close and Personal with the `print` Statement

You've already seen **print** at least a zillion times in this book. Here, though, we focus on some of the lesser-known options and escape sequences that you can specify within a **print** statement.

```
USAGE="usage: print1.ksh"                        # escape sequences
 print "Ring a bell: \a"
# Notice how the \b causes print to overwrite the 'k'.
 print "Overwrite the k: Back\bspace"
# Use the -r option to turn off the special significance of the
# backslash.
 print -r "Interpret \b literally: Back\bspace"

# Use the -- option to turn off the special significance of minus signs
# embedded in text.
 print -- "-5 + 7 is +2"  # need the -- option to print this correctly

# Backslashes are a pain to output because they have special
# significance to the KornShell. To avoid trouble, place the text
# inside a pair of single quotes and specify the -r (or -R) option:
print -r 'The \ is difficult to output.'
# or place the text inside a pair of double quotes and specify \\:
 print "The \\ is difficult to output."
```

Executing This Script

```
$ print1.ksh # you'll hear a bell ring when you run this script
Ring a bell:
Overwrite the k: Bacspace
Interpret \b literally: Back\bspace
-5 + 7 is +2
The \ is difficult to output.
The \ is difficult to output.
```

BEWARE: Bad Options in `print` Statement

At some point or another, you're bound to encounter this cryptic error message:

```
print: bad option(s)
```

Let me guess: You were trying to print some text that started with a minus sign (-), weren't you?

To avoid this error message, use the double minus sign option (--) of print.

BEWARE: Wildcards Within Strings

Suppose that you assign input to a variable and then try to print the variable, but instead of getting the expected output, the **print** statement starts printing all sorts of gibberish that looks like filenames or directory names. The culprit could be wildcards inside the input string. For example, consider the following innocent-looking code:

```
USAGE="usage: wildstr.ksh"        # wildcards in input
 print "Enter a line: "
 read line
 print $line
```

Let's run it and feed it an input string containing wildcards; for example:

```
$ wildstr.ksh
Enter a line: The *s shine bright
The my_mistakes numbers scores words shine bright
```

Uh oh, the **print** statement expanded *s into the list of all objects in the current directory that end with the letters. If that's a problem, you can tell the Korn-Shell not to *glob* the input. If you're not familiar with the term, globbing is a verb (I glob, you glob, the script globs) that means "try to expand that pattern into a pathname." We've seen several instances (particularly within **for** loops) where glob is a many-splendored thing; however, in some instances (for example, in script wildstr.ksh) globbing is a nuisance. To turn off globbing, put this statement somewhere before the **print** statement:

```
set -o noglob
```

Use the following statement to turn globbing back on:

```
set +o noglob
```

An alternative to globbing (at least in the wildstr.ksh script) would be simply to recode the print $line statement as:

```
print "$line"
```

Getting Fancy Output with the printf Statement

If the **echo** statement is a Model-T Ford and the **print** statement is a rugged truck, then the **printf** statement is the temperamental sportscar of the lot—sexy, stylish, and almost guaranteed to put your script in the repair shop for brief periods. Let's pop the hood and take a look at the little devil.

For you C programmers out there—yes, the **printf** statement of the KornShell is similar to the **printf** function of the standard C library. The syntax is slightly different, but basically the KornShell **printf** is a superset of the C **printf**.

Here's a sample bit of code that demonstrates an easy use of **printf**:

```
integer score=93
printf "results = %d\n" $score
```

Running this code yields the output:

```
results = 93
```

Right after the word **printf**, you must supply a *format string*, which is everything between a pair of double quotes. The format string can contain any combination of conversion specifiers, escape sequences, and text. In the previous example,

- The %d is a *conversion specifier*; **printf** outputs the value of the argument that corresponds to this conversion specifier. Conversion specifiers begin with a percent sign %. The character(s) following the % describes the data type of the variable that is to be output and also may describe other characteristics of the output.

- The \n is an *escape sequence*; **printf** outputs the value of the escape sequence; for example, \n symbolizes a newline character, so **printf** outputs a newline. Escape sequences begin with a backslash \.

- The *text* is results = ; **printf** outputs all text verbatim.

The tricky element in a format string is the conversion specifier. Typically, you specify one conversion specifier for every argument that you want to output. For example, in the following **printf** example, the format string contains three conversion specifiers to correspond with the three integer arguments:

```
integer x=2
integer y=3
integer z=5
printf "The first three primes are %d, %d, and %d\n" $x $y $z
```

Running this code yields the output:

```
The first three primes are 2, 3, and 5
```

The first conversion specifier corresponds to the value of **x**, the second to the value of **y**, and the third to the value of **z**.

At this point, you might be saying, "Why bother with **printf**? After all, **print** is much easier to use." Fair enough, but note that **printf** can provide finer control over what gets printed. For example, in the conversion specifier, you can put a number between the % and the d to control the number of spaces the printed integer occupies; for example:

```
integer distanceA=385
integer distanceB=17
integer distanceC=45329
printf "%5d\n%5d\n%5d\n" $distanceA $distanceB $distanceC
```

Running this code yields:

```
  385
   17
45239
```

Notice how nicely the data lines up. In the preceding **printf** statement, the conversion specifier %5d told **printf** to print the values in five spaces. Since most of those values were less than 5 digits, **printf** padded the output with leading blank spaces.

Integers aren't the only kinds of values that **printf** can output. For example, you can use the %f conversion specifier to output the value of float variables:

```
float approximate_pi
(( approximate_pi = 22 / 7 ))
printf "%f\n" $approximate_pi
```

Running the preceding code yields the output:

```
3.142857
```

You can place information between the % and the f to control how **printf** outputs the floating-point value, for example:

```
printf "%.2f\n" $approximate_pi  # output 2 digits past decimal pt.
```

Running the preceding code yields:

```
3.14
```

When using an integer or floating-point conversion specifier, you can omit the dollar sign preceding a variable name. For example, the following are equivalent:

```
printf "%d\n"  quest    # okay to omit $ in front of quest
printf "%d\n" $quest
```

BEWARE: print and printf Handle Newlines Differently

By default, the **print** statement outputs a newline. To suppress the newline, use the **-n** option.

By default, the **printf** statement does *not* output a newline. To output a newline, put a \n in the text.

Table 12-1. Example `printf` Statements That Output Integer Values

integer y=573	Output	Comments
printf "%d" y	573	Prints as a base 10 (decimal) integer
printf "%o" y	1075	Prints as an octal integer
printf "%x" y	23d	Prints as a hexadecimal integer
printf "%+d" y	+573	Prefixes positive integers with a plus sign
printf "%#x" y	0x23d	Prefixes hex numbers with 0x
printf "%5d" y	573	Prints value of **y** so that it consumes five spaces
printf "%7d" y	573	Prints value of **y** so that it consumes seven spaces
printf "%1d" y	573	Even though the field width is 1, **printf** still prints the complete value of **y**.
printf "%*d\n" 7 y	573	Prints value of **y** so that it consumes seven spaces

Table 12-2. Example `printf` Statements That Output Floating-Point Values

float ab=35.289	Output	Comments
printf "%f" ab	35.289000	Prints without using scientific notation
printf "%e" ab	3.528900e+01	Prints using scientific notation
printf "%g" ab	35.289	Prints in the most efficient manner
printf "%8g" ab	35.289	Prints so that the value of **ab** consumes 8 spaces; because 35.289 consumes 6 spaces, prefix the value with two leading blank spaces.
printf "%1g" ab	35.289	Prints the complete value.
printf "$%.2f" ab	$35.29	Prints two digits past the decimal point, rounding as necessary. The dollar sign is printed verbatim.

Table 12-3. Example `printf` Statements to Output String Values

str="Lime Tree"	Output	Comments
printf "%s" "$str"	Lime Tree	Prints the string
printf "%11s" "$str"	Lime Tree	Pads with leading blanks to consume 11 spaces
printf "%3s" "$str"	Lime Tree	Still prints the whole string
printf "%.3s" "$str"	Lim	Prints only the first three characters
printf "%q" "$str"	'Lime Tree'	Encloses output in a pair of quotes
printf "%P" '^..$'	??	Converts the UNIX regular expression into the equivalent KornShell pattern
printf "%P" '..'	*??*	Assumes *arg* is a regular exp. to match entire line

Redirecting Standard Output with >

This script demonstrates one way of sending output to a file.

By default, the KornShell sends output to standard output, which usually is the monitor. You can redirect standard output by specifying the > symbol followed by a filename. If you do specify the > symbol when you invoke the script, all commands that produce output will write the output to the specified file.

```
USAGE="usage: redirect_output.ksh > filename"  # redirecting stdout

read a_string           # gather input from standard input
print "$a_string"       # write to standard output

read a_number           # gather input from standard input
print "$a_number"       # write to standard output
```

Executing This Script

There are no prompts in this script. After typing the name of the script, you must enter a string and then an integer. If the script contained prompts, they too would be written to the specified file rather than to the monitor.

```
$ redirect_output.ksh  # no output redirection
Silent sand.
Silent sand.
175
175

$ redirect_output.ksh > stuff  # redirect output to file stuff
Silent sand.
175
```

Let's check file stuff just to make sure that the data really did end up there:

```
$ cat stuff  # cat is the UNIX command that displays a file
Silent sand.
175
```

BEWARE: "But It Was Right There a Second Ago!"

You can wipe out a file in the wink of an eye with output redirection. For example, just watch this:

```
$ redirect_output.ksh > file_that_took_days_to_create
Silent sand.
175
```

It is my unfortunate duty to inform you that the former contents of your beloved file_that_took_days_to_create have been replaced by "Silent Sand. 175." You had a backup version, didn't you? You, er, didn't?

Let's replay this unfortunate incident, shall we? This time we'll do it the play-safe way.

```
$ set -o noclobber # turn on the noclobber option
$ redirect_output.ksh > file_that_took_days_to_create
ksh: file_that_took_days_to_create : file already exists
```

By turning on the **noclobber** option, we're telling the KornShell not to overwrite any existing files when we redirect output with >. Therefore, when we tried to write to file_that_took_days_to_create, the KornShell wouldn't allow it.

If you really do want to overwrite the file anyway, use >| in place of >; for example:

```
$ redirect_output.ksh >| file_that_took_days_to_create
Silent sand.
175
```

If you're the squeamish type, you probably should put the **set -o noclobber** statement in your KornShell start-up script. Otherwise, you might not remember until it's too late.

Another way to protect a file is to deny write permission to anyone (including yourself) on the directory in which the file resides. For example, suppose file_that_took_days_to_create is in a directory named important. You can protect the file_that_took_days_to_create and all other files in directory important by turning off write permission on important as follows:

```
$ chmod -w important
```

Appending with >>

The following script demonstrates how to append data to the end of a file with the >> operator. The script adds all the integers stored in a file named `values` and then appends the sum to the end of `values`.

If you specify >>*file* and *file* doesn't exist, the KornShell will create it. In a sense, the paranoid KornShell user may wish to use >> in place of > because >> never overwrites anything.

```
USAGE="usage: append.ksh filename"   # appending to a file

 integer running_total=0
 integer number

# Read data as long as there is data.
 while read number
 do
    ((running_total += number))    # keep a running tally
 done < $1

# Append the total to the end of the file that is symbolized by $1
 print "TOTAL: $running_total" >> $1
```

Executing This Script

Use a text editor to store some integers into a file named `numbers.txt`.

```
$ cat numbers.txt
3
7
6
```

Now run the script:

```
$ append.ksh numbers.txt
```

What happened to file `numbers.txt`?

```
$ cat numbers.txt
3
7
6
TOTAL: 16
```

Mixing < and >

The following script shows how one loop can read from one file and write to another.

```
USAGE="usage: redirect_io.ksh"  # using both < and > in a loop

print -n "Pathname of input file: "
read input_file
print -n "Pathname of output file: "
read output_file

# Read each line of the input file and write the first word of each
# input line to the output file.
while read first_token rest_of_line
do
   print "$first_token"
done < $input_file > $output_file        # redirect input and output
print "Done!"
```

Executing This Script

Use a text editor to put some text into a file named poetry.txt. Here's what I put into poetry.txt:

```
$ cat poetry.txt
Now you see a trick that I've never seen.
But wait! Am I lying? Is this part of some scheme?
For how can I who rely on matching hand to eye
still use my hands when my eyes are denied?
```

Now run the script as follows:

```
$ redirect_io.ksh
Pathname of input file: poetry.txt
Pathname of output file: first_words.txt
Done!
```

The preceding script created a file named first_words.txt that should contain the first word of every line; let's verify:

```
$ cat first_words.txt
Now
But
For
still
```

Pipes

The pipe operator (|) tells the KornShell to take the output from one command and use it as the input to another command. For example, the following three command lines:

```
$ command1 > /tmp/file # redirect output to a file named /tmp/file
$ command2 < /tmp/file # redirect input; get it from /tmp/file
$ rm /tmp/file         # delete /tmp/file
```

are equivalent to the following pipeline:

```
$ command1 | command2  # command1's output becomes command2's input
```

Switching to real commands, consider the following sequence:

```
$ ls -l > mylist          # redirect output to file mylist
$ grep 'Nov 14' < mylist  # redirect input
$ rm mylist               # remove temporary file
```

The following single pipeline is equivalent to the preceding three command lines:

```
$ ls -l | grep 'Nov 14'   # pipelines are more efficient
```

Some beginners find the concept of pipes a little daunting, perhaps because experts tend to use them with abandon. Try to imagine a metallic tube (a pipe) connecting two commands. Imagine that data flows out of the command on the left and into the command on the right.

A single line can contain multiple pipes. For example, the following example uses three pipes to connect four commands:

```
$ egrep '^dog ' canine_journal | sort | uniq | wc -l
17
```

The preceding pipeline counts the number of unique lines in file canine_journal that start with the word dog. Here's how the data flowed through the pipeline:

- The output of the grep command becomes input to the sort command.

- The output of the sort command becomes input to the uniq command.

- The output of the uniq command becomes input to the wc command.

- The output of the wc command goes to the terminal.

A rule of thumb: only the first command in a pipeline takes a filename argument.

Streams

Imagine yourself at a picnic on a gentle summer day. It's a hot day so you dip your toes in a nearby stream. The cold water flows from a mountain lake past your toes and out towards the sea. The water flows in one direction.

Now picture yourself running a KornShell script on a dark, depressing winter's night. The KornShell script generates output. It is almost as if that output flows from the script to your monitor. In fact, you might say that this flow is a kind of output data *stream*. Furthermore, an input data stream seems to carry data from the keyboard into your script.

Each KornShell script provides the following three default streams (all of which can be redirected):

- An input stream named *standard input* and numbered 0. By default, the standard input stream flows from the keyboard to your script.

- An output stream named *standard output* and numbered 1. By default, the standard output stream flows from your script to the monitor.

- An output stream named *standard error* and numbered 2. By default, the standard error stream flows from your script to the monitor.

By default, the **print** statement sends data on stream number 1, and the **read** statement gathers data from stream number 0. However, both **print** and **read** take an optional argument named **-u** that allows you to specify the stream number that you are writing to or reading from. For example, to send data out on the standard error stream (number 2), you specify **print -u2.**

In addition to these three default streams, you can use the **exec** statement to create other input and output streams. Figure 12-1 shows a script with five streams: three output and two input. In addition to streams 0, 1, and 2, the script supports an output stream (number 3) that carries data from the script to fileB and an input stream (number 4) that carries data from fileA to the script.

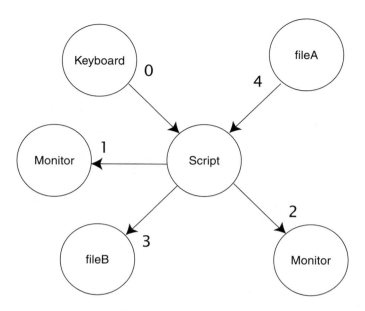

Figure 12-1. Input and Output Streams of a Typical Script

Redirecting Standard Error

By convention, all user programs, operating system commands, KornShell statements, and KornShell scripts are supposed to send error messages to the standard error stream. By default, the standard error stream flows to the monitor. However, the standard output stream also flows to the monitor. Therefore, by default, error messages and regular output are interspersed. When writing an interactive script, it's usually helpful to have error messages go to the monitor. However, there will be times when it would be better to send the error messages and regular output to different destinations.

To redirect the standard output stream, you use the operator >. To redirect the standard error stream, use the same > operator but precede it with the stream number, which is 2.

Here's a script for C programmers. It compiles C source code and produces two compilation reports: a brief report written to standard output and a detailed report (complete with error messages) written to standard error.

```
USAGE="usage: std_err.ksh C_file1 ... [C_fileN] 2> error_file"
# demonstrates standard error stream

 for file in "$@"  # all the files specified on the command line
 do
   print -n      "$file: "  # write name of file to standard output
   print -n -u2  "$file: "  # write name of file to standard error

# Compile the source code. The cc command automatically sends its
# error messages to standard error.
   cc -c $file

# The cc command also returns an error status (not to be confused with
# an error message) that symbolizes the success or failure of the
# compilation. An error status of 0 means that there were no compiler
# errors; a nonzero error status means that there were compiler errors.
   if (($? == 0))
   then   # write text to standard output and standard error
     print      "no errors."
     print -u2  "no errors."
   else   # write text to standard output only
     print      "errors, see error message file."
   fi
 done
```

Executing This Script

This script won't work unless you can feed it some files of C source code as input. By convention, compilable C source code filenames end with the .c suffix. So, the pattern *.c should match all C source code files in the current directory.

For best results, redirect the standard error stream when you invoke the script. The phrase 2> mistakes.txt redirects the standard error stream to the file named mistakes.txt.

```
$ std_err.ksh *.c 2> mistakes.txt   # redirect standard error stream
events.c:  no errors.
boffo.c:  errors, see error message file.
start.c:  no errors.
```

Now let's read the "detailed report" stored in file mistakes.txt:

```
$ cat mistakes.txt
events.c: no errors.
boffo.c:
(0143)      ab7="arf"
******* Line 143 of "boffo.c": "ab7" has not been declared.
start.c: no errors
```

BEWARE: Redirecting Standard Output and Standard Error to Same File

KornShell users often redirect standard output and standard error to different streams. For example, the following command line redirects standard output to file good and standard error to file bad:

```
$ zulu_peaceniks.ksh  > good  2> bad
```

Sometimes it is useful to redirect both standard output and standard error to the *same* file. To accomplish this, your first impulse might be to type:

```
$ zulu_peaceniks.ksh > medium 2> medium
```

However, the preceding command line will have a deleterious effect because regular output and regular error messages will overwrite each other in medium. The resulting medium may well be a jumble.

To redirect both standard output and standard error to file medium, you would enter:

```
$ zulu_peaceniks.ksh > medium 2>&1
```

The phrase 2>&1 tells the KornShell to redirect stream number 2 (standard error) to wherever stream number 1 (standard output) is going. Because stream number 1 is going to medium, stream number 2 also will go to medium. Regular output and error messages won't overwrite each other in medium.

Order is important. The following command line sends stream 2 to the terminal and stream 1 to medium:

```
$ zulu_peaceniks.ksh 2>&1  > medium
```

The KornShell analyzes operands from left to right. Therefore, the KornShell analyzes the 2>&1 prior to analyzing the > medium. When the KornShell analyzes the 2>&1, stream 1 is flowing to the terminal. Therefore, stream number 2 also heads to the terminal. Then the KornShell analyzes > medium, which tells the KornShell to redirect stream number 1 to medium. However, the redirection of standard output (> medium) is too late to influence stream number 2, which is already winging its way to the terminal.

Opening Files with exec

The following script explicitly uses the **exec** statement to open an input stream from file poem to the script. The stream number is 8. If you're used to programming in the C language, then you might find the **exec** statement analogous to the **fopen** function of the C library. (If you haven't programmed too much, you might find the next few examples rather difficult.)

```
USAGE="usage: open_one_stream.ksh"  # opening a file with exec

# Use exec to open a file for reading.
 exec 8< poem.txt          # make file descriptor 8 a synonym for "poem.txt"
# We have now opened a stream from the file "poem.txt"
# to our KornShell script.

# Read the first three lines of this file.
 read -u8 first_line  # read the first line of the file
 read -u8 second_line
 read -u8 third_line
 print "$first_line $second_line $third_line"

# Using read without -u8 won't work quite as well.
 read first_line < poem.txt  # this reads the first line
 read second_line < poem.txt # this also reads the first line
 read third_line < poem.txt  # this also reads the first line
 print "$first_line $second_line $third_line"
```

Executing This Script

Use a text editor to place the following sophomoric lines inside file poem.txt:

```
$ cat poem.txt
A blue wave thunders.
Sand swirls in a summer storm.
Now all is quiet.
```

Now run the shell script:

```
$ open_one_stream.ksh
A blue wave thunders. Sand swirls in a summer storm. Now all is quiet.
A blue wave thunders. A blue wave thunders. A blue wave thunders.
```

Using exec to Do I/O on Multiple Files

The following script demonstrates a fairly sophisticated use of **exec.** This script does a line-by-line comparison of two text files (vaguely like the UNIX diff command). If line N in the first file matches line N in the second file, the script writes line N to a file named match.txt. However, if line N in the first file does not match line N in the second, the script writes both nonmatching lines to a file named nomatch.txt.

All together, the script uses **exec** to open four different streams (the two input files, output file match.txt, and output file nomatch.txt).

```
USAGE="usage: open_four_streams.ksh file1 file2"  # complex exec
 if (($# != 2))   # if user forgets command line arguments, stop script
   then
      print "$USAGE"
      exit 1
   elif [[ (-f $1) && (-f $2) && (-r $1) && (-r $2) ]]
# Both objects must be readable regular files.
   then    # use exec to open four files
      exec 3< $1          # open $1 for input
      exec 4< $2          # open $2 for input
      exec 5> match.txt   # open file "match.txt" for output
      exec 6> nomatch.txt # open file "nomatch.txt" for output
   else    # if user enters bad arguments, stop script
      print "$USAGE"
      exit 1
 fi

 while read -u3 lineA  # read a line out of $1
 do
    read -u4 lineB    # read a line out of $2
    if [[ "$lineA" = "$lineB" ]]  # compare the two input lines
    then   # send matching lines to "match.txt"
       print -u5 "$lineA"
    else   # send nonmatching lines to "nomatch.txt"
       print -u6 "$lineA; $lineB"
    fi
 done

 print "Done!"
```

Executing This Script

Use a text editor to create two different files. Ideally, the two files should be similar, though not identical, and both files should have the same number of lines. I created files named poemA.txt and poemB.txt. Here are their contents:

```
$ cat poemA.txt
I can juggle my hat
and this marble so round
and a tiny tot's shoe
that I saw on the ground.

$ cat poemB.txt
I can juggle my hat
and this marble I found
and a tiny tot's shoe
that I saw on the ground.
```

Now let's run the script:

```
$ open_four_streams.ksh poemA.txt poemB.txt   # compare the two poems
Done!
```

Running the script produced two files: match.txt and nomatch.txt. Here are their contents:

```
$ cat match.txt       # these lines match
I can juggle my hat
and a tiny tot's shoe
that I saw on the ground.

$ cat nomatch.txt   # these lines don't match
and this marble so round; and this marble I found
```

As currently written, the script assumes that both input files contain exactly the same number of lines. You might try experimenting with the script to get it to handle files having different numbers of lines. You also might try combining the two **read** statements through a Boolean operation. Here are a couple of statements to try out:

```
while read -u3 lineA || read -u4 lineB

while read -u3 lineA && read -u4 lineB
```

Closing Streams

If you don't explicitly close a stream, the KornShell will close it for you when the script ends. However, usually it is best to keep streams open for only a short time. Your operating system imposes a limit on the number of streams that a process can open. As you bump up against that limit, you will have to close some streams.

To close a stream, use the syntax:

```
exec number<&-    # to close an input stream
exec number>&-    # to close an output stream
```

The following script opens an input stream, prints the file's second line to standard output, then closes the file. The script repeats this procedure for every regular file in the current directory.

```
USAGE="usage: close_stream.ksh"  # opening and closing streams

for object in *             # list of objects in current directory
do
  if [[ -f $object ]] && [[ -r $object ]]
  then                      # analyze regular readable files only
    print -n "$object: "
    exec 3< $object         # open file $object for reading
    read -u3 first_line     # read the first line of this file; ignore it
    read -u3 second_line    # read the second line of this file
    print "$second_line"    # print second line to standard output
    exec 3<&-               # close stream number 3
  fi
done
```

Executing This Script

```
$ close_stream.ksh  # print second line of each object in current dir.
apple: granny smith's closed higher today.
matching: and a tiny tot's shoe
poetry: allergic syllables sneezed into a dusty haiku.
sky: generally blue except around dawn or dusk
whatever: Like, that is so 5 minutes ago
```

Using $(...) to Assign the Output of a Command to a Variable

By default, the KornShell writes the output of every script, user program, or operating system command to standard output. As shown earlier in this chapter, you can redirect standard output to a file. It turns out that you also can redirect standard output to a variable. In other words, you can tell the KornShell to suppress writing output to a file or to the monitor and write it into a variable instead. To accomplish this feat, use this syntax:

variable=$(*command*)

The following script explores some of the things that you can do with this syntax.

```
USAGE="usage: cmd_out.ksh file word1 word2" # capturing command output

# Specifying $(date) tells the KornShell to run the date command
# and insert the output of the date command in the text.
 print "Today's date is $(date)"  # call date command
# You can also assign the output of the date command to a variable.
 date_variable=$(date)    # call date command again
 print "Today's date is $date_variable"

# The grep command returns the lines of a file that contain a
# certain word. We can assign all these lines to a variable.
 lines_containing_pattern=$(grep "$2" $1)
 print "\nHere's where the word $2 appears in file $1:"
 print "$lines_containing_pattern"

# grep -c  returns a count of the number of lines
# containing a certain word.
 frequency_of_word1=$(grep -c "$2" $1)
 frequency_of_word2=$(grep -c "$3" $1)
 if (( frequency_of_word1 > frequency_of_word2 ))
 then
   print "\n$2 appears in more lines than $3."
 elif (( frequency_of_word1 < frequency_of_word2 ))
 then
   print "\n$3 appears in more lines than $2."
 else
   print "\n$3 and $2 appear in the same number of lines."
 fi
```

Executing This Script

Using a text editor, put some text into a file. Here's the text that I used:

```
$ cat my_text.txt
sunflower sam
ate peanuts and jam
while sunflower sue
had nothing to do.
```

Now, we'll run the script, specifying the name of the file my_text.txt as the first argument, and two words from the file, sunflower and peanut, as the second and third arguments, respectively.

```
$ cmd_out.ksh my_text.txt sunflower peanut
Today's date is Fri Feb 22 10:55:26 EST 1998
Today's date is Fri Feb 22 10:55:27 EST 1998

Here's where the word sunflower appears in file my_text:
sunflower sam
while sunflower sue

sunflower appears in more lines than peanut.
```

Here Documents

An alternative to storing input data in a file is to store that input right in the script or right on the command line; in essence, to store it right *here*. Such input is called a *here document*. The syntax of a command invoked with a here document is as follows:

> *command invocation_arguments <<word*
> *line1 of data*
> *...*
> *lineN of data*
> *word*

That is, you invoke the command as you would invoke any other command but you place *<<word* at the end of the command invocation, where *word* is any group of one or more characters. The *<<word* ending tells the KornShell that a here document follows. The here document can contain as many lines as you want. You terminate a here document by specifying the same *word* that you started it with. Make sure that *word* is flush left; that is, don't allow any white space to the left of *word*. Also, don't put anything to the right of *word*.

The KornShell treats the lines of data in the here document as standard input to the *command*. For example, the following **cat** command gets its standard input from a here document and sends its output to a file named mandu.

```
$ cat > mandu <<EOD
The rain of Maine
Is greeted with disdain.
EOD
```

The contents of file mandu are:

```
$ cat mandu
The rain in Maine
Is greeted with disdain.
```

You can use variables or positional parameters inside here documents; for example, consider the following:

```
$ place="Spain"

$ cat > mandu <<EOD
The rain in $place
Is greeted with disdain.
EOD
```

If you want to turn off the special meaning of the $, ', or \ inside a here document, precede those characters with a backslash, for example:

```
$ cat > money <<EOD
Here is a donation of \$100
EOD
```

The contents of file money are:

```
Here is a donation of $100
```

Some utilities such as the UNIX ex utility rely on here documents to provide a sort of primitive user interface. For such utilities, the here document consists of a group of instructions for the command to run. For such utilities, you can think of the syntax as being more like this:

> *command invocation_arguments <<word*
> *instruction1 to command*
>
> *...*
>
> *instructionN to command*
> *word*

REFERENCE

exec — *Open, close, or copy a stream.*

Syntax

exec *number action target*

where:

number	must be a nonnegative integer. Numbers greater than 9 must be enclosed within braces; for example, {12}. The number 0 corresponds to standard input, the number 1 corresponds to standard output, and the number 2 corresponds to standard error.
action	is one of the I/O redirection operators shown in Table 12-4. Do not put any white space between *number* and *action*.
target	is the pathname of a file, the number of another stream, or a minus sign (–). A minus sign signifies that you are closing a stream. If action is <& or >&, then target cannot be a pathname.

Quick Summary

Use the **exec** statement to do the following:

- Open or close a stream

- Duplicate input or output streams

Table 12-4. I/O Actions

Action	Does this
<	Redirects standard input to *target*
<&	Duplicates input stream
> or >|	Redirects standard output to *target*
>&	Duplicates output stream
>>	Appends output
<>	Opens stream for both input and output; useful in opening two-way communications
<&	Closes an input stream
>&	Closes an output stream

read — *Gather input from the keyboard or from a file.*

Syntax

read *[options] var1 [...varN]*   **read** *[options] var?prompt*

where:

options are zero or more of the following:

-A
: assigns input to array *var1*. The **read** statement will assign the first input token to *var1*[0], the second input token to *var1*[1], and so on until there are no more input tokens. If you specify **-A**, the **read** statement will not assign any input tokens to variables other than *var1*.

-d *char*
: gathers input up to *char*. If you do not specify **-d**, the **read** statement gathers input up to the first newline. For example, if you specify **-d:** and the input line is Mr. Green: enter your vote, the **read** statement sees Mr. Green as valid input but ignores enter your vote.

-n *num*
: assigns the first *num* bytes of input to *var*. (Not all versions of Korn-Shell support this option.)

-p
: reads input from the coprocess.

-r
: by default (if you don't specify **-r**), the **read** statement interprets the backslash character (\) at the end of a line to indicate that the line logically continues on the next physical line. That is, the \ means that the text was too big to fit on one physical line, so it was continued on the next. If you do specify **-r,** each input line is exactly one physical line long, even if it ends with a backslash.

-s
: places the input from this **read** statement into your history file. (See Chapter 16 for information on the history file.) By default (if you don't specify **-s**), the KornShell does not write input into the history file.

-t *seconds*
: forces the user to provide input within the specified number of *seconds*. If the user does not finish entering input within the time limit, the **read** statement returns an exit status of 1 and does not alter the value of *var1 ... varN*.

-u *number*
: if you don't specify **-u**, the KornShell reads from the standard input stream. If you specify **-u** followed by a *number*, the KornShell reads from the file symbolized by *number*. (Use the **exec** statement to associate *number* with a file.) By the way, setting *number* to 0 causes **read** to gather input from the standard input stream.

In addition to *options*, the command line contains either of the following:

var1... [varN]   is one or more variables separated by white space. (Do not put commas between the variables.)

var?prompt   is the name of one (and only one) variable, followed by a question mark (?), followed by a prompt. If the prompt contains more than one word, you must enclose it in a pair of single or double quotes. If you specify a prompt, the KornShell will write the prompt to standard output and then gather the input. Don't put any white space between *var* and ?, or between ? and *prompt*.

Quick Summary

Use the **read** statement to gather input and assign the input to one or more variables. When you issue a **read** statement, here's what happens:

- First, **read** identifies the source of input. The source will be standard input (the default), an alternate file (specified by **-u**), or the coprocess (specified by **-p**).

- Second, **read** gathers from the source of input a virtual line of input (the default), a physical line of input (if **-r** is specified), or everything on the virtual line up until the first occurrence of *char* (if **-d** *char* is specified).

Finally, the KornShell divides the line into tokens and assigns the first token to *var1*, the second token to *var2*, and so on. If the number of tokens in the input line exceeds the number of variables, the KornShell assigns all remaining tokens to *varN*. If you have not specified any *variables* as arguments to **read**, the Korn-Shell assigns input to the reserved variable named **REPLY.** The definition of a token depends on the value of the **IFS** variable, which is detailed on page 289.

REFERENCE

print — *Write output to the screen or to a file.*

Syntax

print *[options] [text]*

where:

options are zero or more of the following:

-f   transforms this **print** statement into a **printf** statement.

-n   suppresses writing a newline at the end of text. If you do not specify -n, **print** will write a newline at the end of text.

-p   writes text to a coprocess.

-r   turns off the special significance of the backslash (\). The backslash is the escape character of the KornShell. (See the list of escape sequences in Table 12-5.) For example, if you put a \t in *text*, **print** ordinarily writes a tab. However, if you want **print** to write an actual backslash and an actual t instead of writing a tab, use the -r option.

--   (two minus signs in a row). Ordinarily, you will want **print** to interpret anything beginning with a minus sign as an option. For example, usually you want **print** to interpret -n as an option. If, however, you actually want **print** to output the two character sequence -n, you must use the -- (two minus signs) option. Therefore, the entire statement would look like this: print -- -n

-R   this option is something like a combination of the -r option and the -- option. Like the -r option, -R turns off the special meaning of the backslash. Like the -- option, -R turns off the significance of the minus sign. However, unlike the -- option, -R still honors the significance of the -n option. That is, if -n appears after -R on the command line, the **print** statement will suppress the trailing newline at the end of text.

-s   writes a copy of text into the history file. See Chapter 16 for a brief description of the history file.

-u*num*   if you do not specify -u or if you specify -u1, **print** writes *text* to standard output. If you specify -u2, **print** writes *text* to standard error. If you specify -u followed by a *num* other than 1 or 2, the KornShell writes *text* to the stream symbolized by *num*. However, you can only specify a value of *num* other than 1 or 2 if you have previously defined *num* in an **exec** statement. Do not specify a *num* corresponding to an input stream. For example, you cannot set *num* to 0.

In addition, you can optionally specify:

text   the information that you want to output. You can optionally enclose *text*
               in a pair of single or double quotes. See page 21 for complete details
               about quoting. The *text* can include zero, one, or many of the escape
               sequences shown in Table 12-5. If you don't specify *text*, **print** writes a
               blank line.

Table 12-5. Escape Sequences

Escape sequence	What it does
\a	Rings the bell on your terminal
\b	Prints the backspace character; the character that follows \b will overwrite the character that precedes \b
\c	Prints everything preceding it and suppresses the printing of everything that follows it; suppresses concluding newline
\E	Is the escape character, $'\x1b'.
\f	Prints a formfeed character; if the output is sent to a printer, the formfeed character tells the printer to start printing on a new page
\n	Prints a newline character (also known as a linefeed character)
\r	Prints a carriage return character
\t	Prints a horizontal tab
\v	Prints a vertical tab
\\	Prints a backslash; in other words, you have to specify two backslashes in order to get one printed
\0*number*	Prints the character whose octal ASCII value is *number*; for example, print "\0124" will output T because octal ASCII value 124 corresponds to T

Quick Summary

Use the **print** statement to write output to the terminal or to a file. When you
issue a **print** statement, the KornShell first identifies the output destination. In
other words, the KornShell figures out where it's supposed to write the output.
The destination will be standard output (the default), an alternate file (specified
by **-u**), or the coprocess (specified by **-p**). Then, the KornShell writes *text* to the
output destination.

REFERENCE

printf — *Superset of ANSI C printf.*

Syntax

printf *format_string [arg1 ... argN]*

where:

format_string	a string encased in a pair of quotes. The string can contain any combination of plain text, conversion specifiers, and escape sequences (see Table 12-5 on page 249). All plain text is printed verbatim.
arg	anything that the KornShell can evaluate. Typically, *arg* is a variable name but also could be a constant or a mathematical expression.

Quick Summary

Use **printf** to output *format_string*, substituting *arg1* for the first conversion specifier in *format_string*, substituting *arg2* for the second conversion specifier in *format_string*, and so on.

printf — *To output integer values.*

Conversion specifiers for integer values take the syntax:

%[flag][field_width]specifier

where:

flag	is optional; you can specify one of the following:

	+	if the value to be printed is positive, prefix it with a plus sign; if the value to be printed is negative, prefix it with a minus sign.
	blank	if the value to be printed is positive, prefix it with a blank space; if the value to be printed is negative, prefix it with a minus sign.
	–	left-justify this value within its field; the size of the field depends on the value of *field_width*.
	#	if the specifier is **o** (octal), prefix the value with **0**; if the specifier is **x** (hexadecimal), prefix the value with **0x**.
	0	if the specifier is **d** (decimal), prefix the value with leading zeroes.

field_width	is optional; you can specify either of the following:

	number	prints the value of *arg* so that it takes up *field_width* spaces. Specifying a small value of *field_width* does not cause **printf** to truncate the value of *arg*. For example, if *arg* is 375 and you specify a *field_width* of 1, printf still prints 375.
	*	sets the field width to the value of the next *arg*.

specifier	is mandatory for printing integers; specify one of the following:

d	prints the integer as a signed decimal (base 10) number.
o	prints the integer as signed octal (base 8) number.
u	prints the integer as an unsigned decimal (base 10) number.
x	prints the integer as unsigned hexadecimal (base 16) number, using lowercase letters (a–f).
X	prints the integer as unsigned hexadecimal (base 16) number, using uppercase letters (A–F).

REFERENCE

printf — *To output float values.*

Syntax

Conversion specifiers for floating-point values take the syntax:

%[flag][field_width][precision]specifier

where:

flag	is optional; you can specify one of the following:	
	+	if the value to be printed is positive, prefix it with a plus sign; if the value to be printed is negative, prefix it with a minus sign.
	blank	if the value to be printed is positive, prefix it with a blank space; if the value to be printed is negative, prefix it with a minus sign.
	–	left-justify this value within its field; the size of the field depends on the value of *field_width*.
	#	display radix point; if specifier is **g** or **G**, pad to *precision* with leading zeroes.
	0	prefix the value with leading zeroes to consume *field_width* spaces.
field_width	is optional; you can specify one of the following:	
	number	print the value of *arg* so that it takes up *field_width* spaces. Specifying a small value of *field_width* does not cause **printf** to truncate the value of *arg*. For example, if *arg* is 673.4 and you specify a *field_width* of 1, **printf** still prints 673.4.
	*	set the field width to the value of the next *arg*.
precision	is optional; you can specify either of the following:	
	.*number*	if specifier is **e, E,** or **f**, print *number* digits past the decimal point. If specifier is **g** or **G**, print number significant digits.
	.*	set the precision to the value of the next *arg*.

specifier   is mandatory for printing floats; you must specify one of the following:

        e or **E**   always use expanded (scientific) notation; **printf** represents the exponent with an **e** (if you specify **e**) or an **E** (if you specify **E**).

        f   never use expanded notation.

        g or **G**   use expanded notation when most efficient; otherwise, don't use expanded notation. If using expanded notation, **printf** represents the exponent, with an **e** (if you specify **g**) or an **E** (if you specify **G**).

printf — *To output strings and patterns.*

Conversion specifiers for string values take the syntax:

%[*field_width*][*chars_to_print*]*specifier*

where:

field_width	is optional; you can specify either of the following:	
	number	print the value of *arg* so that it takes up *field_width* spaces, padding the value of *arg* with leading spaces as necessary. Specifying a small value of *field_width* does not cause **printf** to truncate the value of *arg*. For example, if *arg* is "rhino" and you specify a *field_width* of 2, **printf** writes "rhino" not "rh".
	*	set the field width to the value of the next *arg*.
chars_to_print	is optional; you can specify either of the following:	
	.*number*	if specifier is **q** or **s**, print *number* characters of the string *arg*. For example, if *arg* is "rhino" and you specify a *precision* of 2, **printf** writes "rh".
	.*	set the precision to the value of the next *arg*.
specifier	is mandatory for printing strings or patterns; you must specify one of the following:	
	c	print *arg* as a character.
	P	if *arg* is a UNIX regular expression, convert it to a Korn-Shell pattern and then print it. Regular expressions are a special form of wildcards used by UNIX utilities like egrep and awk, and to a lesser extent by grep, sed, and vi.
	q	print *arg* as a string, encasing the string inside a pair of single quotes.
	s	print *arg* as a string.

13 Manipulating Strings

This chapter details string manipulation in the KornShell.

If You're New to Programming . . .

The string is the primary data type of the KornShell. Just about everything is a string, including individual letters, phrases, sentences, and pathnames. Even numbers are strings, assuming that you haven't declared them as integers or floats. Using KornShell, you can do almost anything imaginable with strings, including formatting text into nicely columned reports.

Once you get the hang of it, this is a blast; a great opportunity to embrace your inner nerd.

If You're an Experienced Programmer . . .

Some users think of the KornShell as a string manipulation language first and a command processor second. If the KornShell is a little weak on the mathematical front, it more than makes up for it on the string processing arena. You can slice and dice strings in the KornShell far easier than in other languages.

KornShell 93 introduces several new string manipulation features not found in KornShell 88, including:

- Search and replace operators. In KornShell 88, you typically had to call an outside program (such as sed or ex) to do search and replace. With KornShell 93, you can keep it all within the KornShell.

- Substring operators. KornShell 93 lets you assign chunks of one string to another string. For example, you can ask KornShell 93 to assign characters 5 through 17 of string variable **x** to string variable **y**.

Uppercase and Lowercase

The following script demonstrates how to convert strings to all uppercase or to all lowercase. Use the **typeset -u** attribute to convert a string to all uppercase. Use the **typeset -l** attribute to convert a string to all lowercase.

```
USAGE="usage: U_and_lc.ksh"  # upper and lowercase strings

# Ordinary string input.
 print -n "Enter a string: "
 read a_string
 backup_string=$a_string
 print "\nOriginal string: $a_string"

# Convert a_string to all uppercase.
 typeset -u a_string
 print "All uppercase: $a_string"

# Convert a_string to all lowercase.
 typeset -l a_string        # turn on lowercase attribute; turn off
                            # uppercase attribute
 print "All lowercase: $a_string"

# Reassign original string to a_string. Before reassigning, turn
# off lowercase attribute of a_string; if we don't turn this off,
# then value of a_string will be all lowercase.
 typeset +l a_string
 a_string=$backup_string
 print "Return to original string: $a_string"
```

Executing This Script

```
$ U_and_lc.ksh
Enter a string: The Rain in Spain.

Original string: The Rain in Spain.
All uppercase: THE RAIN IN SPAIN.
All lowercase: the rain in spain.
Return to original string: The Rain in Spain.
```

A script that asks, "What's your favorite kind of pet?" should be prepared for users to enter: **DOG**, **Dog**, or **dog**. To handle such uncertainty, the script should convert (using **typeset -u** or **typeset -l**) user responses to all one case. With user responses guaranteed to be in one case, comparisons are much easier.

Left Justification

This shell script demonstrates the **typeset** -**L**[*n*] and **typeset** -**LZ**[*n*] attributes. You can use these attributes to:

- Make nice, neat output columns (with -**L***n*) when you're writing a report.

- Copy (with -**L***n*) the first *n* characters of a string to another string. This is useful when you're only interested in the first *n* characters and want to ignore the rest of the string.

- Strip leading zeros (-**LZ** or -**LZ***n*) from strings.

The KornShell also supports string attributes **typeset** -**R**[*n*] for those wishing to right-justify strings and **typeset** -**RZ**[*n*], which right-justifies and fills leading spaces with zeroes.

```
USAGE="usage: left_just.ksh" # typeset -L and typeset -LZ
# Declare three strings with -Ln attribute. This will not influence
# the read statement, but will influence the print statement.
 typeset -L10 first_name    # output width will be 10 characters
 typeset -L8 middle_name    # output width will be 8 characters
 typeset -L15 last_name     # output width will be 15 characters


# Gather input names from a file and write them to standard output in
# three neat columns. The first column will use up 10 characters, the
# second column 8, and the third 15.
 while read first_name middle_name last_name
 do
    print "$first_name $middle_name $last_name"
 done < file_of_names.txt


# Another use of left justification is to isolate a substring and
# assign it to another string. Here, we declare a string variable
# named middle_initial. If we try to assign a string value to
# middle_initial, only the leftmost character in the string value will
# actually be assigned.
 typeset -L1 middle_initial
 print -n "\nEnter a middle name: "
 read middle_name
# Assign to middle_initial the first character of middle_name.
 middle_initial=$middle_name
 print "Middle initial -- $middle_initial"


# Finally, we can use typeset -LZ to strip leading zeros.
 typeset -LZ1 month day
 print -n "\nEnter today's date in numerical form (e.g., 04 07 62): "
 read month day year    # North American-style date
 print "$month-$day-$year"
```

Executing This Script

Using a text editor, place some names inside of a file named `file_of_names`.

```
$ cat file_of_names.txt  # here's my file of names
Hugo Killer Whale
Flipper The Dolphin
Cher Melissa Stanislawski
Liberace Rosencrantz Smith
Incredible Howard Hulk
```

The data in `file_of_names` isn't formatted into nice, neat columns, so let's have the script do that for us:

```
$ leftjust.ksh
Hugo       Killer    Whale
Flipper    The       Dolphin
Cher       Melissa   Stanislawski
Liberace   Rosencra  Smith
Incredible Howard    Hulk

Enter a middle name: Joyce
Middle initial -- J

Enter today's date in numerical form (e.g., 04 07 62): 01 05 98
1-5-98
```

Notice that the input word "Rosencrantz" was truncated to "Rosencra" because "Rosencrantz" was longer than eight characters.

Concatenating Strings

You can concatenate (append) multiple strings to create a new string. For example, the following script concatenates four strings and assigns the results to a variable named **complete_name**.

```
USAGE="usage: append_string.ksh"   # concatenate one string to another

read first_name?"Enter first name: "
read middle_name?"Enter middle name: "
read last_name?"Enter last name: "

# Concatenate this information and provide appropriate prefixes and
# white space. The white space will become part of complete_name.
complete_name="Ms. $first_name $middle_name $last_name"
print "Full name -- $complete_name"
```

Executing This Script

```
$ append_string.ksh
Enter first name: Marilyn
Enter middle name: Joyce
Enter last name: Tucker
Full name -- Ms. Marilyn Joyce Tucker
```

Reading an Entire File into One String Variable

The following syntax assigns the entire contents of *filename* to *string_variable*:

string_variable=**$(<** *filename***)**

Note that the KornShell will assign every character in the file (including white space and any other **IFS** characters) to *string_variable*.

When I first saw this syntax, I thought, "Cute trick, but not too useful." Having learned the C language prior to KornShell, I was more comfortable analyzing text files character-by-character or line-by-line. Only after many years of writing Korn-Shell scripts did I finally catch on to just how powerful this "trick" really was.

The following script compares two files. The script doesn't perform a line-by-line comparison *a la* diff. Rather, the script simply determines whether the two files are identical. As such, this script is a KornShell kin to the POSIX cmp command (except that, unlike the POSIX cmp, cmp.ksh cannot compare binary files).

```
USAGE="usage: cmp.ksh file1 file2"  # read contents of file into variable

# Store file1 in variable contents1
 contents1=$(< $1)

# Store file2 in variable contents2
 contents2=$(< $2)

# Compare the two string variables
 if [[ "$contents1" == "$contents2" ]]
 then
    exit 0   # files are the same
 else
    exit 1   # files are different
 fi
```

Executing This Script

Suppose that joyous.txt and happy.txt have the same contents:

```
$ cmp.ksh joyous.txt happy.txt
$ print $?   # Examine error status
0
```

Further suppose that joyous.txt and melancholy.txt have different contents:

```
$ cmp.ksh joyous.txt melancholy.txt
$ print $?   # Examine error status
1
```

Search and Replace Overview

The KornShell offers four different ways to perform search and replace operations on strings. In a search and replace operation, the KornShell searches a string for a pattern. If the pattern is found, the KornShell replaces it with a replacement string. Table 13-1 shows the four KornShell search and replace operations.

Table 13-1. KornShell Search and Replace Operations

Operation	What it does
${*string_var//search_pattern/replacement_string*}	Replaces all occurrences of *search_pattern* in *string_var* with *replacement_string*.
${*string_var/search_pattern/replacement_string*}	Replaces the first occurrence of *search_pattern* in *string_var* with *replacement_string*.
${*string_var/#search_pattern/replacement_string*}	If *string_var* begins with *search_pattern*, replaces the first occurrence of *search_pattern* with *replacement_string*.
${*string_var/%search_pattern/replacement_string*}	If *string_var* ends with *search_pattern*, replaces the last occurrence of *search_pattern* with *replacement_string*.

A few things to note about these operations:

- *string_var* must be either a positional parameter or a string variable.

- Most scripts assign the results of these operations to another string variable.

- These operations do not change the value of *string_var*.

Let's look at these operators in action.

```
thoroughgood="50 dates in 50 states"
n=${thoroughgood//50/85}   # n becomes "85 dates in 85 states"
n=${thoroughgood/50/75}    # n becomes "75 dates in 50 states"
n=${thoroughgood/#50/65}   # n becomes "65 dates in 50 states"
n=${thoroughgood/%50/55}   # n becomes "50 dates in 50 states"
```

Note that the final example, the one using the % operator, does not find anything to replace because **thoroughgood** did not end with the string 50.

The preceding search and replacement operations do not alter the value of variable **thoroughgood**.

Search and Replace Practical Example

Here's a script that performs a friendly search and replace on any pattern inside the specified file. As such, it is a kind of verbose sed command.

```
USAGE="usage: search_and_replace.ksh"  # friendly sed

 print -n "What file are you searching? "
 read input_filename
 output_filename=$input_filename.corrected
 if [[ ! -f $input_filename ]] || [[ ! -r $input_filename ]]
 then
   print -u2 "$input_filename is not a regular file or is not readable."
   exit 1
 fi

 print -n "Change this pattern: "
 read search

 print -n "To this: "
 read replace

# Read entire input file into a string variable; then perform a search
# and replace operation on the string variable.
 original=$(< $input_filename)
 modified=${original//$search/$replace}
 print -R "$modified" > $output_filename
```

Executing This Script

Before running this script, I created a short text file named mystory.txt containing:

```
$ cat mystory.txt
This jacket is reversable
and reversable is flexible.

$ search_and_replace.ksh
What file are you searching? mystory.txt
Change this pattern: reversable
To this: reversible
```

The properly spelled version of mystory.txt is written to mystory.txt.corrected:

```
$ cat mystory.txt.corrected
This jacket is reversible
and reversible is flexible.
```

Isolating a Portion of a String

Sometimes it is useful to isolate a subset of a string. The KornShell provides two related operators to do just that.

The following syntax isolates *length* characters of *string* beginning with the character at position *start*:

${*string*:*start*:*length*}

And the following syntax isolates the characters in *string* from the character at position *start* until the last character in *string*:

${*string*:*start*}

Input files often are organized by token; for instance, the first token contains one kind of information, the second contains another kind of information, and so on. Some input files are organized by columns. For example, consider an input file containing names. Some names contain two tokens (for example, John Smith), some three (John Jacob Smith), and some far more (Mr. John Jacob Jingleheimer Smith Nah Nah Nah Nah Nah Nah Nah). Such an input file would be best organized by columns, where the first names must start at a particular column, the middle names at another column, and the last names at yet another column.

```
USAGE="usage: substring.ksh"    # isolating a subset of a string

while read line
do
   name=${line:0:25}   # get first 25 characters of line
   comments=${line:38} # get characters from position 38 to the end
   print "$name $comments"
done < database.txt
```

Executing This Script

Consider a file named database.txt organized into nice, neat columns:

```
$ cat database.txt
Matilda Evergreen        509-555-1439 Telekinetic heroine
Aunts' Sponger & Spike   617-555-1348 Misanthropic to the max
Dr. William Wonka        499-555-8752 Sweet
```

Running substring.ksh yields the contents of specified columns:

```
$ substring.ksh
Matilda Evergreen        Telekinetic heroine
Aunts' Sponger & Spike   Misanthropic to the max
Dr. William Wonka        Sweet
```

Removing the Leftmost Characters in a String with

The following script demonstrates the # operator, which deletes a substring from the left side (the beginning) of a string. Actually, the # operator doesn't really change the value of the string. Use # to find out what a string would look like if a chunk of it were removed.

```
USAGE="usage: remove_left.ksh" # demonstrates the # removal operator
 animal="tiger"
# The following two lines are synonymous:
 print "The full string -- $animal"
 print "The full string -- ${animal}"

# Delete substrings from the left portion of the string.
 print "Remove the 't' -- ${animal#t}"
 print "Remove the 'ti' -- ${animal#ti}"
 abbrev="tig"
 print "Remove the '$abbrev' -- ${animal#$abbrev}"
 print "Try (unsuccessfully) to remove the 'iger' -- ${animal#iger}"

# You can also delete a pattern.
 print "\nRemove the first two characters -- ${animal#??}"
 print "Remove up to and including the first 'e' -- ${animal#*e}"

# Remove tokens (words) from the string.
# Pattern "* " matches everything up to and including the first space.
 cats="lions and tigers"
 print "\nThe full string -- ${cats}"
 print "Remove the first token -- ${cats#* }"
 print "Remove the first two tokens -- ${cats#* * }"
```

Executing This Script

```
$ remove_left.ksh
The full string -- tiger
The full string -- tiger
Remove the 't' -- iger
Remove the 'ti' -- ger
Remove the 'tig' -- er
Try (unsuccessfully) to remove the 'iger' -- tiger

Remove the first two characters -- ger
Remove up to and including the first 'e' -- r

The full string -- lions and tigers
Remove the first token -- and tigers
Remove the first two tokens -- tigers
```

Removing the Rightmost Characters in a String with %

Use the % operator to remove a substring from the end (the right side) of a string.

```
USAGE="usage: remove_right.ksh"  # demonstrates the substring operator %

animal="tiger"
abbrev="ger"

print "The full string -- ${animal}"
# Delete substrings from the right characters in a string.
print "Remove the 'r' -- ${animal%r}"
print "Remove the 'er' -- ${animal%er}"
print "Remove the '$abbrev' -- ${animal%$abbrev}"
print "Try (unsuccessfully) to remove the 'tige' -- ${animal%tige}"

# You can also delete a pattern.
print "\nRemove the last two characters -- ${animal%??}"
print "Remove the characters beginning with 'g' -- ${animal%g*}"

cats="lions and tigers"
print "\nThe full string -- ${cats}"
print "Remove the last token -- ${cats% *}"
print "Remove the last two tokens -- ${cats% * *}"
```

Executing This Script

```
$ remove_right.ksh
The full string -- tiger
Remove the 'r' -- tige
Remove the 'er' -- tig
Remove the 'ger' -- ti
Try (unsuccessfully) to remove the 'tige' -- tiger

Remove the last two characters -- tig
Remove the characters beginning with 'g' -- ti

The full string -- lions and tigers
Remove the last token -- lions and
Remove the last two tokens -- lions
```

An Application of %

Filenames are strings, so you can use the substring deletion operators to parse filenames. For example, you can use the % operator to help you change filenames. The
following script changes all filenames with the suffix .shd to the suffix .shadow:

```
USAGE="usage: rename.ksh"   # using % to parse filenames

for old_file_name in *.shd  # list all objects ending in '.shd'
do

  # Strip the '.shd' suffix and replace it with '.shadow'.
  new_file_name=${old_file_name%.shd}.shadow

  # mv is the UNIX command that renames a file.
  mv $old_file_name $new_file_name
  if (($? == 0))  # examine error status of mv command
  then       # mv was successful
    print "Changed $old_file_name to $new_file_name"
  else       # mv was unsuccessful
    print "Could not change $old_file_name to $new_file_name"
  fi

done
```

Executing This Script

```
$ rename.ksh
Changed jean_marc.shd to jean_marc.shadow
Changed mick.shd to mick.shadow
Changed tim.shd to tim.shadow
```

Versus

The following script demonstrates the difference between # (delete first occurrence) and ## (delete up to and including last occurrence).

```
USAGE="usage: remove_far_left.ksh" # difference between # and ##

 simple="abcdabcd"
# If your pattern does not contain any wildcards, then the # and ##
# operators produce identical outcomes.
 print "The full string -- ${simple}"
 print "Remove the 'ab' with # -- ${simple#ab}"
 print "Remove the 'ab' with ## -- ${simple##ab}"

# If the pattern does contain wildcards, then the # and ##
# operators may produce different results. Notice that the letters
# 'ab' appear twice in 'abcdabcd'. Using the # operator causes the
# KornShell to delete the first occurrence of *ab.
 print "\nRemove '*ab' with # -- ${simple#*ab}"
# Using the ## operator causes the KornShell to remove all characters
# through the last occurrence of *ab.
 print "Remove '*ab' with ## -- ${simple##*ab}"

# The pattern '* ' matches any group of characters that ends with
# a blank space. It is a very useful pattern for dividing a sentence
# into words.
 phrase="I always get the last word."
 print "\nThe full string -- ${phrase}"
 print "Removing the first word yields -- ${phrase#* }"
 print "Removing all but the last word yields -- ${phrase##* }"
```

Executing This Script

```
$ remove_far_left.ksh
The full string -- abcdabcd
Remove the 'ab' with # -- cdabcd
Remove the 'ab' with ## -- cdabcd

Remove '*ab' with # -- cdabcd
Remove '*ab' with ## -- cd

The full string -- I always get the last word.
Removing the first word yields -- always get the last word.
Removing all but the last word yields -- word.
```

% Versus %%

The following script demonstrates the difference between % (delete last occurrence) and %% (delete up to and including first occurrence).

```
USAGE="usage: remove_far_right.ksh"  # difference between % and %%

 phrase="I always get the first word."
 print "The full string -- ${phrase}"

# This next use of % tells the KornShell to start at the end of
# the string and delete the first occurrence of the pattern ' *'.
# That is, working backwards (from right to left), delete every
# character until the first blank space in the string.
 print "Removing the last word yields -- ${phrase% *}"

# Using %% instead of % tells the KornShell to delete the longest
# occurrence of ' *'.
 print "Removing all but the first word yields -- ${phrase%% *}"

oz="Lions and tigers and bears"
print "\nThe full string -- ${oz}"
print "Delete from last 'and*' to end of line -- ${oz%and*}"
print "Delete from first 'and*' to end of line -- ${oz%%and*}"
```

Executing This Script

```
$ remove_far_right.ksh
The full string -- I always get the first word.
Removing the last word yields -- I always get the first
Removing all but the first word yields -- I

The full string -- Lions and tigers and bears
Delete from last 'and*' to end of line -- Lions and tigers
Delete from first 'and*' to end of line -- Lions
```

Using # on Numbers

You can use the substring deletion operators (#, #, %, and %%) on a string of numbers just as you can use these operators on a string of letters.

Here's a script that takes longer to explain than to execute. In the United States, phone numbers are 10 digits long, where the first 3 digits are an area code. If the caller and person being called are within the same area code, the caller uses only the last 7 digits of the phone number. If the caller and person being called are in different area codes, then the caller must dial all 10 digits.

```
USAGE="usage: remove_num_strings.ksh"  # parsing numerical strings

while read a_phone_number  # read in one phone number at a time
do

  # Assume that the caller is within the 617 area code.
  # Delete leading '617-'; leave all other area codes intact.
  dial_this=${a_phone_number#'617-'}
  print "Please dial ${dial_this}"

done < phone_numbers.txt
```

Executing This Script

Use a text editor to enter some 10-digit phone numbers into a file named phone_numbers.txt. Here's my list:

```
$ cat phone_numbers.txt
929-555-4567
617-555-3598
427-555-4322
909-555-0082
617-555-1298
```

Now run remove5.ksh, gathering input data from phone_numbers.txt:

```
$ remove_num_strings.ksh
Please dial 929-555-4567
Please dial 555-3598
Please dial 427-555-4322
Please dial 909-555-0082
Please dial 555-1298
```

By the way, I set the middle three digits of all the example phone numbers to 555 for legal reasons only. If you want to play with this script, you can use any numbers you like.

Deleting a Substring from the Middle of a String

Because you can delete a substring from the beginning or end of a string, it is only natural to wonder how to delete a substring from the middle of a string. In older versions of the KornShell, this procedure was painful. However, with KornShell 93, you merely perform a search and replace operation. That is, you search for the substring to delete and then replace that substring with the null string.

```
USAGE="usage: remove_middle.ksh" # delete substring from middle of string

oz="Lions and tigers and bears"
print "The original string -- $oz"

substring_to_remove=" and tigers"
replacement_string=""
safer_oz=${oz/$substring_to_remove/$replacement_string}
print "The modified string -- $safer_oz"
```

Executing This Script

```
$ remove_middle.ksh
The original string -- Lions and tigers and bears
The modified string -- Lions and bears
```

Pruning Branches from Pathnames

A pathname is itself a string. Therefore, you can use the substring deletion operators on pathnames. These operators are very useful for isolating branches (directories) in a long pathname.

The KornShell reserved variable **PWD** holds the pathname of the current directory, and the KornShell reserved variable **HOME** holds the pathname of the home
(login) directory.

```
USAGE="usage: remove_branches.ksh"    # using # on pathnames

print "Home directory -- $HOME"
print "Current directory -- $PWD"

relative=${PWD#$HOME/}
print "Same dir. relative to HOME -- $relative"
```

Executing This Script

First run `remove_branches.ksh` from a directory somewhere underneath your **HOME**
directory; for example:

```
$ remove_branches.ksh
Home directory -- /usr/barry
Current directory -- /usr/barry/book/text/ch9
Same dir. relative to HOME -- book/text/ch9
```

Now navigate to a different directory, one not underneath the **HOME** directory, and
rerun `remove_branches.ksh`; for example:

```
$ cd /seuss/samiam
$ remove_branches.ksh
Home directory -- /usr/barry
Current directory -- /seuss/samiam
Same dir. relative to HOME -- /seuss/samiam
```

Since **PWD** does not begin with the contents of **HOME**, the phrase ${PWD#$HOME/} won't
delete anything.

Matching Multiple Strings on the Same Line

Suppose your task is to search through a file and find all lines containing the words *fish* and *bicycle*. If you are on a system that contains egrep and you are well-versed in UNIX-style regular expressions, you could solve the problem without using the KornShell. However, the KornShell does provide a couple of fairly easy ways to solve such a problem. One solution is to connect a couple of tests with the Boolean AND operator (&); for example:

```
if [[ $line == *fish* ]] && [[ $line == *bicycle* ]]
```

Another way is to use a KornShell wildcard with an embedded Boolean AND operator (&), as shown in the following example:

```
USAGE="usage: multiple_matches.ksh"    # AND inside wildcards

while read line
do
    if [[ "$line" == +(*fish*&*bicycle*) ]]
    then
        print "$line"
    fi
done < velodrone.txt
```

Executing This Script

Assume that the following text is stored in file velodrone.txt:

```
$ cat velodrone.txt
round and round the fishies go.
peddling their bicycles to and fro.
fish need bicycles, yes they do,
like fish need water, and I need you.
```

Running the script yields the following:

```
$ multiple_matches.ksh
fish need bicycles, yes they do
```

The wildcard in the preceding script basically means find all lines that match both the pattern *fish* and the pattern *bicycle*. If you placed an OR operator (|) where the AND operator (&) appeared, every line in velodrone.txt would have been matched because every line contains either fish or bicycle, or both.

Finding the Length of a String

The "length" of a string is the number of characters it contains. Use the following syntax to find the length of a string:

   length=**${#***string***}**

   The following script reads each line from a file, one line at a time. The script then calculates the length of each line.

```
USAGE="usage: strlen.ksh" # finding string length

# By setting IFS to a null string, we are ensuring that read won't
# ignore leading white space in the input line.
IFS=''

while read -r line    # read one line at a time from the input file
do
   # Write length of line, then two blanks, and then the text of the line:
   print "${#line}  $line"
done
```

Executing This Script

Use a text editor to enter the following atrocious verse into a file named `vogon.txt`:

```
$ cat vogon.txt
     Haiku to Autumn

Crimson crackling leaves.
Pumpkins on a frosty fence.
Rotting grapes smell sweet.
```

Now we'll preface each of these lines with a character count:

```
$ strlen.ksh < vogon.txt
20       Haiku to Autumn
0
26  Crimson crackling leaves.
28  Pumpkins on a frosty fence.
28  Rotting grapes smell sweet.
```

Notice that the blank spaces preceding the word `Haiku` on the first line are counted as part of the length.

Parsing Strings into Words

Sometimes it's useful to parse input text into words. This dandy little script parses a text file into words, sorts the words in alphabetical order, and then writes the sorted list (one word per line) to standard output.

```
USAGE="usage: parse_into_words.ksh file"  # parse file into words

# Make sure script has a file to analyze.
 if (( $# == 0 ))
 then
   print "You must specify a text file."
   exit 1
 else
   file_to_examine=$1
 fi

# Declare a string variable named contents; the -l option forces all
# values assigned to contents to be converted to lowercase.
 typeset -l contents

# Set IFS to all the characters that can separate two words.
 IFS=$' \t\n,.;!?'

# Assign all of the input file to the variable named contents.
 contents=$(< $file_to_examine)

# Assign each word to a positional parameter.
# Sort the positional parameters.
 set -s $contents

# Write each positional parameter to standard output, one per line
 for word in $*
 do
   print $word
 done
```

Executing This Script

Using a text editor, write some text into a file. Here's what I used:

```
$ cat bad_poem.txt  # cat is the UNIX utility that displays a file
        Why, Oh Why?
Why, oh why,
Do we never hear ourselves snore?
```

Running the script yields an alphabetized list of words used in bad_poem.txt:

```
$ parse_into_words.ksh bad_poem.txt
do
hear
never
oh
oh
ourselves
snore
we
why
why
why
why
```

The following pipeline returns a count of the number of unique words appearing in a text file:

```
$ parse_into_words.ksh bad_poem.txt | uniq | wc -l
      8
```

The uniq utility removes redundant words. That is, if a word appears more than once in the output file, uniq will remove all but the first occurrence. The wc -l utility counts the number of lines in the output file. Because each line contains exactly one unique word, the number of lines should equal the number of unique words. Thus, bad_poem.txt consists of an eight-word vocabulary.

Parsing Strings into Characters

The easiest way to parse a passage of prose into individual characters is to rely on the array subset operator described on page 263. The following script uses this operator to count the number of times the specified character appears in an input file.

```
USAGE="usage: parse_into_chars.ksh file"  # parse file into chars
 if (( $# == 0 ))
 then
   print "You must specify a text file."
   exit 1
 else
   file_to_examine=$1
 fi

print -n "What character would you like to count: "
read scrutinized_character

contents=$(< $file_to_examine)
total_chars_in_this_file=${#contents}

integer counter=0
for (( position=0; position < $total_chars_in_this_file; position++ ))
do
   next_char=${contents:$position:1}  # get next character from file
   if [[ "$next_char" == "$scrutinized_character" ]]
   then
      ((counter++))  #
   fi
done
print "This passage contains $counter $scrutinized_character's."
```

Executing This Script

Let's count all the y's in file bad_poem.txt (whose contents appear on the previous page):

```
$ parse_into_chars.ksh bad_poem.txt
What character would you like to count: y
This passage contains 4 y's.
```

Specifying Default Values

The KornShell provides four *parameter expansion modifiers*. These modifiers examine *strings* to see if they are set, unset, or null, and then take an appropriate action depending on the outcome. In this context, *string* means any string variable or positional parameter. A *null* string is a positional parameter or string variable whose value is "" (an empty string); for example:

```
str1="Rain" # str1 is not null
str2=""     # str2 is null
```

An *unset* string is any of the following:

- A positional parameter whose value has not been set

- The name of a variable that has never been explicitly or implicitly declared

- A variable declared with **typeset** that has no value assigned to it

- A string variable explicitly unset by the **unset** statement

For example, the following statement sets positional parameters **$1**, **$2**, and **$3**, but unsets any positional parameter greater than **$3**:

```
set apple banana carambola
```

Similarly, the following sets the value of variable **str3**:

```
str3="Snow and Sleet."
```

And the following statement unsets variable **str3**:

```
unset str3
```

Table 13-2 summarizes the parameter expansion modifiers. By the way, if you're testing a string to see if it's unset, the colon after the string is optional. If you're testing a string to see if it's null, the colon is required.

Table 13-2. Parameter Expansion Modifiers

Operation	If string is set and is not null	If string is unset or null
var = **$**{*string*:*-expr*}	*var*=${*string*}	*var*=*expr*
var=**$**{*string*:=*expr*}	*var*=${*string*}	*string*=*expr* *var*=*expr*
var=**$**{*string*:+*expr*}	*var*=*expr*	*var* becomes null
var=**$**{*string*:?*expr*}	*var*=${*string*}	the KornShell writes *expr* to standard error

For example, consider the influence of the parameter expansion modifier
var=${*string*:-*expr*} on two different variables:

```
str1="Rain"          # str1 is set and is not null
str2=""              # str2 is set, but is null
r1=${str1:-"Dry"}    # assign "Rain" to r1; nothing happens to str1
r2=${str2:-"Wet"}    # assign "Wet" to r2; nothing happens to str2
```

The following example script demonstrates the parameter expansion modifiers:

```
USAGE="usage: prom_mod.ksh [shoe_color]" # parameter expansion modifiers
# If user enters an argument on the command line, then $1 will be set.
# If user does not enter an argument on the command line, then $1 will
# be unset. If $1 is set, then the KornShell will assign $1 to color,
# but if $1 is unset, the KornShell will assign "white" to color.
 color=${1-"white"}
 print "You have selected $color shoes"

read choice?"Enter corsage choice (or press <RETURN> for default):"
# If user enters <RETURN>, then choice will be null.
# If choice is null, then the KornShell assigns "gardenia" to choice.
# If choice is not null, then the KornShell leaves choice alone.
 flower=${choice:="gardenia"}  # modifies both flower and choice
 print "You have selected a $flower"

 read music_choice?"Enter your choice of music: "
# If user enters <RETURN>, then music_choice will be null.
# If music_choice is null, the KornShell prints an error message
# and then exits the script. If music_choice is not null, then the
# KornShell assign $music_choice to variable music.
 music=${music_choice:?"You have to pick something! Bye."}
 print "You picked $music"
```

Executing This Script

```
$ prom_mod.ksh          # pick all the defaults, go with the flow
You have selected white shoes
Enter corsage choice (or press <RETURN> for default): <RETURN>
You have selected a gardenia
Enter your choice of music: <RETURN> # uh oh, not a good choice
prom_mod.ksh[23]: music_choice: You have to pick something! Bye.

$ prom_mod.ksh purple   # avoid defaults, be creative
You have selected purple shoes
Enter corsage choice (or press <RETURN> for default): thorny rose
You have selected a thorny rose
Enter your choice of music: The Beatles
You picked The Beatles
```

Parsing PATH

The KornShell variable **PATH** (and its cousins **CDPATH** and **FPATH**) holds a set of directories. For example, the following statement assigns a set of three directories to **PATH:**

```
PATH=/bin:$HOME/bin:.
```

Notice that the colon (**:**) separates the directory names.

How would you parse **PATH?** After all, its assigned value does not contain any white space. Actually, there are many ways to parse **PATH.** One way is to use the substring deletion operators. Another way, shown in the following script, is to rely on the fact that the **for** statement uses **IFS** to parse a string into individual list items.

```
USAGE="usage: parse_path.ksh"  # influence of IFS on for loops

PATH=:/usr/bin:/bin:$HOME/bin # assign three dirs to PATH

# The PATH variable uses the colon as a field separator. Therefore,
# assign the colon to IFS.
IFS=':'
print "The current PATH consists of: "
for directory in $PATH  # for will parse PATH based on IFS
do
   print "\t$directory"
done
```

Executing This Script

```
$ parse_path.ksh
The current PATH consists of:
    /usr/bin
    /bin
    /users/ryan/bin
```

Practical Application: Extracting Comments From C Source Code

The C programming language and the UNIX operating system go together like ants and picnics. Here's a script that shows off string manipulation operators. Its purpose: to copy all the comments from a C source file into a separate file. This script will not alter the contents of the input C source code file.

```ksh
USAGE="usage: c_comments.ksh file.c"  # copy C comments to a file

suffix=".comments" # file containing comments will have this suffix

pathname_of_C_file=${1:-"main.c"}  # default to main.c
if [[ ! -f $pathname_of_C_file ]] || [[ ! -r $pathname_of_C_file ]]
then
  print -u2 "$pathname_of_C_file doesn't exist or isn't readable."
  exit 1
fi

contents=$(< $pathname_of_C_file)  # copy entire file into a variable
while :
do
  length=${#contents}

 # Remove everything up to start of next comment.
  contents=${contents#*\/\*}   # notice that contents has changed

 # Remove everything past the end of this comment
  comment=${contents%%\*\/*}

 # Determine when there are no more comments
  new_length=${#contents}
  if (( new_length == length ))
  then
     break  # no more comments
  else
     print -R "$comment"      # output the comment
  fi
done > $pathname_of_C_file$suffix
```

Executing This Script

Suppose an uninspired C source code file named main.c contains:

```
$ cat main.c  # display the contents of main.c
#include <stdio.h>

/* This program contains some nifty C comments, some
   of which span multiple physical lines. */
int
void main(void)
{
  /* This program declares 2 variables. */
  long x, rt=0;

  for (x=0; x<50; x++)  {  /* Loop to execute 50 times. */  {
   /* Get rid of this for production code. */  printf("c\n");
      rt += ((x * x) - (x * 2));
  }

  /* Output conclusions. */
   printf("Total: %ld\n", rt);
}
```

Now run the script:

```
$ c_comments.ksh main.c # copy comments of math.c to math.c.comments
```

The preceding script creates a file named main.c.comments, which contains all the comments of math.c.

```
$ cat main.c.comments  # display the contents of the comments file
 This program contains some nifty C comments, some
    of which span multiple physical lines.
 This program declares 2 variables.
 Loop to execute 50 times.
 Get rid of this for production code.
 Output conclusions.
```

String Manipulation Summary

In all of the operations shown in Table 13-3, the operation will not modify the *string*, *search_pattern*, *replacement_string*, *pattern*, *start*, and *length* operands.

Table 13-3. String Manipulation Operators

Operation	What it does
r=$\{*string*//*search_pattern*/*replacement_string*\}	Replaces all occurrences of *search_pattern* in *string* with *replacement_string*; assigns results to *r*.
r=$\{*string*/*search_pattern*/*replacement_string*\}	Replaces the first occurrence of *search_pattern* in *string* with *replacement_string*; assigns results to *r*.
r=$\{*string*/#*search_pattern*/*replacement_string*\}	If *string* begins with *search_pattern*, replaces the first occurrence of *search_pattern* with *replacement_string*; assigns results to *r*.
r=$\{*string*/%*search_pattern*/*replacement_string*\}	If *string* ends with *search_pattern*, replaces the last occurrence of *search_pattern* with *replacement_string*; assigns results to *r*.
r=$\{*string*#*pattern*\}	Starting from beginning of *string*, removes the first occurrence of *pattern* from *string*; assigns results to *r*.
r=$\{*string*##*pattern*\}	Starting from beginning of *string*, removes the longest occurrence of *pattern* from *string*; assigns results to *r*.
r=$\{*string*%*pattern*\}	Removes the last occurrence of *pattern* from *string*; assigns results to *r*.
r=$\{*string*%%*pattern*\}	Removes the longest last occurrence of *pattern* from *string*; assigns results to *r*.
r=$\{#*string*\}	Assigns the length of string to *r*.
r=$\{*string*:*start*:*length*\}	Assigns *length* characters of *string*, beginning at character *start*, to *r*.
r=$\{*string*:*start*\}	Assigns every character in *string* from *start* to the end of string to *r*.

14 KornShell Reserved Variables

This chapter details all of the KornShell's reserved variables.

If You're New to Programming ...

You've probably noticed that certain words (for example, **print, for**, and **while**) have special meaning to the KornShell. All of these words are KornShell statements. The KornShell also reserves many variable names (for example, **PATH** and **PS1**) and gives these variables special meaning. You don't have to memorize every reserved KornShell variable. Just browse through the chapter quickly and take a few mental notes. Then, as your experience grows, you can return here and find what you need.

Many reserved variables have limited use within scripts and are primarily intended to make the KornShell command line easier to use.

Notice that nearly all of the reserved variables have uppercase names. To avoid confusion, you usually should give variables that you define—the **x**'s and **y**'s of your scripts—lowercase names. That way, it will be almost impossible for you to reuse a reserved variable name by mistake.

If You're an Experienced Programmer ...

The KornShell's reserved variables fall into two general categories:

- Reserved variables whose values the KornShell automatically sets and updates. For example, the KornShell automatically assigns a random number to **RANDOM**.

- Reserved variables whose values the KornShell does not automatically set. Instead, KornShell users or system administrators set the values. System administrators typically set values in the /etc/profile start-up file. Users typically set values in $HOME/.profile or the environment file, though users could also set values on the shell command line or in a shell script.

The rightmost column of Table 14-1 indicates who *usually* sets the value of the variable. For example, **.sh.edcol** is marked "KSH" to tell you that the KornShell usually sets it; the **PS1** variable is marked "U" because the user usually sets it, and the **LANG** variable is marked "SA" because the system administrator usually sets it.

Table 14-1. KornShell Reserved Variables

Variable	What it holds	Default value	Who usually sets its value?
`.sh.edchar`	In a **KEYBD** trap, the character(s) triggering the trap	None	KSH
`.sh.edcol`	In a **KEYBD** trap, the position of the character within the current line	None	KSH
`.sh.edmode`	In a **KEYBD** trap, the escape character, if you were in the text insert mode of vi when the **KEYBD** trap happened	ESCAPE or NULL	KSH
`.sh.edtext`	In a **KEYBD** trap, the character(s) on the current line	None	KSH
`.sh.name`	In a discipline function, the name of the variable being scrutinized	None	KSH
`.sh.subscript`	In a discipline function, the array subscript of the variable being scrutinized	None	KSH
`.sh.value`	In a discipline function, the value of the variable being scrutinized	None	KSH first, then U
`.sh.version`	A string containing the date on which this design of the KornShell was first built	None	KSH
CDPATH	Directories that **cd** searches	None	U
COLUMNS	Number of characters that can fit on a line	80	U or SA
EDITOR	Pathname of command line editor	`/bin/ed`	U or SA
ENV	Pathname of start-up script	None	U or SA
FCEDIT	Pathname of history file editor; obsolete: use **HISTEDIT** instead	`/bin/ed`	U or SA
FIGNORE	Filename pattern that KornShell should ignore when doing pattern matching	None	U
FPATH	Path of autoloaded functions	None	U
HISTCMD	Current command line number	None	KSH
HISTEDIT	Pathname of history file editor	`/bin/ed`	U or SA
HISTFILE	Pathname of history file	`$HOME/.sh_history`	U or SA
HISTSIZE	Number of accessible commands in history file	128	U or SA

Table 14-1. (Continued)

Variable	What it holds	Default value	Who usually sets its value?
HOME	Login directory	None	SA
IFS	Set of characters that act as token delimiters	Blank, tab, and newline	U
LANG	Locale	POSIX	SA
LC_ALL	Locale (overrides **LANG**, **LC_COLLATE**, **LC_CTYPE**, and **LC_NUMERIC**)	None	SA
LC_COLLATE	Locale for sorting strings	None	SA
LC_CTYPE	Locale for character classes such as `[[:char:]]`	None	SA
LC_NUMERIC	Locale for determining how decimal points will be handled	None	SA
LINENO	Current line number within script or function	None	KSH
LINES	Number of lines this window can display at one time	24	U or SA
MAIL	Pathname of master mail file	None	SA
MAILCHECK	Frequency at which the KornShell checks for receipt of new mail	600 (seconds)	U or SA
MAILPATH	Pathnames of master mail files	None	SA
OLDPWD	Previous current directory	None	KSH
OPTARG	Name of argument to a switch	None	KSH
OPTIND	Option's ordinal position on command line	None	KSH
PATH	Pathname of directories the KornShell searches for commands, scripts, or programs	Usually /bin:/usr/bin	SA, then U
PPID	PID of parent	None	KSH
PS1	Command line prompt	$	U
PS2	Prompt for command that extends more than one line	>	U
PS3	Prompt of **select** statement	#?	U
PS4	Debug mode prompt	+	U
PWD	Current directory	None	KSH
RANDOM	A random integer	None	KSH

Table 14-1. (Continued)

Variable	What it holds	Default value	Who usually sets its value?
REPLY	Input that hasn't yet been assigned	None	KSH
SECONDS	Number of seconds since the KornShell was invoked	None	KSH
SHELL	Controls creation of restricted KornShell	None	SA
TERM	Type of terminal you're using	None	SA or U
TMOUT	Turn off (time out) an unused KornShell	0 (unlimited)	U or SA
VISUAL	Command line editor	`/bin/ed`	U or SA
$	PID of current process	None	KSH
!	PID of background process	None	KSH
?	Exit status of most recent KornShell statement, system command, or user program	None	KSH
- (minus)	Option flags	None	KSH
_ (underscore)	Miscellaneous data	None	KSH

The remainder of this chapter details these reserved variables.

`.sh.edchar`, `.sh.edcol`, `.sh.edmode`, `.sh.edtext`

The KornShell automatically sets values for these variables when a **KEYBD** signal is trapped:

- `.sh.edchar`, which holds the identity of the last character or the last key sequence typed.

- `.sh.edtext`, which holds the line currently being typed.

- `.sh.edmode`, which usually holds a NULL character but will hold an escape character if you are in command mode of `vi`.

- `.sh.edcol`, which holds the position within the current line. So, when a user types the first character, the KornShell will set `.sh.edcol` to 0; when the user types the second character, the KornShell will set `.sh.edcol` to 1; and so on.

The KornShell issues a **KEYBD** signal whenever a user types a character (or, possibly, a sequence of characters, such as **CONTROL-C**). Through clever programming, you can trap the key(s) the user types and then treat those keys in whatever fashion you desire. For example, you could set a trap so that whenever a user typed a character, the KornShell would display the typed character's ASCII value instead of the character itself. For instance, if a user typed the letter B, the KornShell would display 66 (the ASCII value of letter B) instead of B.

For details about the **KEYBD** trap and the four associated variables, see page 321.

`.sh.name`, `.sh.subscript`, **and** `.sh.value`

The KornShell automatically sets values for these variables when a discipline function is called:

- `.sh.name`, which holds the name of the variable that triggered the discipline function.

- `.sh.subscript`, which holds the name of the array subscript when the associated array triggered the discipline function.

- `.sh.value`, which holds the value of the variable that triggered the discipline function. A discipline function can assign a new value to `.sh.value`. If it does, the KornShell will assign this value to the trigger variable.

See page 180 for an overview of discipline functions.

`.sh.version`

The `.sh.version` variable holds a string identifying the version of the KornShell. The "version" of the KornShell contains the date that this *design* of the KornShell was first built. For example, one of the KornShells I'm using has a version of:

```
$ print ${.sh.version}
Version M-12/28/93f
```

Thus, even though this KornShell was actually built (compiled, linked, and so on) in late 1997, the first functioning prototype of this KornShell was built in late 1993.

ENV

The **ENV** variable holds the pathname of a start-up script that the KornShell will call every time you:

- Start up a new KornShell

- Run a KornShell script

For details, see Chapter 11.

FIGNORE

The **FIGNORE** variable holds a pattern. When you issue a command that causes the KornShell to expand wildcards, the KornShell will ignore files that match the pattern assigned to **FIGNORE**; for example:

```
$ ls [a-z]*     # all objects beginning with a lowercase letter
lemon       lemon.bak      orange      orange.bak
$ FIGNORE=*.bak   # ignore all objects whose names end in .bak
```

Now when you issue a command containing a wildcard, the KornShell ignores all objects whose names end in `.bak`:

```
$ ls [a-z]*     # all objects beginning with a lowercase
lemon       orange
```

Note that **FIGNORE** only influences commands having wildcards. For example, since the following command does not contain any wildcards, ls continues to report on files ending with `.bak`:

```
$ ls
91      98      lemon      lemon.bak      orange      orange.bak
```

$? — Error Status

Every KornShell statement and script, every operating system command, and every user program returns an *error status* (or *exit status*). The KornShell automatically assigns the error status to variable **$?**.

The error status is an integer that symbolizes the success or failure of the statement, script, command, or program. Generally speaking, an error status of 0 indicates success, and a nonzero error status indicates failure. Unfortunately, some commands are careless in setting the error status, so you can't always depend on **$?** being an accurate barometer of success or failure.

HISTFILE, HISTSIZE, HISTEDIT, HISTCMD, and FCEDIT — History File

The KornShell supports several variables to control the history file.

The **HISTFILE** variable holds the pathname of the history file. The default value of **HISTFILE** is $HOME/.sh_history. So, for example, if your login **(HOME)** directory is /usr/julie, the history file will be stored in pathname /usr/julie/.sh_history.

If you are working on a dumb terminal that does not support multiple windows, there is seldom any reason to change the value of **HISTFILE.** If you are working on a terminal that supports multiple windows, you might want to create multiple history files, one for each window running a KornShell. If you do *not* create separate history files, all the commands you execute in different windows will be archived in one central history file. Some users like this, but others find it rather confusing. If you'd like a different history file for each window, put the following two lines in your Korn-Shell start-up file:

```
export HISTFILE=$HOME/.history$$
```

(See "$$, $!, and PPID—Process ID" on page 307 for an explanation of **$$**.)

The **HISTSIZE** variable holds an integer representing the number of commands that you can access from the history file. For example, if you specify the following:

```
HISTSIZE=50
```

in your $HOME/.profile start-up script, the KornShell allows you to read, edit, or execute any of the 50 most recently issued commands. If you don't specify a value of **HISTSIZE,** the KornShell allows you to read, edit, or execute any of the 128 most recently issued commands. By the way, once the KornShell has been invoked, modifying the value of **HISTSIZE** won't alter the number of commands that you can access.

You can use the **hist -s** command (or its alias, **r**) to edit commands from the history file and then re-execute them. Of course, in order to edit a command, you'll need a text editor. You may specify the text editor when you invoke the **hist** command; for example, the following command tells **hist** to use the text editor stored at pathname /usr/ucb/vi when editing command number 238:

```
$ hist -e /usr/ucb/vi 238
```

It quickly will become annoying to keep reminding **hist** what your favorite editor is. To get around having to use hist -e every time, just assign the pathname of your favorite editor to the **HISTEDIT** variable. For example, the following command tells the KornShell to do command line editing with vi:

```
$ HISTEDIT=/usr/ucb/vi
```

Now that **HISTEDIT** is set, you can edit command number 238 in a more civilized manner, to wit:

```
$ hist 238
```

In case you're wondering, hist -e takes precedence over the value of **HISTEDIT**. For example, if you set **HISTEDIT** to vi and specify hist -e /usr/ucb/emacs, the KornShell will invoke emacs (not vi) to edit the command line. **FCEDIT** does the same thing as **HISTEDIT**; however, we recommend using **HISTEDIT**.

HISTCMD holds the current command number. Thus, with each command you execute on the KornShell command line, the KornShell automatically increments **HISTCMD** by one. You can assign any nonnegative integer value to **HISTCMD**.

IFS — Parsing Lines into Tokens

IFS is an acronym for *internal field separator*. Its primary purpose is to define a token for those statements **(read, for, select)** or commands that need to parse information into tokens.

We detail the **IFS** variable on page 216. Briefly, **IFS** holds a set of characters, where each character is a token delimiter. The default set of characters is all three white space characters (space, tab, newline). For many KornShell scripts, the default set of characters is just fine. However, you could assign a completely different set of characters to **IFS**; for example:

```
$ IFS='Zz'  # assign two letters to IFS
$ read one two three four five
zebras in zoos go zzoom.
```

Table 14-2 shows how the **read** statement would parse the input line.

Table 14-2. How the read Statement Parses the Input Line

Variable	Is assigned this value	Explanation
one	" "	Everything from start of line to first z
two	"ebras in "	Everything after first z up until next z
three	"oos go "	Everything from z in zoos up until first z in zzoom.
four	" "	Everything between two z's in zzoom
five	"oom."	Everything after last z until end of line

When writing the values of all the positional parameters with the following statement:

```
print "$*"
```

the first character in **IFS** separates the values. See "The IFS Variable" on page 216 for an example.

You often have to assign white space characters to **IFS**. One way to do this is simply to type the white space characters inside a pair of single quotes. For example, the following command assigns a blank, a tab, and a newline to **IFS**:

```
$ IFS='
'
```

Because it is impossible to "see" the white space, you just kind of have to take my word for it. A better way of assigning invisible characters is to assign escape sequences (see page 376) inside **IFS**. However, in order to assign escape sequences to **IFS**, you must preface the initial single quote with a dollar sign ($). For example, the following command assigns a blank, a tab, and a newline to **IFS**:

```
$ IFS=$' \t\n'  # there's a blank space just before the \t
```

LANG, LC_ALL, LC_COLLATE, LC_TYPE, **and** LC_NUMERIC

These five reserved variables are useful for internationalizing your scripts. The term *internationalization* often is abbreviated I18N because of the 18 letters between the starting *I* and the closing *N* in this very long word. The goal of I18N is to simplify the coding of programs that must run in multiple countries.

I've got to warn you that there are entire books (long ones with moldy covers) devoted to this topic. The central problem tackled by these books is how other countries screw up perfectly good "Americentric" principles. For instance, consider the following KornShell character class:

```
[[:alpha:]]
```

But what exactly is an alpha? Americans know that an **alpha** is any of the 26 "real" letters from A to shining Z. However, the French understand an **alpha** to include not only the Roman 26, but also those *très charmant* accent marks that can transform a modest hotel into a thousand-franc-a-night *hôtel*. Japanese programmers, with their plethora of alphabets, must wonder which *kanas* form an **alpha**, or whether *kanji* characters are themselves considered **alpha**.

If you're writing a KornShell script that will run in different locales, do you have to redefine **alpha** for every locale? Fortunately, the answer is no. You write the code only once. The KornShell looks at the value of the appropriate locale variables to figure out what an **alpha** is. For example, if a locale variable defines the locale as German, the KornShell understands an alpha to be any character in the German alphabet. And if that same KornShell scripts runs in a French locale, the KornShell will understand an **alpha** to be any character in the French alphabet. *Esta wunderbar, n'est-ce pas?*

Character classes such as [[:alpha:]] aren't the only part of the KornShell influenced by locale. For example, some cultures use a dot for a decimal point, while others use a comma.

The KornShell supplies different locale variables to control different aspects of I18N. For example, by setting I18N variables appropriately, you could request a Dutch-style definition of [[:alpha:]] with British-style decimal points.

On to the I18N variables themselves. There are five of them:

* **LC_NUMERIC**, which controls the way that decimal points will be displayed.

* **LC_COLLATE**, which controls how the KornShell sorts strings.

* **LC_CTYPE**, which controls the definition of character classes (such as [[:alpha:]]).

* **LANG**, which (if set) overrides the value of all other I18N variables. The default value of **LANG** is POSIX, which is a sort of American locale.

* **LC_ALL**, which (if set) overrides the value of all other I18N variables, including **LANG**. Thus, **LC_ALL** is the most powerful of the five.

For example, the simplest way to run your program in the French language locale of France is to put the following in a start-up file:

```
export LC_ALL=fr-fr
```

It would be a wonderful world if these variables also magically translated the text strings in your script.

LINENO — Current Line Number

The KornShell sets **LINENO** to the current line number within the script. The top line in the script has a **LINENO** value of 1, the second has a **LINENO** value of 2, and so on. If you place **LINENO** inside a function, the KornShell sets **LINENO** to the current line number relative to the beginning of the function. The KornShell considers the function's starting brace ({) to have a **LINENO** value of 1. Thus, in the following script, the **print** statement in function happy has a **LINENO** value of 2.

Note that *all* lines, even blank lines and comments, are included in **LINENO**'s count. If you put multiple statements (separated by semicolons) on one line, **LINENO** still counts that as only one line.

```
USAGE="usage: LINENOex.ksh"      # LINENO reserved variable

function happy
{
   print "Greetings from Line $LINENO of $0"
}

function friendly
{
 # Comments and blank lines are also included in the count.

   print "Hello again."
   print "Greetings from Line $LINENO of $0"
}

happy      # call function happy
friendly  # call function friendly
print "Greetings from Line $LINENO of $0"
```

Executing This Script

```
$ LINENOex.ksh
Greetings from Line 2 of happy
Hello again.
Greetings from Line 5 of friendly
Greetings from Line 18 of LINEN0_ex.ksh
```

MAIL, MAILPATH, and MAILCHECK — **Electronic Mail**

Of all the contributions that e-mail has made to our planet, I'd have to say that the best is that no e-mail system has ever opened fire on any of its coworkers.

There are two basic kinds of mail storage systems. In one, the mail system appends all incoming mail to the user's master mail file. In the other mail storage system, each piece of incoming mail gets stored in its own separate file. If your mail storage system is the latter, then **MAIL, MAILPATH,** and **MAILCHECK** do not have any influence. (The remainder of this section assumes that you are using the master mail file storage system.)

If all your electronic mail ends up in one master mail file, then the system administrator or user should set **MAIL** equal to the pathname of that master mail file; for example:

```
MAIL=/usr/spool/mail/paul
```

On the other hand, some users belong to multiple mail systems and have multiple master mail files. For these users, the system administrator or user should set **MAILPATH** equal to the pathnames of all of the master mail files. For example, if user "paul" has two different master mail files, the following assignment tells **MAILPATH** about both of them. (Use a colon to separate each pathname.)

```
MAILPATH=/usr/spool/mail/paul:/uucp/paul
```

If both **MAIL** and **MAILPATH** are set, **MAILPATH** has precedence over **MAIL.**

Assuming that **MAIL** or **MAILPATH** have been set, you can assign an integer value to **MAILCHECK.** The **MAILCHECK** variable determines how often (in seconds) the KornShell will check for new mail. For example, the following command tells the KornShell to check the mailboxes or mail files every five minutes (300 seconds):

```
MAILCHECK=300
```

If no new mail arrived during those 300 seconds, the KornShell keeps quiet about it. If mail did arrive, KornShell announces its arrival with a jolly:

```
You have mail in $_
```

where KornShell replaces **$_** with the name of the master mail file that received the mail.

OPTARG and OPTIND — **Values Associated with** getopts

Chapter 9 details both of these variables. Briefly, the **getopts** statement automatically sets **OPTARG** to the following:

- The name of an invalid switch

- The name of an argument to a valid switch

The value of **OPTIND** usually is an argument to a **shift** statement. See the `getopts6.ksh` example on page 157 for details.

PATH, CDPATH, and FPATH — Search Directories

Each of these three variables—**PATH**, **CDPATH**, and **FPATH**—holds a different list of directories. Under certain circumstances, the KornShell will search through these lists in order to find:

- A certain program or shell script to execute (**PATH**)

- A certain directory to move to (**CDPATH**)

- A certain autoloaded function (**FPATH**) (see Chapter 10)

PATH, CDPATH, and **FPATH** influence only implicit pathnames; they have no influence over explicit pathnames. On UNIX systems, an *explicit pathname* begins with any of the following character sequences:

- /

- ./

- ../

An *implicit pathname* does not begin with one of the preceding character sequences. For example, contrast the following pathnames:

```
/usr/ng/myscript    # explicit pathname, begins with /
myscript            # implicit pathname
./vi                # explicit pathname, begins with ./
vi                  # implicit pathname
../games            # explicit pathname, begins with .
games/solitaire     # implicit pathname
```

An explicit pathname also can begin with any variable whose value begins with the character sequences /, ./, or ../; for example, assuming that the value of **HOME** is /usr/mar, then:

```
$HOME/heart/is      # explicit pathname, $HOME begins with /
heart/is            # implicit pathname
```

Now that we've gotten that out of the way, we can concentrate on **PATH.** Let's start by setting **PATH** equal to three directories: . (the current directory), /bin, and $HOME/bin. Here's the assignment:

```
$ PATH=.:/bin:$HOME/bin
```

If we try to execute a script by typing its explicit pathname, for instance:

```
$ /usr/quentin/title.ksh
```

the KornShell will try to execute whatever is stored at /usr/quentin/title.ksh and ignore **PATH.** However, if we type the following implicit pathname:

   $ **goo**

the KornShell will search the directories of **PATH** one by one until it finds goo. The quest is illustrated in Figure 14-1.

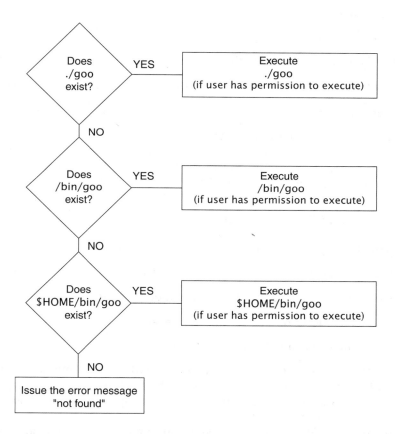

Figure 14-1. The KornShell Searches the PATH Directories for an Implicit Pathname

    CDPATH is similar to **PATH** in that it holds a list of directories; however, **CDPATH** influences only the **cd** (change directory) statement. The **cd** statement takes an explicit or implicit pathname as an argument. If you specify an explicit pathname, **cd** ignores **CDPATH.** If, however, you specify an implicit pathname, **cd** looks for a subdirectory by that name in the list of directories of **CDPATH.**

    Let's explore **CDPATH** through some examples. First, let's assign a list of directories to **CDPATH** as follows:

```
$ CDPATH=.:$HOME/my_book:/usr/jan
```

If you issue an explicit pathname such as:

```
$ cd /usr/beth
```

then **cd** ignores **CDPATH** and simply tries to change the current directory to /usr/beth. Suppose, though, that you specify an implicit pathname argument instead, such as:

```
$ cd chapter8
```

In this case, **cd** will search for directory chapter8 in the following order:

1. Does ./chapter8 exist? If yes, change current directory to it.

2. Does $HOME/my_book/chapter8 exist? If yes, change current directory to it.

3. Does /usr/jan/chapter8 exist? If yes, change current directory to it.

There is no default value for **CDPATH**. If **CDPATH** isn't set and you issue a **cd** statement, the KornShell searches for directories underneath the current directory.

If you do specify a list of directories for **CDPATH,** it is almost always a good idea to include the current directory in that list.

PS1, PS2, PS3, **and** PS4 — **Prompts**

The KornShell provides four variables to define the four kinds of prompts:

*   **PS1**, which describes the command line prompt

*   **PS2**, which describes the line continuation prompt

*   **PS3**, which describes the prompt for **select** statements

*   **PS4**, which describes the prompt seen in debug mode

The KornShell uses the value of the variable **PS1** as the command line prompt. When you first invoke the KornShell, the prompt stares back at you. After every command finishes running, the command line prompt greets you. The command line prompt is set to the value of **PS1.**

The default KornShell command line prompt for users is a dollar sign $ followed by a space; the default KornShell command line prompt for the root user is the pound symbol # followed by a space. If you don't like the default prompt, you can change it by assigning a new value to **PS1.** Typically, KornShell users specify the command line prompt in their start-up script (see Chapter 11), although you can redefine the prompt at any time. For example, if you find the dollar sign a little too boring, you can change it by assigning a new value to **PS1**; for example:

```
$ PS1='Hey There Good Looking: ' # change PS1
Hey There Good Looking:          # here's the new prompt
```

Go ahead and try it—make up your own witty prompts.

Some Popular Command Line Prompts

Most beginners treat the prompt as a lifeless lump of clay, an inert and frequently profane text string. Yet the prompt can be a lot more than that.

Set the prompt to the current command number (see Chapter 17 for an explanation of command numbers):

```
$ PS1='! Korn> ' #change prompt
25 Korn> pwd       # prompt is now 25 Korn>
/usr/shannon/ftn/programs
26 Korn> cd /usr/shannon
27 Korn> # the KornShell automatically increments command number
```

Set the prompt to the current directory:

```
$ PS1='$PWD '            # change PS1
/usr/mel x=3             # the prompt contains the current directory
/usr/mel cd /usr/joan/teach # when you change directories...
/usr/joan/teach          # the prompt changes
```

Set the prompt to the current directory relative to the **HOME** directory:

```
$ print $PWD              # what's the current directory?
/usr/shannon/ftn/programs
$ print $HOME             # what's the home directory?
/usr/shannon
$ PS1='${PWD#$HOME/}: '   # change prompt
ftn/programs/:            # here's the new prompt
```

Set the prompt to the rightmost directory name:

```
$ print $PWD              # what's the current directory?
/usr/shannon/ftn/programs
$ PS1=' ${PWD##*/}: '     # change prompt
programs:        # the new prompt is the rightmost directory name
```

Set the prompt to the number of seconds since you started up the KornShell:

```
$ PS1='$SECONDS: ' # change prompt
3.41: scr.ksh # the new prompt tells us how old the KornShell is
5.95:          # 2.54 seconds elapsed since the previous prompt
```

Set the prompt to the PID of the current process and the PID of the most recently invoked background process:

```
$ PS1=''$$ $!: ' # change prompt
186: print "hi"   # 186 is the PID of the current process
hi
186: myscript&    # start a background process
[1]   215         # 215 is the PID of the background process
186 215:          # prompt changes to include the background PID
```

BEWARE: Common Mistakes in Setting Prompts

When assigning a value to a prompt, it is a really good idea to enclose that value inside a pair of single quotes. In fact, if the prompt string you are assigning contains a variable whose value will change, it is a necessity to enclose that prompt in single quotes. For example, suppose you want your prompt to be the number of seconds since this KornShell started.

```
PS1=$SECONDS      # wrong, prompt will never change
PS1="$SECONDS "   # wrong, prompt will never change
PS1='$SECONDS '   # right, prompt will update every time
```

You always should specify at least one character of white space at the end of the prompt string. If you don't, the user's input will bump smack against the prompt.

```
PS1='Go'     # wrong, no space after Go
PS1='Go '    # right, space after Go
```

If you put an exclamation point in the string you assign to **PS1**, the KornShell will display the command number as part of the prompt. However, suppose you want a literal exclamation point to appear as part of your prompt. In this case, you must specify two exclamation points in a row; for example:

```
$ PS1='Enter your command, now!! '
Enter your command, now!
```

Assigning a value to **PS3** or **PS4** from the KornShell command line will not change those prompts *unless* you export the variable.

PS2 is the line continuation prompt. Its default value is the > character. The KornShell displays the line continuation prompt when you do not complete a command on one line. For example, the following **for** loop requires four lines, so the KornShell will display **PS2** three times:

```
$ for object in b*
> do
>   print "\t$object"
> done
```

Just to get cute, I'll make **PS1** and **PS2** as literal as possible:

```
$ PS1='Command Starts Here: '
$ PS2=' and continues here: '
Command Starts Here: for object in b*
and continues here: do
and continues here:    print "\t$object"
and continues here: done
```

The line continuation prompt (**PS2**) often appears when I didn't expect it. *"Hey, I typed the whole command on one line; why is the line continuation prompt appearing?"* Often, the culprit is an unmatched single- or double-quote; for example:

```
Command Starts Here: print "and here we are
and continues here: what? 1 forgot to finish that line?"
```

PS3 is the variable controlling the prompt within a `select` statement. See Chapter 8 for some examples.

PS4 is the debug prompt. Actually, calling **PS4** a "prompt" is somewhat misleading because it doesn't actually prompt the user to enter input. Instead, when you debug your script (by specifying `set -x` or `ksh -x`), the KornShell precedes the name of the command being executed with the value of **PS4**. By default, the value of **PS4** is a plus sign (**+**). You may wish to change your debug prompt so that it equals **LINENO.** That way, the KornShell will display the line number of the command being executed. Another fun thing to do is to have **PS4** print the number of seconds elapsed since the script started running, like this:

```
SECONDS=0    # reset SECONDS
PS4='$SECONDS: '
export PS4
```

Remember to export **PS4**. If you don't export it, the debug prompt won't change.

HOME, PWD, and OLDPWD — Login, Current, and Previous Directories

PWD holds the name of the directory you're currently in. **OLDPWD** holds the name of the directory you just left; for example:

```
$ print $PWD       # print name of current directory
/usr/ignatov/clubs/seven
$ cd /rastelli/sticks  # change current directory
$ print $PWD       # print new current directory
/rastelli/sticks
$ print $OLDPWD    # print previous current directory
/usr/ignatov/clubs/seven
$ cd $OLDPWD       # change current directory to previous directory
```

By the way, when used as an argument to **cd**, the – character is a synonym for **$OLDPWD**. Thus, the following command changes directory to the previous directory:

```
$ cd -
```

HOME holds the name of a special directory, typically the directory you log into. Usually, the system administrator sets the value of **HOME** for you; however, you may choose to redefine it. If you specify the **cd** statement without specifying an argument, **cd** sets the current directory to **HOME**. Also, on most UNIX systems, you can use the tilde ~ character to symbolize the **HOME** directory; for example:

```
$ cd $HOME       # return to your login directory
$ cd             # same as previous command
$ cd ~           # same as previous command
```

On most UNIX systems, the phrase *~username* refers to the **HOME** directory of *username*; for example:

```
$ cd ~steve       # change to steve's HOME directory
```

Don't confuse the **PWD** reserved variable with the **pwd** statement, for example:

```
$ PWD             # wrong; PWD is a variable, not a command
ksh: PWD: not found

$ pwd             # right, pwd is a command
/usr/ignatov/clubs/seven
```

It is legal to assign a value to **PWD,** but you really shouldn't do it. Changing the value of **PWD** does not actually change the current directory; it just causes confusion.

Changing the current directory within a script does not change the current directory of the shell or the process that called that script. For example, consider the following simple script:

```
USAGE="usage: PWD_ex.ksh new_dir" # PWD variable

cd $1
print "Current directory is $PWD"
```

Executing This Script

Before running the script, let's find the current directory:

```
$ print $PWD      # find the current dir
/rastelli/sticks
```

Now let's run the script:

```
$ PWD_ex.ksh /usr/arthur/juggle # call the script
Current directory is /usr/arthur/juggle
```

Did the script change the current directory of the shell?

```
$ print $PWD            # find the current dir after calling the script
/rastelli/sticks
```

No, it did not. See Chapter 11 for more information.

RANDOM — Random Integer Generator

Every time you access **RANDOM**, the KornShell sets its value to a different random integer between 0 and 32,767. If you are accustomed to other high-level languages, you might pretend that **RANDOM** is a function call that returns a random number.

In some other programming languages, the default behavior of the random number generator is to provide the same set of random integers every time you run the program. However, the default behavior of the KornShell **RANDOM** variable is to provide a different set of random integers every time you run the program. If you do want the KornShell to provide the same set of random integers every time you run the program, you need to seed **RANDOM** by assigning a constant to it.

```
USAGE="usage: RANDOMex.ksh" # RANDOM
 function throw_two_dice
 {
   ((dice1 = (RANDOM % 6) + 1)) # random number from 1 to 6
   ((dice2 = (RANDOM % 6) + 1)) # random number from 1 to 6
   ((total = dice1 + dice2))    # random number from 2 to 12
   return $total
 }
 ################################################################
 # Script starts executing at next statement.
 # By default, RANDOM provides truly random numbers.
 throw_two_dice
 print "Truly random roll: $?"

 # If you want to generate the same random number each time
 # you run the script, set RANDOM to a constant.
 RANDOM=2 # seed random number generator to a constant
 throw_two_dice
 print "Same every time: $?"

 # If you want to generate a different set of random numbers
 # each time you run the script, then set RANDOM to $$ or to SECONDS.
 RANDOM=$SECONDS
 throw_two_dice
 print "Truly random roll: $?"
```

Executing This Script

```
$ RANDOMex.ksh
Truly random roll: 7
Same every time: 6
Another truly random roll: 10

$ RANDOMex.ksh
Truly random roll: 4
Same every time: 6
Another truly random roll: 3
```

REPLY, -, and _ — Miscellaneous Input Repository

The KornShell sets the values of three reserved variables, **REPLY**, -, and _, to hold various input information.

The KornShell sets the value of **REPLY** to the following:

- Whatever the user inputs in a **select** statement. See Chapter 8 for an example.

- Whatever the user inputs to a **read** statement that does not contain a target variable. See Chapter 12 for an example.

No other event can influence **REPLY.**

Although it looks like a typo, the underscore character _ is a KornShell reserved variable. The KornShell sets this value according to the following rules:

- The final token of the most recently executed KornShell statement, Korn-Shell script, operating system command, or user program. Every time you invoke anything (either in a script or on the KornShell command line), the KornShell automatically assigns a new value to the _ variable. For example, suppose that you issue the command ls -l. In this case, the KornShell automatically assigns -l to the _ variable because -l is the last token on the command line. Suppose you issue another command, say, read pints quarts. Now the KornShell assigns the value "quarts" to the _ variable. Incidentally, the starting value of the _ variable is the pathname of the script. In other words, before the KornShell executes any commands in a script, the KornShell assigns **$0** to the _ variable.

- The name of the master mail file that received mail. See the description of **MAILCHECK** earlier in this chapter.

And as if naming a variable _ weren't bad enough, the KornShell also provides a variable named - (that's right, a minus sign). The KornShell automatically sets the value of this variable to a string of letters in which each letter represents a different KornShell invocation command. When I invoke the following command on a command line, I get:

```
$ print $-
ims
```

The response, ims, indicates that the KornShell itself was invoked with three options (i, m, and s). Of the many documented and undocumented invocation options that **$-** might return, the most interesting is the i option. The i stands for interactive and will be present in **$-** whenever you're on the KornShell command line. Within a script, the value of **$-** will never contain i. Thus, if your .profile script needs to do one thing for the KornShell command line and another thing for KornShell scripts, this start-up script should test the value of **$-** to see if it contains i.

SECONDS — Elapsed Time

The KornShell sets **SECONDS** to the number of seconds elapsed since you invoked the KornShell; for example:

```
$ print "I invoked this KornShell $SECONDS seconds ago."
I invoked this KornShell 1338.248 seconds ago.
```

If you use **SECONDS** inside a script, **SECONDS** measures the number of seconds elapsed since the script began executing.

On older versions of KornShell, the value of **SECONDS** is an integer. Beginning with KornShell 93, **SECONDS** became a floating-point value. So, you now get a much more precise reading on how much time you've squandered. Progress marches on.

If you set **SECONDS** to some numerical value, **SECONDS** begins counting from the specified value. For example, the following script resets **SECONDS** to zero in order to restart a timer:

```
USAGE="usage: stopwatch.ksh"  # demonstrates SECONDS

# How fast can you type?
 print "Type the following and I'll time you:"
 print "The quick brown fox jumped over the lazy dog."
 read first_typing_test
 printf "It took you %.1f seconds to type that passage.\n" $SECONDS

 print "\nNow try to type the following:"
 print "QWERTY may be slower, but I can't be retrained."
 SECONDS=0          # reset our timer
 read second_typing_test
 printf "It took you %.1f seconds to type that passage.\n" $SECONDS
```

Executing This Script

```
$ stopwatch.ksh
Type the following and I'll time you:
The quick brown fox jumped over the lazy dog.
The quick brown fox jumped over the lazy dog.
It took you 7.5 seconds to type that passage.

Now try to type the following:
QWERTY may be slow, but I can't be retrained.
QWERTY may be slow, but I can't be retrained.
It took you 6.7 seconds to type that passage.
```

SHELL

Ignore this variable unless you want to create a *restricted KornShell,* generally known as rksh. As the name implies, a restricted KornShell is a KornShell implementation that prevents (restricts) the user from doing certain things. Specifically, users running in a restricted KornShell are not allowed to do any of the following:

- Change the current directory. (In other words, the **cd** command won't work.)

- Change the value of the **SHELL, ENV,** or **PATH** variables.

- Invoke a program (including operating system utilities) by specifying the explicit pathname of that program.

- Redirect output with >, >|, <>, or >>.

However, if a user working in a restricted KornShell invokes a KornShell script, the script will run normally. That is, a restricted KornShell does not restrict KornShell scripts.

Warning: Setting up a bulletproof restricted environment is difficult! Do you really need to do it?

There are two ways to create a restricted KornShell. One is to invoke the program named rksh. Another is by setting the **SHELL** variable. This variable holds a pathname. If the leafname of this pathname contains the letter r, the system invokes a restricted KornShell. Otherwise, the system invokes a regular (nonrestricted) Korn-Shell. For those unfamiliar with this term, the *leafname* of a pathname is the last (rightmost) component of the pathname. For example, the following assignment in a start-up script will cause the system to invoke a restricted KornShell:

```
SHELL=/usr/bin/rksh    # leafname (rksh) contains letter r
```

However, the following assignment in a start-up script will cause the system to invoke a regular (nonrestricted) KornShell:

```
SHELL=/usr/bin/ksh     # leafname (ksh) does not contain letter r
```

By the way, many users think that the KornShell automatically assigns **SHELL** the pathname of the KornShell currently in use. However, the KornShell does not do this. If you're in the KornShell and want to find the pathname of the current Korn-Shell, type the following:

```
$ print $0
/bin/ksh
```

TERM, COLUMN, LINES — **Terminal Characteristics**

Each implementation of the KornShell provides several variables to define the shape, size, characteristics, and identity of the terminal or virtual terminals (windows) that you are using. The KornShell itself makes only scant use of these variables, but other software may depend on them.

On some implementations of the KornShell, the values of the **COLUMNS** and **LINES** variables control how the **select** statement outputs menu entries.

The **TERM** variable holds a string identifying the kind of terminal on which you are working. For instance, I set the **TERM** variable on my terminal as follows:

```
export TERM=xterm
```

The value xterm indicates that the terminal is running a standard window of the X windows system.

On UNIX systems, the file /etc/termcap contains cryptic descriptions of all the terminals that can run on your UNIX system along with the correct values for **TERM**.

Certain UNIX utilities, such as vi, depend on **TERM** for a description of the terminal's characteristics.

TMOUT — **Time Out an Unused KornShell**

The default value of **TMOUT** is 0, meaning that KornShell users can wait an infinite amount of time between entering commands. If you'd like to force users to move it or lose it, then assign an integer value to **TMOUT**. For example, let's set the timeout period to two minutes (120 seconds) by issuing the following command:

```
$ TMOUT=120
```

If at any point during the KornShell session, the user goes two minutes without issuing a command, the KornShell will issue the message:

```
shell will time out in 60 seconds
```

Once the message appears, the user has another minute to enter a command. If the user does not, the KornShell ends its session. If the user does enter a command, the KornShell time out clock starts ticking anew. Keep in mind that the clock starts when the user *invokes* the command; it does not start when the user simply begins *typing* a command. Something else to keep in mind—the KornShell has no qualms about timing you out of a session even when background processes are running.

On some systems, particularly systems with dumb terminals, the system automatically logs out users when the KornShell dies. Thus, **TMOUT** can be effective in automatically logging out users who've forgotten to log themselves out.

Some systems support a screen time out variable, which temporarily darkens the monitor (to save electricity and wear-and-tear on the screen) or runs a screen saver program when user input stops. Despite a certain conceptual resemblance, the Korn-Shell **TMOUT** and the screen timeout variable are unrelated.

Though it may cause undue stress on users, you can use **TMOUT** within a script to encourage users to type faster. When a KornShell script reaches a **read** or a **select** statement, the KornShell will pause to await user input. If the user fails to hit a carriage return before the specified number of **TMOUT** seconds, then the KornShell essentially skips over the **read** or **select** statement, assigning a null string to the argument(s) of **read** or **select**. For example, consider the following high-strung script:

```
USAGE="usage: TMOUTex.ksh"

TMOUT=4
print "Enter your name and be quick about it: "
read name

if [[ -z $name ]]
then  # name holds the null string
    print "Type faster next time!"
else  # name probably holds a non-null value
    print "Thank you for your quick response, $name"
fi
```

Executing this Script

```
$ TMOUTex.ksh
Enter your name and be quick about it:
Goldilocks<RETURN>
Thank you for your quick response, Goldilocks
```

But suppose the next user didn't type quite as fast:

```
$ TMOUTex.ksh
Enter your name and be quick about it:
Rapunz
Type faster next time!
```

VISUAL and EDITOR — Command Line Text Editors

Use **VISUAL** or **EDITOR** to specify a text editor for KornShell command lines. (See Chapter 16 for an explanation of command line text editors.)

Some users think they have to specify the full pathname at which the text editor is stored; for example, /usr/ucb/vi or /bin/vi. In reality, the KornShell command line text editors are built into the KornShell itself. In other words, if you assign **VISUAL** the value /usr/ucb/vi, the KornShell will not actually use the vi editor stored at /usr/ucb/vi. Instead, the KornShell interprets only the last few characters of the value of **VISUAL:**

- If the last two characters are vi, the KornShell will use vi-style command line editing.

- If the last five characters are emacs, the KornShell will use emacs-style command line editing.

- If the last five characters are gmacs, the KornShell will use gmacs-style command line editing.

The value you assign to **VISUAL** does not restrict your choices for regular text editing. For example, if you set **VISUAL** to emacs, you can still use vi (or any other text editor) to edit a text file.

Note that **EDITOR** serves the same purpose as **VISUAL**; however, as far as the KornShell is concerned, **VISUAL** has precedence over **EDITOR**. In other words, if you assign a value to both **VISUAL** and **EDITOR**, the KornShell will ignore the value of **EDITOR**. Note that **EDITOR** defaults to /bin/ed (an editor so primitive that a Carbon-14 test is required to pin down its age), but **VISUAL** has no default.

By the way, besides the KornShell, several other UNIX commands rely on the value of the **EDITOR** variable.

$$, $!, and PPID — Process ID

Casually speaking, a *process* is an executing program. (If you need a more formal definition, get a life.) Operating systems keep track of processes by associating a unique identification number, usually called a *PID*, with each process. The PID is more than just an interesting piece of trivia; certain statements (for example, **kill**) require a PID as an argument.

The KornShell provides three reserved variables that hold PIDs:

- **$$**, which holds the PID of the current process.

- **$PPID**, which holds the PID of the parent process of the current process. The parent process is the process that invoked the current process.

- **$!**, which holds the PID of the most recently invoked background process (even if that process isn't currently running). See "Background and Foreground" on page 309 for an explanation of background processes.

Here's a script that exercises two of these variables:

```
USAGE="usage: pid_ex.ksh"  # demonstrates $$ and $PPID

print "The PID of the current process is $$"
print "The PID of the parent process is $PPID"
```

Executing This Script

Before invoking `pid_ex.ksh`, let's find out what the PID of the KornShell is. (Remember, an executing KornShell is itself a process.)

```
$ print "The PID of my KornShell is $$"
The PID of my KornShell is 225
```

Now, we'll invoke the script from the KornShell, thus making the KornShell into the script's parent:

```
$ pid_ex.ksh
The PID of the current process is 234
The PID of the parent process is 225
```

UNIX users can use the `ps` command (with appropriate switches) to obtain PIDs and PPIDs. However, parsing the complicated `ps` output format from within a script can be a bit of a chore. Also, different versions of `ps` take different switches, so writing a portable shell script that uses `ps` can be downright tricky.

But I Have More Variables Than That

The `set` statement returns a list of all the variables currently set in your environment. If you look at this list, you'll no doubt see the names of variables not described in this chapter. That's because this chapter only describes variables that have special meaning to the KornShell. However, shocking as it may seem, it turns out that other programs besides the KornShell also run on your system. Many of these other programs rely on their own environment variables. For example, many UNIX systems define a variable named **LD_LIBRARY_PATH** that contains a list of directories that the UNIX runtime system searches to find shared libraries.

15 Foreground, Background, and Signaling

This chapter explains the difference between foreground and background, and then details signaling. Beginners probably can skip over the signaling parts.

Background and Foreground

Consider the following session on the KornShell command line:

```
$ ls -Rl      # UNIX utility
$ stats       # program to average five billion floating-point numbers
$ my_script # KornShell script
```

You may think to yourself, Hey, those three commands ran in the KornShell. However, it would be more accurate to think, Hey, those three commands ran in the KornShell's *foreground*. It is an easy mistake to make because, by default, all commands run in the foreground. The foreground can execute only one command at a time.[1] When that command finishes executing, the KornShell prompts you to enter another one, and so you do until you end the KornShell session.

The problem with the foreground is that a lengthy program can tie up your terminal for hours or even days. For example, if you invoke stats on Monday, you might not be able to invoke my_script until Tuesday. To solve this problem, the KornShell lets you run commands in the *background*. Background commands run off in their own little world without disturbing the foreground. When the background command finishes running, the KornShell can send you a short message to tell you that it's done. By running time-consuming commands in the background, the foreground is freed up for interactive commands.

Although only one command at a time can run in the foreground, you can concurrently run multiple background commands. Not all KornShell implementations support job control. Generally speaking, if your operating system supports job control, so will your KornShell.

To run a command in the background, simply append an ampersand (&) to the command line; for example:

---

1. One could argue that a pipeline (that is, a command line containing a pipe operator) executes multiple commands at one time.

```
$ stats &  # run stats in the background
```

If you want `stats` to continue running after you log out (yes, it's possible), preface the entire command with the word **nohup** (short for do **no**t **h**ang **up**); for example:

```
$ nohup stats &   # run stats in background even after log out
```

Scripts running in the background cannot be interactive. In other words, a background script has to take all of its input from a file or from a pipe because background scripts cannot gather input from the keyboard.

By default, scripts running in the background send their standard output and standard error to the terminal. There you are sitting at the keyboard, having a quiet moment composing some pastoral poetry, when whammo, the output of the payroll process starts spilling into your verse on the quiet power of cows. So, when running a script in the background, you usually should redirect standard output and standard error so that they write their output to a file or to a pipe, never to the terminal. So, for example, a typical background invocation might look this:

```
$ typical_script.ksh < input_data > the_answer 2> bad_stuff &
[1] 405
```

Notice the numbers (for example, [1] and 405) that the KornShell displays when you run a command in the background. The first number is called a *job number*. The KornShell assigns job number 1 to the first background process, job number 2 to the second background process, and so on. The second number is called a *process identifier* or *PID*. The KornShell displays the job number and PID because you may need one of them as an argument to a job control statement. Table 15-1 lists all the KornShell job control statements.

Table 15-1. Job Control Statements

Statement	What it does
bg	Resumes a stopped job, running it in the background. The stopped job originally could have been a foreground job or a background job.
disown	Prevents a background job from being terminated when you log out.
fg	Moves a background job to the foreground.
jobs	Lists information about all current background jobs.
kill	Lists all legal signals on this system, or sends a signal to a foreground or background job. (We detail signals in the next section.) One common use of **kill** is to terminate a background job.
wait	Waits for a specified background job to finish executing. For example, suppose that `scriptA` depends on the results of `scriptB`. In this case, you could use **wait** to tell the KornShell to hold off executing `scriptA` until `scriptB` finishes.

You can have the KornShell send you a message when your background job finishes executing. To do so, turn on the **monitor** option by issuing the following:

```
$ set -o monitor   # turn on the monitor option
```

When Should You Run a Job in the Background?

Terminals that support multiple windows are rapidly replacing single-window dumb terminals. If your terminal does support multiple windows, chances are good that you can run multiple KornShells concurrently. If that's the case, then you may not want to run your scripts, even the time-consuming ones, in the background at all. Instead, you might find it easier to run your time-consuming scripts in separate windows. On the other hand, if you're still singing those VT100 blues, the background will help you get a lot more work done.

Up until now, we've concentrated on running time-consuming programs in the background. However, there are other kinds of programs known as *servers* or, in UNIX slang, *daemons*, that typically run in the background. A server provides a resource (a service) to a requesting process (called a *client*) running on this system or another system. Generally speaking, clients access servers sporadically. The servers lurk in the background and listen for service requests from clients. For example, most UNIX systems run a server called telnetd. This server runs quietly in the background using minimal system resources until a client makes a telnet request. When that happens, the telnetd server temporarily uses a lot of resources.

The operating system probably starts several servers based on the information inside its login scripts. Other software packages, such as X windows, also may start up servers. Users may be asked to start up servers (such as license servers) before running certain programs.

Another use of the background is for running scripts that need to access information sporadically. For example, once a minute, the following script requests information about disk space and writes it to a file named /tmp/disk_log.

```
USAGE="usage: sporadic.ksh" # loop once a minute

while :      # loop until system administrator kills script
do
  df . >> /tmp/disk_log     # write disk usage to /tmp/disk_log
  sleep 60  # suspend script for 60 seconds
done
```

This would be an ideal script to run in the background even after you log out. Here's how to invoke it:

```
$ nohup sporadic.ksh&
```

Signaling

Once you start a script, you usually want it to run to completion. Oh sure, the script may pause from time to time to wait for input, but the general flow is from start to finish.

Suppose, however, that you start the script and suddenly realize, "Wait a second. I didn't want to run that script. It could disrupt the whole balance of power in Europe." Or perhaps after starting a script you think to yourself, "I need to temporarily halt the script so I can see what happened to Andorra and Liechtenstein." In both cases, you need to send a *signal* to the script.

A signal is a number that you send to a script. Because numbers are a little tricky to remember, every system provides an English-like name that corresponds to the number. The number symbolizes your intentions on a scale ranging from "I think there might be a slight problem here" to "Stop that thing no matter what!" Each operating system supports a different set of signals. To get a list of *all* the signals that your system supports, issue the `kill -l` statement; for example:

```
$ kill -l   # get a list of all signal names on your system
HUP
INT
QUIT
ILL
TRAP
...              # and many more
```

In KornShell 88, `kill -l` printed not only signal names but also the corresponding signal numbers. In KornShell 93, `kill -l` prints only signal names. However, the following little KornShell 93 script will print both signal numbers and signal names.

```
USAGE="usage: signal_list.ksh n" # list first n signals

for (( i = 1; i <= $1; i++ ))
do
# The following statement prints signal name and corresponding
# signal number.
   print "$i: $(kill -l $i)"
done
```

Executing This Script

```
$ signal_list.ksh 5
1 HUP
2 INT
3 QUIT
4 ILL
5 TRAP
```

How to Send a Signal to a Script

The method you use to send a signal to a script depends on whether the script is running in the foreground or in the background.

You usually send signals to foreground scripts by pressing the **CONTROL** key in combination with some other key. For this to work, the key sequence must have been predefined to correspond to a signal. Unfortunately, each system predefines keys in a different way. Often, though, you can generate:

- A **QUIT** signal by typing **<CONTROL>**

- An **INT** signal by typing **<CONTROL>c** or by pressing **<DELETE>**

- A **STOP** signal by typing **<CONTROL>z**

- A **CONT** signal by typing **<CONTROL>y**

I want to reemphasize that your system might not support the preceding key definitions. Also, many applications change the way that the system handles special keys. For example, pressing the **<DELETE>** key from within an emacs session will not cause the emacs session to terminate.

Most systems permit you to specify your own key definitions. If you're working on the UNIX operating system, you can use the stty command to define keys. Unfortunately, the syntax of stty is not standard across different versions of the UNIX operating system.

To send a signal to a background script, use the **kill** statement. The **kill** statement takes the following syntax:

kill *-signal job_name*

The *signal* can be either the name of the signal (for example, **QUIT**) or the signal number (for example, 3). For *job_name,* enter the job number (preceded by a %), the PID of the background process, or the name of the script (preceded by a %). For example, suppose that you invoke payroll in the background as follows:

```
$ payroll &
[1] 405
```

Here are several ways to send a **QUIT** signal to this job:

```
$ kill -QUIT 405 # 405 is the PID
$ kill -3 405    # -3 is the number corresponding to QUIT
$ kill -QUIT %1  # 1 is the job command number
$ kill -QUIT %payroll # specify the full name of command...
$ kill -QUIT %pa     #...or just the start of the command name
$ kill -QUIT %%  # send a signal to the most recently invoked job,
                 # which may or may not be payroll
```

Sending a signal is only half the battle. The other half is writing a program that responds to that signal.

Writing Scripts That Respond to Signals

By default, every signal (except for **STOP** and **CONT**) received by a script will terminate the script. However, you can use a **trap** statement to "catch" a specific signal and take appropriate action. The action your script takes is completely up to you. You might ignore the signal altogether or you might do something elaborate such as call a secondary signal-handling script.

You can set traps on more than one signal. Perhaps your script will take one action if it receives a **QUIT** signal and another if it receives a **HUP** signal.

You may be wondering if it's possible to set up so many traps that it becomes impossible to kill your script. In fact, it is always possible to kill a rampaging script (as long as you own the job running it) by sending it a **KILL** signal, which always corresponds to signal number 9. The KornShell will ignore any traps that you set for the **KILL** signal. The **KILL** signal is a kind of programming back door or, to pick another metaphor, a way to prevent painting yourself into a corner.

Catching Signals

The following script sets traps on two different signals, **INT** and **QUIT**.

```
USAGE="usage: trap_ex1.ksh"  # setting traps on INT and QUIT

# The script will respond to an INT signal by printing the value of c.
 trap 'print "Received INT signal; c = $c"' INT
# The script will respond to a QUIT signal by printing the value of rt.
 trap 'print "Received QUIT signal; rt = $rt"' QUIT

 integer c=0
 integer rt=0

 for ((c=0; c < 10000; c++))
 do
   ((rt += c))
 done
 print "The (misleading) final answer is $rt"
```

Executing This Script

We could run `trap_ex1.ksh` in either the background or foreground, but running it in the background makes the demonstration a little easier to follow. Here goes:

```
$ trap_ex1.ksh&       # start up script in background
[1] 6551              # KornShell assigns it job number 1
$ kill -INT %1        # send INT signal to trap_ex1.ksh
Received INT signal; c= 1578
$ kill -QUIT %1       # send QUIT signal to trap_ex1.ksh
Received QUIT signal; rt = 17931066
The final answer is 50005000
```

Start `trap_ex1.ksh` again, but this time send it a **HUP** signal. Because `trap_ex1.ksh` doesn't trap the **HUP** signal, the script will immediately die.

```
$ trap_ex1.ksh&
[1] 6552
$ kill -HUP %1        # send a HUP signal and trap_ex1.ksh will die
[1] + Hangup
```

A Trap That Calls Another Script

The following script, trap_ex2.ksh, sets a trap on the **INT** signal. If the script is running and you send it an **INT** signal, then trap_ex2.ksh calls (as a dot script) another script named interupt.ksh. The interrupt.ksh script asks the user whether to continue running the script. If the user says yes, trap_ex2.ksh starts running again (right where it left off before the **INT**erruption). If the user says no, both trap_ex1.ksh and interupt.ksh stop running.

```
USAGE="usage: trap_ex2.ksh" # call another script in response to signal
 integer c=0
 integer rt=0
 print "The PID of this process is $$"
# Invoke interrupt.ksh as a dot script; pass it these two arguments:
#     1) the PID of this process
#     2) the value of variable c
 trap '. interrupt.ksh $$ $c' INT

 for ((c=0; c < 50000; c++))
 do
   ((rt += c))
 done
```

```
USAGE="usage: interrupt.ksh PID number" # script called by trap_ex2.ksh

 print "The script is now stopped and the current value of c is $2"
 print "Do you want to continue? "
 read response
 if [[ $response = [Yy]* ]]
 then
   print "Okay then, the script will continue where it left off."
 else
   print "I'll stop then."
   kill -KILL $1              # send signal to trap_example1 to terminate
 fi
```

Executing This Script

Let's run trap_ex2.ksh in the foreground. Running it in the background makes it difficult for interrupt.ksh to correctly perform the read response statement.

```
$ trap_ex2.ksh    # run script in foreground
<CONTROL>c        # send an INT signal
The PID of this process is 1175
The script is now stopped and the current value of c is 753
Do you want to continue?
Yes
Okay then, the script will continue where it left off.
<CONTROL>c          # send another INT signal
The script is now stopped and the current value of c is 1392
Do you want to continue?
No
I'll stop then.
Killed
```

Trapping Whenever a Script Exits

Whenever a script terminates, the KornShell automatically issues an **EXIT** signal. This signal is issued whether the script terminated naturally or as a result of receiving another signal.

Many scripts create temporary files that should be removed when the script terminates. The best way to remove such temporary files is to trap the **EXIT** signal.

```
USAGE="usage: trap_EXIT.ksh"  # trapping the EXIT signal

temporary_file="fad.$$"
trap 'rm $temporary_file' EXIT
# Generate a file containing a bunch of random integers.
integer data_points=500
for (( c=1; c<data_points; c++ ))
do
    print $RANDOM >> $temporary_file
done

# Average all the integers in $temporary_file
integer number
integer running_total=0
while read number
do
    (( running_total += number ))
done < $tempoary_file
(( average = running_total / data_points ))
print "average is $average"
```

Executing This Script

First, let the script run to the end:

```
$ trap_EXIT.ksh
average is 16917
```

If you examine the current directory, you will find no fad files.

Invoke the script a second time, but send a signal that will cause the script to terminate before it reaches the end:

```
$ trap_EXIT.ksh
<CONTROL>c
```

Again, if you examine the current directory, you won't find any fads.

If you comment out the **trap** statement and run the script a third time, you'll discover that the fad file is still around after the script terminates.

Trapping Whenever Error Status Becomes Nonzero

The KornShell sends a special signal named **ERR** to your script whenever something goes "wrong" inside your script. By wrong, I mean that a child process of this script returns a nonzero exit status.

As you may recall, all programs and scripts return an exit status. The KornShell automatically assigns this exit status to **$?**. By convention, a **$?** value of 0 means that the command executed properly, and a **$?** value other than zero means that there was an error. If you set a trap on **ERR**, the KornShell will execute your error routine whenever a child process causes **$?** to become nonzero.

If a KornShell statement running inside the script returns **$?**, the KornShell does not throw an **ERR** signal. For example, the **while read** statement returns a nonzero exit status upon reaching the end of input, but this does not trigger an **ERR** signal.

```
USAGE="usage: trap_err_signal.ksh"  # trapping on ERR (error)
# If user enters a bad filename, suggest some alternatives before
# exiting.

trap 'typeset -L1 f=$filename;
      print "Perhaps you meant one of these files instead:" $f*
      exit 1' ERR

print -n "Enter a filename: "
read filename
cat $filename 2> /dev/null

print -n "\nEnter another filename: "
read filename
cat $filename 2> /dev/null
```

Executing This Script

Consider a directory that contains several files:

```
$ ls
trap_err_signal.ksh    uncle              vexing
umbrella               unicorn            volition
```
You trigger the **ERR** signal by providing a filename other than one of the preceding six files. To get helpful feedback from the trap response, enter a filename that starts with **u** or **v** but is not one of the actual filenames:

```
$ trap_err_signal.ksh    # run this script in the foreground
Enter a filename: unicorn
hello from unicorn.      # the contents of file "unicorn"

Enter another filename: vile    # triggers the error signal
Perhaps you meant one of these files instead: vexing volition
```

Writing Your Own Debugger

The KornShell sends a **DEBUG** signal to your script after every statement in the script is expanded and just before it executes. Your script can trap the **DEBUG** signal in order to create a do-it-yourself debugger. Trapping on the **DEBUG** signal hurts performance, so when you finish debugging, take the trap out of your code.

If you want to write the line number at which the **DEBUG** trap was encountered, print the value of the reserved variable **LINENO**.

```
USAGE="usage: trap_debug_signal.ksh"   # the DEBUG signal

 trap 'print Line $LINENO: x = $x' DEBUG

 integer x=5    # Line 5
 integer y=0    # Line 6

 while (( x <= 15 ))  # Line 8
 do
    (( x += 5 ))   # Line 10
    (( y += x ))   # Line 11
 done
```

Executing This Script

```
$ trap_debug_signal.ksh
Line 5: x =
Line 6: x = 5
Line 8: x = 5
Line 10: x = 5
Line 11: x = 10
Line 8: x = 10
Line 10: x = 10
Line 11: x = 15
Line 8: x = 15
Line 10: x = 15
Line 11: x = 20
Line 8: x = 20
```

Notice that the first line of script output does not have a value for **x**. Remember that the script receives the **DEBUG** signal just *before* executing line 5. So, at that point in the script, no value has been set for **x**.

By the way, if you run the preceding script on KornShell 88, you'll get different results. That's because KornShell 88 sends the **DEBUG** signal just after executing the line. So, for example, the first line of output for the preceding script would show a value of 5 for variable **x**.

Trapping KEYBD **Signals**

Every time you type a character (or a key sequence like **Esc-X**), the KornShell sends a **KEYBD** signal. If you trap the **KEYBD** signal, the KornShell automatically assigns values to the following four reserved variables:

- **.sh.edchar**, which holds the identity of the last character or key sequence typed.

- **.sh.edtext**, which holds the contents of the current input line.

- **.sh.edmode**, which usually holds a NULL character but will hold an escape character if the user is in command mode of vi.

- **.sh.edcol**, which holds the position within the current line. So, when the user types the first character, the KornShell will set **.sh.edcol** to 0; when the user types the second character, the KornShell will set **.sh.edcol** to 1; and so on.

Note that the **KEYBD** signal is sent only when users provide interactive input. If a script gathers input from a file, the **KEYBD** signal is not sent.

```
USAGE="usage: keybd_trap.ksh"

# If the first character on an input line is a lowercase letter, the
# trap will convert the letter to uppercase.  Otherwise, the trap
# will simply ignore the typed character.
 trap 'if [[ ${.sh.edchar} == [a-z] ]] && [[ ${.sh.edcol} == 0 ]]
      then
            typeset -u substitute
            substitute=${.sh.edchar}
            .sh.edchar=$substitute
      fi' KEYBD

print -n "Enter a name: "
read name
print "$name"
```

Executing This Script

```
$ keybd_trap.ksh
Enter a name: Danny  # I typed danny, but the trap changed the d to D
You entered: Danny
```

With an extremely sophisticated **KEYBD** trap, you could even create your own text editor.

REFERENCE

trap — *Respond to signals, errors, and exits.*

Syntax

trap *[response]* *[event1 ... eventN]*

where:

response   is either one of the following:

        'cmd' is the name of one or more programs, shell scripts, or Korn-Shell statements. If more than one, use a semicolon to separate each one. Enclose *cmd* inside a pair of single quotes. If you want the KornShell to disregard a particular *event*, just specify a pair of single quotes as the *response*.

        – a minus sign tells the KornShell to restore the prior trap actions for *event1...eventN*.

event1...eventN is one or more of the following. (If you specify more than one, separate them with blank spaces.

       signal any of the signal numbers or signal names returned by the **kill -l** command. The KornShell executes *response* when one of the *signals* is received.

       CHLD the KornShell executes *response* whenever a background command terminates or stops.

       DEBUG the KornShell executes *response* after every command. You can use **DEBUG** to create a do-it-yourself debugger.

       ERR the KornShell executes *response* whenever **$?** is nonzero. You can use **ERR** to produce your own error messages or perhaps to take corrective action on certain errors.

       EXIT the KornShell executes *response* whenever a function, a
       or 0 script, or the KornShell session itself ends. For example, you can trap **EXIT** to delete the history file at the end of your KornShell session. In a script, you can trap **EXIT** to delete any temporary files that the script created.

       KEYBD the KornShell executes *response* whenever a key is typed unless the typed key is part of certain text editing commands. For example, if **HISTEDIT** is set to **vi** and you type **<ESCAPE>/** to initiate a search, typing the search string itself will not generate any **KEYBD** traps.

Quick Summary

Use **trap** to define a *response* to certain *events*. If you specify **trap** without any arguments, the KornShell lists the names of all *events* for which a trap has been set.

You can place **trap** statements inside scripts or inside KornShell start-up files. For example, to trap the end of a KornShell session (a trap on the **EXIT** signal), you would ordinarily place the **trap** statement inside the $HOME/.profile start-up file.

16 Command Line Editing and the History File

Although the focus of this book is KornShell scripts, much of your work actually will be done on the KornShell command line, typing in commands and such. This short chapter explains how to use command line editing features of the KornShell to simplify command line sessions and to reduce typing.

What Is Command Line Editing?

When writing a book, a typewriter is no match for a computer running a good text editing program. However, when it comes to editing the command line itself, many terminals are about as ineffective as typewriters. That is, many terminals provide no real way to edit the command line other than to hit the delete key a whole bunch of times.

The KornShell supports *command line editing* features, which allow you to edit the command line in much the same way you would edit a text file. If you already know how to edit a text file with vi or emacs, you're all set. You can select either of these to be your command line text editor. Actually, if you select one of them, say vi, you won't get *all* the features of vi but you will get enough of vi to edit command lines as comfortably as you would edit text files.

Not only can you edit the current command line, but you also can edit commands that you've previously issued.

What Is a History File?

Every time you enter a command on the KornShell command line, the KornShell automatically stores a copy of that command in the *history file*. In other words, the history file contains a record of all the commands that you have invoked.

As the name implies, the history file is, in fact, a file. However, the history file is not a regular text file; you cannot edit it with a text editor. Instead, you access the information in the history file through the **hist** statement. By default, the history file is located at pathname $HOME/.sh_history. To place the history file in a different pathname, assign that different pathname to the **HISTFILE** variable.

Listing Previous Commands

The **history** statement lists recently issued commands. The **history** statement does not re-execute these commands; it simply provides a record of what happened.

How far back can **history** go? Well, that depends on the size of the history file, which is determined by the **HISTSIZE** variable. For example, if **HISTSIZE** is set to 400, the history file holds the 400 most recently issued commands. By default, the **history** statement lists the 15 most recently issued commands.

```
$ history  # list the 15 most recent commands (plus the current one)
158     print ${x#*e}
159     pwd
...  (12 lines omitted for space reasons)
172     set --
173     history

$ history 142 144     # list commands 142 through 144
142     y="bon jour"
143     print $x$y
144     print "hello $x $y"

$ history -r 142 144  # list 142 through 144 in reverse order
144     print "hello $x $y"
143     print $x$y
142     y="bon jour"

$ history -2  # list the previous two commands (and the current one)
174     history 142 144
175     history -r 142 144
176     history -2

$ history set  # list from most recent set command to present
172     set --
173     history
174     history 142 144
175     history -r 142 144
176     history -2
177     history set
```

The preceding examples reflect the state of my history file at the moment I was writing this page. Your history file will undoubtedly contain different commands and different command line numbers.

Re-Executing Previous Commands

The one-letter statement, **r**, re-executes a previously issued command. We'll start by issuing a few UNIX commands just to fill up the history file:

```
214 $ cc main.c math.c io.c strings.c
215 $ exit_status=$?
216 $ sleep 1
```

To repeat execution of the most recently issued command, type:

```
$ r      # repeat execution of the last command (216)
sleep 1
```

You can repeat a command by number:

```
$ r 214
cc main.c math.c io.c strings.c
```

or by name:

```
$ r sleep  # repeat most recent command starting with sleep
sleep 1
```

You don't even have to enter the entire name, just a letter or two ought to do the trick:

```
$ r sl      # repeat most recent command starting with sl
sleep 1
```

You can do a substitution in the repeated command by using the -s option to r. For example, the following command repeats command 214, substituting cond.c for math.c:

```
$ r -s math.c=cond.c 214
cc main.c cond.c io.c strings.c
```

BEWARE: Can't Use r on Multiple Commands

You cannot use **r** to re-execute multiple commands; for example, this won't work:

```
222 $ r 214 215  # try to re-execute command numbers 214 and 215
ksh: fc: bad number  # you can only re-execute one command
```

However, you can use the **hist** command to edit *and then* re-execute multiple commands. (See the following section for examples.)

Editing Previous Commands, Then Executing Them

Use the **hist** statement to edit a previously issued command or group of commands, and then to execute the edited command(s). Before issuing your first **hist** statement, you should tell the KornShell what editor you want to use. To do so, assign your choice of editor (either vi or emacs) to the **HISTEDIT** variable. For example, if you prefer vi, you need to issue the following command, typically inside your $HOME/.profile start-up file:

```
HISTEDIT=vi
```

Suppose the following lines are in your history file:

```
270     read name?"Enter your name: "
271     length_of_name=${#name}          # find length of name
272     if (( $length_of_name < 12 ))
        then
           print "You have a short name."
        fi
```

To modify the most recently issued command (272) and then re-execute the results, enter:

```
$ hist        # edit, then re-execute most recent command
```

The preceding command will place you in the vi editor, but instead of editing a file, you'll be editing the four lines that originally appeared in command number 272. You can use vi to add, delete, or modify any of the commands. End your session as you would end any vi session (usually, by typing ZZ). After you end the editing session, the KornShell will store the results as command number 273 of the history file. The KornShell then will attempt to execute command number 273.

The **hist** statement is not limited to the most recent command; for example, you can edit a command by number:

```
$ hist 271    # edit, then re-execute, command number 271
```

or by name:

```
$ hist read   # edit, then re-execute, the most recent read command
```

Probably the best part of **hist** is that you can use it to group commands into a sort of virtual KornShell script. For example, commands 270 through 272 are related; you can edit them as a group by typing:

```
$ hist 270 272    # edit 270, 271, & 272, then re-execute
```

While in vi or emacs, you can save your virtual KornShell script to disk, thus making it into a real KornShell script.

The Thing You're Going to Do Anyway

As I crisscross this great country (four time zones, yet only one POSIX locale!) preaching the wonders of KornShell, I often get into lively discussions about command line editing that go something like this:

STUDENT: Lovely sweater, Mr. Cleaver.

ME: Thanks, Eddie, but my name isn't Mr. Cleaver.

STUDENT: Yes sir, but I was wondering.

ME: Yes, Eddie?

STUDENT: In DOS, I just hit the up arrow key and the previous commands pop into the shell.

ME: (*chuckling knowingly*) Well, that's DOS, Eddie. The guy who wrote DOS didn't even graduate from college.

CLASS: (*laughs dutifully*)

STUDENT: So, can I do that in the KornShell?

ME: But why would you want to do that, Eddie? If you need to re-execute a really old command, do you really want to hit the up arrow key 40, 50, 60 times? Wouldn't it be a lot simpler just to use the KornShell **r** statement?

STUDENT: Well, maybe—but how about if you just tell me how to do that up arrow thing, so that I can, er, compare and contrast.

ME: (*growing increasingly exasperated*) Oh, come now, that old up arrow thing is totally ancient. The KornShell provides a far superior...

SMART STUDENT IN BACK OF ROOM: Escape-k. I read it in his notes. If HISTEDIT is set to vi, all you have to do is hit escape, then every time you hit k, the previous command will get loaded in, and every time you hit j, you go forward through the history file.

STUDENT: (*hitting a blizzard of k's*) Hey, it works. Thanks, Mr. Cleaver!

ME: Wait a sec...

OTHER STUDENT: What if HISTEDIT is set to emacs?

SMART STUDENT IN BACK OF ROOM: "In emacs, control-p goes backwards and control-n goes forwards."

OTHER STUDENT: (*trying it out*) Thanks, this is great.

ME: Great? Why, this is positively antediluvian. You may as well go back to pen and paper. (*The clatter of students pounding escape-k and control-p is so loud that no one can hear me.*)

ENTIRE CLASS: Gee, thanks, Mr. Cleaver!

Pathname Completion

Pathname completion is a command line feature in which the user can type in part of a pathname and let the KornShell fill in the rest. Pathname completion can dramatically reduce typing. Pathname completion has become such an important feature of shells that some UNIX users pick a shell based solely on how it does pathname completion.

To demonstrate pathname completion, imagine that you are in a directory containing three subdirectories: submarine, substantial, and carefree. If you want to change directories to carefree, you could type:

```
$ cd carefree      # go the distance
```

An alternate approach would be to type:

```
$ cd c<Escape>\    # get lazy; rely on pathname completion
```

In other words, you type the first letter of carefree, then the **escape** key, and then the backslash key. The KornShell will complete the pathname for you and display:

```
$ cd carefree      # the KornShell completed the pathname for you
```

Suppose you had wanted to go to substantial instead of carefree. If you type:

```
$ cd s<Escape>\    # ambiguous
```

the KornShell can't complete the pathname because it can't figure out whether you want to go to submarine or substantial. After all, both of them start with an s. Come to think of it, both of them start with sub, so you actually have to type four letters before pathname completion does anything:

```
$ cd subs<Escape>\    # unambiguous
```

The KornShell can provide clues. For example, suppose that you want to know the names of all the subdirectories that start with s. In that case, you could rely on the sequence <Escape>=; for instance:

```
$ cd s<Escape>=    # request a list of subdirectories starting with s
1) submarine/
2) substantial/
$ cd subm<Escape>\ # now you can use pathname completion
```

Though not as glamorous as true pathname completion, wildcards on the command line will also do the trick. For example, the following command will change the current directory to substantial:

```
$ cd subs*
```

Pathname completion handles ambiguities better than wildcarding.

Command Completion

Command completion is closely related to pathname completion. With command completion, you can type in part of a command name and ask the KornShell to help you fill in the rest.

For example, suppose you are on the KornShell command line and you can't remember the name of the POSIX command that does pattern matching. Fortunately, you *do* remember that this command begins with the letters gr. (Okay, this is kind of a contrived example.) So, relying on command completion, you type:

```
$ gr<Escape>=
1) /bin/grep
2) /bin/grap
3) /bin/groups
4) /usr/local/bin/groff
5) /usr/local/bin/grabchars
6) /usr/users/danny/great.ksh
```

Typing the **<Escape>=** sequence causes the KornShell to search all the directories of your **PATH**, listing those files that:

- Begin with the letters gr

- Have execute permission

So the **<Escape>=** sequence acts as a kind of mnemonic device. "Oh yeah, the command I'm looking for is grep."

Not surprisingly, you also can use command completion to save you typing out the full name of a command. The sequence **<Escape>** will complete the command name. However, as with pathname completion, command completion can't guess your intentions when two commands begin with the same letters. For example, if you type:

```
$ gre<Escape>\
```

the KornShell still doesn't know whether you want the grep command or the great.ksh script. Nevertheless, command completion sometimes can save you a bunch of typing; for example, typing the following characters on my (extremely contrived) system:

```
$ zep<Escape>\
```

causes the KornShell to substitute the following:

```
$ zephyr_hills_florida_accounts_receivable.ksh
```

REFERENCE

hist — *List, re-execute, or edit and re-execute previously issued commands.*

Syntax

hist [**-e** *editor*] [**-1nr**] [*cmd_id_range*]   **hist -s** *change_this=to_this [cmd]*

where:

-e *editor*   specify pathname of *editor* to use when editing *cmd_id_range*. If you specify – for *editor,* **hist** will suppress editing of the command line and will simply re-execute *cmd_id_range.*

-1   list the commands in *cmd_id_range,* or, if *cmd_id_range* is not specified, list the 16 commands most recently issued.

-n   suppress command numbers in output listing. The history file labels each command with a unique number. If you do specify **-n, hist** won't display this number. If you don't specify **-n, hist** will display this number.

-r   reverse the order in which **hist** displays or edits commands.

cmd_range   is the command or group of commands to which **hist** applies. The influence of *cmd_range* depends on whether you are listing previous commands or whether you are editing or re-executing previous commands. If you are using **hist** or **history** to list commands and you omit *cmd_range,* the default value is the 16 most recently issued commands. If you are using **hist** to edit or re-execute commands and you omit *cmd_range,* the default value is the most recently issued command. If you don't like these defaults, you can specify a *cmd_range* consisting of one or two values.

If you specify a number for *cmd_range,* **hist** applies to that command number.

If you put a minus sign in front of a number, **hist** applies to the current command number minus that number. For example, if the current command number is **100,** specifying a number of **-5** means that you want to act on command number 95.

If you specify two numbers for *cmd_range,* **hist** applies to all the commands from the first number to the second number inclusive.

If you specify a string for *cmd_range,* **hist** applies to the most recently issued command whose name starts with string.

-s	do a search and replace on *cmd*, then re-execute it.
change_this	the string in *cmd* that you want to replace.
to_this	the replacement string. If there are multiple occurrences of *change_this* in *cmd*, only the first occurrence of *change_this* will be replaced.
cmd	is the command to which **hist** applies. If you specify a number for *cmd*, then **hist** applies to that command number. If you specify a string for *cmd*, then **hist** applies to the most recently issued command whose name starts with the specified string. If you omit *cmd*, **hist** applies to the most recently issued command. You cannot specify multiple command numbers because this form of **hist** only applies to a single command.

Quick Summary

Use the **hist** statement or its aliases to access commands stored in the history file. You can do any of the following with **hist:**

- List previously executed commands

- Re-execute previously executed commands

- Edit, then re-execute, previously executed commands

An alias for **hist -l** is **history**. In other words, you can use **hist -l** or **history** interchangeably.

The alias **r** (short for repeat or redo) is a nickname for **hist -e -.**

If you omit **-e** *editor*, **hist** uses the command line editor stored at variable **HISTEDIT**. If **HISTEDIT** is not set, **hist** uses the editor stored at variable **FCEDIT**. If neither **HISTEDIT** nor **FCEDIT** are set, **hist** uses the editor stored at /bin/ed.

17 Writing CGI Scripts

This chapter explains how to write CGI programs as KornShell scripts. CGI programs are the backbone of Internet programming.

If You're New to CGI Programming . . .

I've been writing these blasted "Intro to the Internet" sections for four years now and would like to state for the record that you already know what the Internet is, your friends already know what the Internet is, your mom already knows what the Internet is, and your dog already knows what the Internet is. So, I now feel safe in chucking out the perfunctory, "Gosh, let me tell you just how big the Internet is" introduction.[1]

You also know that programs such as Netscape Navigator and Microsoft Internet Explorer are known as browsers. And you know that browsers make requests to Web servers, such as www.awl.com. Okay, since we're straight on all that, let's get acquainted with CGI programs.

"What do CGI programs do?"

In theory, a CGI program can do just about anything that any other kind of program can do. In practice, most CGI programs perform two kinds of tasks:

- Analyzing information that users enter into forms

- Generating Web pages on-the-fly, often by accessing data stored in files or databases

---

1. The Internet is so large that if it were laid end-to-end and hammered into a sheet one meter wide, it would reach from here to infinity. And back! Why, that's enough to fill up Yankee Stadium five times!

"Why use CGI programs to generate Web pages?"

HTML editors such as Netscape Composer are terrific for creating *static* Web pages, which are Web pages that are stored on disk and whose content never varies (unless you go back in with an HTML editor and modify the text). By contrast, *dynamic* Web pages are not stored on disk. Instead, they are generated on demand. CGI programs are a good way to generate dynamic Web pages.

"Where do CGI programs run?"

CGI programs must run on the same host as the Web server. Note that there is a protocol called FastCGI that does allow so-called *FastCGI programs* (a variant of CGI programs) to run on a different host than the Web server.

"How do you invoke a CGI program?"

You invoke a CGI program as you would invoke any other Web resource, namely, by specifying its URL. Many hyperlinks point to CGI programs, so you probably have invoked many CGI programs without realizing it.

"Are there special rules for writing CGI programs?"

Yes. CGI programs have to conform to the CGI protocol established by the World Wide Web Consortium.

"What languages can you use to write a CGI program?"

The KornShell.

"Any other languages?"

No.

"Really?"

Well, now that you've jogged my memory, it seems that you actually can use any language, compiled or interpreted, to create a CGI program. If you do use an interpreted language such as Perl, then the Perl interpreter must be installed in such a way that the host Web server can invoke it.

"Are CGI programs portable?"

You have to be careful in coding CGI programs in order to make them truly portable. CGI programs that make operating system commands are unlikely to be portable. Also, CGI programs that expect each Web server to work exactly the same way also may run into porting problems. Nevertheless, the average CGI program has little need to make operating system commands or any reason to trip over Web server dependencies, so the average CGI program will be portable.

"What is the Flow of Data Around a CGI Program? "

Figure 17-1 illustrates the sequence of data movement through a request to run a CGI program. The steps are:

1. When a browser asks to run a CGI script, the Web server intercepts the request.

2. The Web server examines any data the browser may have passed, sets various environment variables, and then invokes the CGI program. Depending on the kind of request the browser made, the Web server may pass information to the CGI program.

3. The CGI program executes, analyzing the information passed by the Web server. Whatever information the CGI program writes to standard output will be sent to the Web server. Usually, the CGI program writes a Web page to standard output.

4. The Web server passes information received by the CGI program back to the browser. If the Web server passes a Web page, the browser will display that Web page.

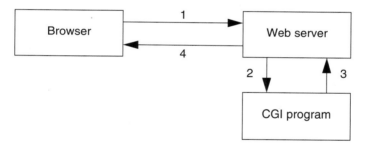

Figure 17-1. Flow of Data Through a Typical CGI Program

"How do CGI programs differ from applets?"

When a browser invokes an applet, the Web server sends the applet binary code to the browser. Then the browser runs this code locally. So, the primary difference is that CGI programs run on the same host as the Web server, but Web applets run on the browser's machine. There are pros and cons to both methods of Web programming.

"Do you need to know HTML to write CGI programs"

Yes, definitely. And to become a really good CGI programmer, you need to become expert in HTML.

If you are new to HTML and don't feel like rushing over to your bookstore just yet, take a look at Appendix B.

If You're an Experienced CGI Programmer . . .

Let's assume that you've gone over to the dark side and used some other language to write a CGI program or two. The good news is that when you switch to the Korn-Shell, your CGI knowledge is entirely transferable. After all, the CGI protocol doesn't change just because you've changed languages.

The KornShell is an excellent choice for CGI programming. The string manipulation features of the KornShell make it fairly easy to parse the name-value pairs passed to CGI programs.

Forms

Most CGI scripts exist to analyze input entered into an *HTML form*. Basically, an HTML form is any entity that enables a user to supply input. Types of entities you can put into forms include:

- Text boxes, in which a user can enter any single line of text.

- Password boxes, which are just like text boxes except that the user's input does not appear on the browser screen. Thus, they are useful for gathering passwords.

- Text areas, in which a user can enter multiple lines of text.

- Checkboxes, which allow the user to mark or unmark an entry.

- Radio buttons, in which the user is forced to select one and only one entry from a list of entries.

- Popup lists, which "pop up" to reveal a list from which the user must select one and only one entry. (Popup lists are kissin' cousins of scrollable lists.)

- Scrollable lists, which are like popup lists, except that they don't "pop up." You can configure scrollable lists so that users can select multiple items instead of just one.

- Activation buttons, which the user clicks to cause the form to be submitted to the Web server.

Web pages often contain some combination of the preceding entities. For example, an online store might display a form in which buyers supply various kinds of information. This form might contain:

- A text box to gather the user's name

- Several text boxes, or possibly one text area, to gather the user's street address

- A scrollable list to gather the user's country

- A popup list to gather the user's choice of credit card

- A text box or password box to gather the user's credit card number

The next few pages demonstrate some common forms.

Text Boxes and Password Boxes

The following HTML file, text_forms.htm, generates a text box and a password box. The form part of the file starts with a **<form>** tag, which is explained later. After the **Enter your name** prompt, you'll notice a whole bunch of **<input>** tags. Each **<input>** tag contains a **type** attribute:

- If the type is **"text"** the browser displays a text box. In a text box, the size attribute refers to the width of the text box. The value 22 means that the text box should be wide enough to hold 22 characters of the current font. The **maxlength** attribute identifies the maximum number of characters the user can enter into this text box.

- If the type is **"password"** the browser displays a password box.

- If the type is **"reset"** the browser displays a button. If the user presses this button, then whatever had appeared in the text box or password box gets erased.

- If the type is **"submit"** the browser displays another button. If the user presses this button, the information in the text box or password box is sent to the CGI program.

```
<html>
<head><title>Text Forms</title></head>
<body><h1><center>Text Forms</center></h1></body>

<p>A <em>text box</em> allows the user to enter
a single line of text.
<form method=post action="/cgi-bin/my_cgi_program.cgi">
<strong>Enter your name:</strong>
<input type="text" value=""
       name="color" size=22 maxlength=34>
<input type="reset" value="Clear">
<input type="submit" value="Analyze">
</form>


<br>
<p>A <em>password box</em> is similar to a text box except
that the user's input is replaced by asterisks.
<form method=post action="/cgi-bin/my_cgi_program.cgi">
<strong>Enter your password: </strong>
<input type="password" name="color" size=18>
<input type="reset" value="Clear">
<input type="submit" value="Analyze">
</form>
</body></html>
```

Viewing This HTML File

To view this HTML file, you need to direct your browser to file `text_forms.htm`, which is in directory `ch17` on the CD. When this file is viewed on my browser, `text_forms.htm` looks like the following:

Clicking on either of the Analyze buttons will cause an error because we haven't coded the CGI part of this code.

By the way, there is nothing very secure about information entered into a password box. True, the information typed into the password box doesn't appear on the monitor, but that information usually will get passed to a CGI program as unencrypted text. For secure transmission of sensitive information, your browser needs to encrypt the information sent to the CGI program. If your browser is connected to a "secure" Web server port, your browser will automatically encrypt the data. "Secure" means that the Web server is using the Secure Socket Layer (SSL) protocol to communicate with your browser.

Checkboxes

Checkboxes let the user toggle a setting. The following HTML file, `checkboxes.htm`, contains four different checkboxes.

```
<html>
<head><title>Checkboxes </title></head>
<body><h1><center>Checkboxes </center></h1>

<form method=get action="./yo.cgi">
 <p>What are your favorite sports?
  <p> <input type=checkbox name=sport value="frisbee">Ultimate Frisbee
  <br><input type=checkbox name=sport value="juggling" checked>Juggling
  <br><input type=checkbox name=sport value="scripting">Aerobic Scripting
  <br><input type=checkbox name=sport value="typing">Extreme Typing

 <p><input type=submit value="YES">
</form>
</body></html>
```

Viewing This HTML File

Have your browser open `ch17/checkboxes.htm`. After turning on three of the checkboxes, the preceding HTML file, `checkboxes.htm`, looks like this on my browser:

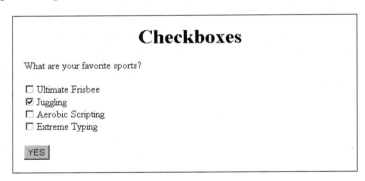

Radio Buttons

In an old-fashioned car radio, when you pushed in one of the radio buttons, the previously selected button would pop out. Thus, only one radio button at a time could be selected. Similarly, only one HTML radio button can be selected at a time.

```
<html>
<head><title>Radio Buttons </title></head>
<body><h1><center>Radio Buttons </center></h1>

<form method=get action="./yo.cgi">
  <p>What is your favorite sport?
    <p><input type=radio name=sport value="frisbee">Ultimate Frisbee
    <br><input type=radio name=sport value="juggling" checked>Juggling
    <br><input type=radio name=sport value="scripting">Aerobic Scripting
    <br><input type=radio name=sport value="typing">Extreme Typing

  <p><input type=submit value="YES">
</form>

</body></html>
```

Viewing This HTML File

Have your browser open ch17/radio.htm. When it is first displayed, the preceding HTML file, radio.htm, looks like this on my browser:

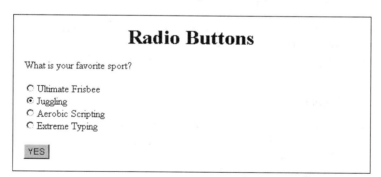

Note that Juggling is the initial choice because the entry for Juggling has the **checked** attribute.

Getting Started Writing CGI Programs

Most CGI programs generate HTML.

You create a CGI program as you would create any KornShell script, namely, by opening a regular text file with any ASCII text editor (such as vi, emacs, or notepad). So, pull up a sharpened number 2 keyboard and enter the following into a file named getting_started.cgi:

```
#!/usr/bin/ksh93

# getting_started.cgi: CGI script to generate some very easy HTML.
# filename is getting_started.cgi
print "Content-type: text/html"
print
print "<head><title>Getting Started with CGI</title></head>"
print "<body><h1>Generated by a CGI Script</h1>"
print "<p>This page was generated dynamically by a CGI script.</p>"
print "</body></html>"
```

Your initial reaction to getting_started.cgi is probably, hey, it looks just like an HTML file except that each line of HTML is encased in a **print** statement. Bingo. When a CGI script runs, all of its standard output will be sent to the user's browser. Thus, the user's browser receives the following HTML:

```
Content-type: text/html>

<head><title>Getting Started with CGI</title></head>
<body><h1>Generated by a CGI Script</h1>
<p>This page was generated dynamically by a CGI script.</p>
</body></html>
```

Executing This CGI Program

The way you execute this CGI program depends on how you have configured your Web server and where you have placed this example. The rest of this chapter arbitrarily picks a local URL of:

```
/cgi-bin/getting_started.cgi
```

You will almost certainly have to specify a different URL. When you access this CGI script in a browser, the browser will display the following Web page:

Generated by a CGI Script

This page was generated dynamically by a CGI script.

CGI RULE 1: First Line of Every Script

All CGI scripts written in KornShell *must* begin by identifying the pathname of the KornShell itself. For example, the system on which `getting_started.cgi` runs has the KornShell installed at pathname `/usr/bin/ksh93`. Therefore, the first line of `getting_started.cgi` is:

```
#!/usr/bin/ksh93
```

If your KornShell is located at a different pathname, then adjust this first line accordingly. Make sure that the pound symbol (#) is flush left on the first line of the script. Make sure the exclamation point (!) is snug against the pound symbol.

CGI RULE 2: First Two Lines of Output

The first two lines of standard output for all CGI scripts that generate HTML should be:

```
print "Content-type: text/html"
print      # outputs a blank line
```

Note that the blank line is required. I can't tell you how many hours I've wasted searching for bugs in CGI scripts only to discover that I forget that stupid blank line.

By the way, not all CGI scripts generate HTML. CGI scripts that generate something other than HTML will output a different content type.

CGI RULE 3: Standard Output Goes to Browser

Whatever a CGI program writes to standard output will be automatically sent to the Web server. The Web server, in turn, will send this stream to the browser that requested the CGI program.

Whatever a CGI program writes to standard error also will be sent to the Web server. However, the Web server will not send this information to the browser. Instead, this information probably will get written to your Web server's error log file.

BEWARE: If Your CGI Script Doesn't Work

Getting that first CGI script to run can be incredibly frustrating. Here are a bunch of suggestions to get you over that hump.

Suggestion one—try to run this CGI script directly on the KornShell command line. For example, here's what should happen when you invoke `getting_started.cgi` on the command line:

```
$ ch17/cgi/getting_started.cgi
Content-type: text/html

<head><title>Getting Started with CGI</title></head>
<body><h1>Generated by a CGI Script</h1>
<p>This page was generated dynamically by a CGI script.</p>
</body></html>
```

The script should run without errors. A common problem is forgetting to balance quotes; did you remember to supply one closing quote for each opening quote? As with all scripts, you must have execute permission in order to run it.

Suggestion two—make sure you've set the permissions on the CGI script so that others can execute it. Most CGI scripts have the permissions set as 755—read, write, and execute permission for the script's programmer, read and execute permission for everyone else. Often, programmers give themselves execute permission but forget to give it to others. On UNIX, the "user" who invokes every CGI script is typically the owner of the Web server program.

Suggestion three—determine whether the Web server requires CGI scripts to go into a directory having a certain name. For example, some Web servers insist that all CGI scripts go into a directory named `cgi-bin`. Examine the CGI scripts already on your system. (Your Web server probably came with a bunch of its own CGI scripts.) If you put your CGI script into one of these "already-working" directories, does it run?

Suggestion four—ensure that you are specifying the right URL when invoking your CGI script. Sometimes, you specify what you think is the URL of a CGI script only to discover (after several hours of struggle) that you have specified an incorrect URL. The local pathname portion of a URL is a slippery beast. For example, given a URL such as:

```
http://www.kornzilla.com/slippery/beast.cgi
```

it is very unlikely that file `beast.cgi` is actually located at the absolute pathname `/slippery/beast.cgi`. More than likely, the Web server maps the directory `/slippery` to some other directory on that system.

A CGI Script Containing More Than Just print Statements

To be honest, there was nothing to be gained by coding getting_started.cgi as a CGI script rather than as a just plain HTML file. So, let's move on to a CGI script that could not be done as a static HTML file—one that must be written as a CGI script.

You can put any statement in a CGI script that you could put in a regular Korn-Shell script. For example, the following script—no big whoop itself—assigns a random number to variable **r** and then prints the value of **r**. The HTML produced by this CGI script could not have been produced by a static HTML file.

```ksh
#!/usr/bin/ksh

# changes_each_time.cgi: CGI script to generate some very easy HTML.
# filename is getting_started.cgi
print "Content-type: text/html"
print
print "<head><title>Random Number Generator</title></head>"
r=$RANDOM
print "<body><h1>$r</h1>"
print "</body></html>"
```

Executing This Script

To run this script, aim your browser at the following URL:

    /cgi-bin/changes_each_time.cgi

Every time you run this CGI script, you should get a different result. So, try running it a few times. Here's the way it looked one of the times I ran it:

26931

File I/O from CGI Scripts

A CGI script can read from input files or write to output files just as any KornShell script would. The following example CGI script reads from and writes to a very simple text file.

You've no doubt seen Web pages that proudly announce, "You are visitor 4,256 to our Website." You can use all sorts of convoluted techniques to count visitors, but we're going to skip all that and go straight to an incredibly easy method.

The incredibly easy technique is to create a simple text file named Webhits whose starting contents are simply the integer:

    1

Then, you write a CGI script that reads the contents of Webhits and displays this number in one of those spiffy, "You are visitor number..." banners. After displaying the banner, your CGI script must increment the previous integer value by 1 and then store the incremented value in Webhits, overwriting the previous contents. So, after the script runs once, the new contents of Webhits will be:

    2

```
#!/usr/bin/ksh93
# counting_web_hits.cgi: CGI script that counts Web hits.

print "Content-type: text/html"
print
print "<head><title>File I/O in CGI Scripts</title></head>"

# Gather current contents of webhits.txt.
read counter < webhits.txt

print "<body><h1>Curling</h1>"
print "<p>This page is dedicated to the sport of curling.</p>"
print "<p>You are visitor $counter to this page."

# Increment counter and write the new value back to webhits.txt
(( counter++ ))
print $counter > webhits.txt
print "</body></html>"
```

Executing This Script

To run this script, aim your browser at the following URL:

    /cgi-bin/count_web_hits.cgi

Every time you run this CGI script, you should get a different result. So, try running it a few times. Here's the way it looked one of the times I ran it:

> # Curling
>
> This page is dedicated to the sport of curling.
>
> You are visitor 12 to this page.

By the way, pressing your browser's Reload or Refresh button will increment the counter, but pressing your browser's Back button will not.

BEWARE: File Permissions

File I/O is a chronic source of problems in CGI programs. The culprit is generally file permission problems.

Here's a typical situation. You write a CGI script that needs to access a file. You run the CGI script from the KornShell command line and it works fine; that is, your CGI script has no trouble accessing the file. Then, you try to access the same CGI script from your browser, but the browser sends back a permission error. When this happens, you have to remember that it is the Web server, not you, invoking the CGI script. So, it is likely that the Web server does not have permission to access the file.

Some modern Web servers can circumvent this problem through SUID bits or certain wrapper programs. The basic idea on these enlightened systems is that, to run a CGI script, the Web server temporarily masquerades as the owner of the CGI script.

Analyzing Form Input: The Get and Post Methods

HTTP provides two mechanisms for passing information from an HTML form to a CGI program:

- Get method

- Post method

The HTML form that calls a CGI script specifies which of the two methods to use. For example, the following form preamble specifies that the Get method be used to call `color1_analyze.cgi`:

```
<form method="Get" action="/cgi-bin/color1_analyze.cgi">
```

And the following form preamble specifies that the Post method be used to call `color2_analyze.cgi`:

```
<form method="Post" action="/cgi-bin/color2_analyze.cgi">
```

In the Get method, the user's input is passed to the called CGI script via the CGI environment variable `QUERY_STRING`. The CGI script evaluates the value of `QUERY_STRING` and takes an appropriate response.

In the Post method, the user's input is passed as standard input to a CGI script. The CGI script reads from standard input and takes an appropriate response.

The Get Method

When an HTML form uses the Get method to call a CGI program, the user's responses to that form are passed to the CGI program in the **QUERY_STRING** environment variable. The CGI program evaluates **QUERY_STRING** and takes an appropriate response.

The following HTML file (`color_pref_get.htm`) generates a simple form:

```
<html>
<head><title>Personality by Color </title></head>
<body>
<center><h1> Personality by Color </h1></center>

<p>This program examines your choice of color and returns
a stunning insight into your personality.

<p>
<form method="get" ACTION="/cgi-bin/color1_get.cgi">
<strong>Pick a color (red, green, blue):</strong>
<input name="color" size=6>
<br>
<input type="reset" value="Clear">
<input type="submit" value="Analyze Me">
</form>

<p>And have a colorful day.

</body>
</html>
```

Notice that the preceding form requests only one piece of data. For such forms, the Web server assigns **QUERY_STRING** a value having the format:

> *name=value*

where:

name	is the **name** option for this part of the form. For example, in the form of `color_pref_get.htm`, the **name** tag is found on the line:

> `<input name="color" size=6>`

value	is the text that the user entered (or the default value if there is a default and the user did not supply a value).

For example, suppose the user entered **Green** as the favorite color. In this case, the Web server assigns **QUERY_STRING** the following:

`color=green`

The called CGI program, `color1_get.cgi`, analyzes the value of **QUERY_STRING**.

```ksh
#!/usr/bin/ksh
# color1_get.cgi: CGI program called by color_pref_get.htm.

# Write the necessary HTML header.
 print "Content-type: text/html"
 print
 print "<html>"
 print "<head><title>Your Personality</title></head>"
 print "<body><h1><center>Your Personality</center></h1>"

# What color did the user provide?  The chosen
# color will be contained in the QUERY_STRING variable.
 name_value_pair=$QUERY_STRING
# Strip away the phrase "color=" from the name_value_pair,
# leaving only the chosen color.
 your_color=${name_value_pair#"color="}

# Now analyze the chosen color, returning an appropriate
# response for each.
 case $your_color in
    "red")  print "<p><font color=$your_color>You are fiery."</font>;;
    "green") print "<p><font color=$your_color>You are pastoral."</font>;;
    "blue") print "<p><font color=$your_color>You are a dreamer."</font>;;
    *) print "<p>You can't follow directions.";;
 esac

# Now print the HTML trailer.
 print "</body>"
 print "</html>"
```

Executing This Script

To run this script, aim your browser at the following URL:

```
ch17/color_pref_get.htm
```

Suppose you respond to the HTML form by typing **green** as your favorite color:

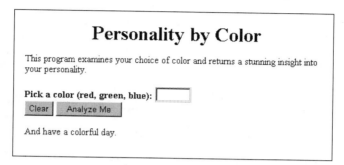

After hitting the Analyze Me button, the CGI program (`color1_get.cgi`) runs and generates the following spiffy screen:

Get Method: Multiple Input Values

If a form passes multiple pieces of information to a CGI script, the **QUERY_STRING** variable will hold multiple name-value pairs, where each pair is separated by an ampersand. So, for a multi-morsel form, **QUERY_STRING** will hold a value having the format:

> *name1=value1&name2=value2&...nameN=valueN*

The following HTML file, advanced_get.htm, displays a form that requests three pieces of data, so three name-value pairs will be passed to the CGI script.

```html
<html>
<head><title>Advanced Personality Test </title></head>
<body>
<center><h1> Advanced Personality Test </h1></center>

<p>Pick your favorites and we'll sort it all out for you.

<p>
<form method="get" ACTION="/cgi-bin/multiple_get.cgi">
<strong>Pick your favorite season:</strong>
<input type="radio" name="season" value="winter">Winter
<input type="radio" name="season" value="spring">Spring
<input type="radio" name="season" value="summer" checked>Summer
<input type="radio" name="season" value="fall">Fall

<p>
<strong>Pick your favorite medium:</strong>
<input type="radio" name="medium" value="tv">Television
<input type="radio" name="medium" value="web" checked>Web

<p>
<strong>Pick your favorite sport:</strong>
<input type="radio" name="sport" value="basketball">Basketball
<input type="radio" name="sport" value="football" checked>Football
<p>
<center><input type="submit" value="Help Me Doc"></center>
</form>
</body>
</html>
```

Suppose the user chooses:

- Winter
- Television
- Football

In this case, the Web server will assign the following to **QUERY_STRING**:

```
season=winter&medium=tv&sport=football
```

The preceding Web page uses the Get method to call a CGI program named `multiple_get.cgi`:

```ksh
#!/usr/bin/ksh93
# multiple_get.cgi: CGI program called by advanced_get.htm

# Write the necessary HTML header.
 print "Content-type: text/html"
 print
 print "<html>"
 print "<head><title>Advanced Personality Results</title></head>"
 print "<body><h1><center>Advanced Personality Results</center></h1>"

# What choices did the user pick?  The choices are all
# contained in the QUERY_STRING variable.

# Extract the user's favorite season from the QUERY_STRING.
 temp=${QUERY_STRING##*"season="}
 favorite_season=${temp%%'&'*}

# Extract the user's favorite medium.
 temp=${QUERY_STRING##*"medium="}
 favorite_medium=${temp%%'&'*}

# Extract the user's favorite sport.
 temp=${QUERY_STRING##*"sport="}
 favorite_sport=${temp%%'&'*}

# Come up with some cogent analysis.
 if [[ "$favorite_season" == "summer" ]] &&
    [[ "$favorite_medium" == "web"    ]] &&
    [[ "$favorite_sport"  == "basketball" ]]
 then
    print "<p>You are mentally sound."
 else
    print "<p>Seek help."
 fi

# Now print the HTML trailer.
 print "</body>"
 print "</html>"
```

Executing This Script

To run this script, aim your browser at the following URL:

```
ch17/advanced_get.htm
```

Your browser should display a Web page. After poking around with the radio buttons, you might end up with something that looks like this:

Advanced Personality Test

Pick your favorites and we'll sort it all out for you.

Pick your favorite season: ○ Winter ○ Spring ● Summer ○ Fall

Pick your favorite medium: ○ Television ● Web

Pick your favorite sport: ○ Basketball ● Football

> Help Me Doc

When finished punching up the buttons, press Help Me Doc, and the CGI program will run. The CGI program will generate a Web page that looks something like this:

Your Advanced Personality Results

Seek help.

The Post Method

The Post method and the Get method both cause a Web server to fling exactly the same name-value pairs to a CGI program. However, in the Post method, the name-value pairs become standard input to the CGI program. In the Post method, the Web server does not set a value for **QUERY_STRING**.

When the Web server passes post data to a CGI program, the Web server *does not* terminate the information with any sort of end-of-data marker. However, the Web server *does* pass an environment variable named **CONTENT_LENGTH** whose value is the number of characters passed to the CGI script. For example, if **CONTENT_LENGTH** is 500, your CGI program ordinarily would read 500 characters from standard input. Or, you can ask your CGI program to read all of standard input and then treat only the first 500 characters as significant.

On your CD, you'll find an HTML file named `color_pref_post.htm` whose contents are identical to `color_pref_get.htm` shown earlier in this chapter. The only difference is in the form preamble. In `color_pref_get.htm`, the form preamble looks as follows:

```
<form method="get" action="/cgi-bin/color1_get.cgi">
```

By contrast, the form preamble of `color_pref_post.htm` calls the post method as follows:

```
<form method="post" action="/cgi-bin/color1_post.cgi">
```

The only difference between `color1_get.cgi` and `color1_post.cgi` is in how they retrieve the user's response. Here is `color1_post.cgi` in its entirety:

```ksh
#!/usr/bin/ksh
# color1_post.cgi: CGI program called by color_pref_post.htm.

# Write the necessary HTML header.
 print "Content-type: text/html"
 print
 print "<html>"
 print "<head><title>Your Personality</title></head>"
 print "<body><h1><center>Your Personality</center></h1>"

# Assign all of standard input to variable raw_input.
 raw_input=$(cat -)

# Clip raw_input, just in case there are some superfluous
# characters at the end.
 name_value_pair=${raw_input:0:$CONTENT_LENGTH}

# What color did the user provide?  The chosen
# color will be contained in the name_value_pair variable.
# Strip away the phrase "color=" from the name_value_pair,
# leaving only the chosen color.
 the_chosen_color=${name_value_pair#"color="}

# Now analyze the chosen color, returning an appropriate
# response for each.
 case $the_chosen_color in
    "red")   print "<p>You are fiery.";;
    "green") print "<p>You are pastoral.";;
    "blue")  print "<p>You are a dreamer.";;
    *) print "<p>You can't follow directions.";;
 esac

# Now print the HTML trailer.
 print "</body>"
 print "</html>"
```

Executing This Script

To run this CGI script, aim your browser at the following URL:

```
/cgi-bin/color1_pref_post.htm
```

The Web page generated by `color1_pref_post.htm` will look identical to the Web page generated by `color1_pref_get.htm`. Similarly, the Web page generated by `color1_post.cgi` will look identical to the Web page generated by `color1_get.cgi`.

To Post or To Get

At this point, you're probably wondering whether the post method or the get method is the way to go. In fact, both post and get have their strengths and weaknesses.

When an HTML form uses the get method to invoke a CGI script, the name-value pairs being passed become part of the URL. For example, suppose you invoke `color_prog_get.htm` and choose `green` as your favorite color. When you press Analyze Me, the URL becomes:

```
/cgi-bin/color1_get.cgi?color=green
```

This URL, including the `color=green` part, will appear in your browser's Location box. So, if you're debugging `color1_get.cgi` and wondering what name-value pairs were actually passed, you simply can look at the Location box. Also, if you bookmark this CGI program, the `color=green` selection becomes part of the bookmark.

By contrast, when an HTML form uses the post method to invoke a CGI script, the name-value pairs being passed *do not* become part of the URL. So, when you invoke `color_pref_post.htm` and choose green as your favorite color, the URL does not contain your choice. The URL is simply:

```
/cgi-bin/color1_get.cgi
```

Thus, with the post method, the user's color preference will not appear in the browser's Location box and will not become part of the bookmark.

Many Web servers have trouble handling extremely long URLs and end up truncating parts of the URL. If the data being passed from a form is very long, the post method is the only way to go.

One way to resolve the debate is to write a CGI program that is flexible enough to handle either a get submission or a post submission. The Web server passes an environment variable named **REQUEST_METHOD** to every CGI program; the value of **REQUEST_METHOD** identifies whether a get method or a post method was used. So, an overachieving CGI program can evaluate the value of **REQUEST_METHOD** and take appropriate action.

Handling Special Characters

The CGI protocol insists that form data passed to CGI scripts be encoded as follows:

- All letters and digits are passed without modification.

- Every blank space is encoded as a plus sign or as %20.

- All characters other than letters, digits, and blank spaces are encoded as a three-character sequence in which the first character is a percent sign and the remaining two are the character's hexadecimal value. For example, the hexadecimal value of a slash (/) is 2F. Therefore, the Web server encodes all slashes as %2F.

For example, suppose the user enters the following text into a text box:

```
Flames to /dev/null.
```

The Web server encodes the preceding text so that the following data is passed to the CGI script:

```
Flames+to+%2Fdev%2Fnull%2E
```

Many CGI scripts need to decode the special characters—that is, to turn all the %NN and + characters back into normal upstanding printable characters. Take, for example, the CGI program that gets called by the following Web page (haiku_contest.htm):

```
<html>
<head><title>Write a Haiku </title></head>
<body>
<center><h1>Write an Anonymous Haiku </h1></center>

<p>
<form method="post" ACTION="/cgi-bin/funky_characters.cgi">
<p>Enter a haiku inside the box.
<p> <textarea name="poetry" rows=3 cols=70> </textarea>
<input type="reset" value="Clear">
<input type="submit" value="I'm so Proud">
</form>
</body>
</html>
```

The CGI script `funky_characters.cgi` runs when a user presses the I'm so Proud button. Here is the source code for `funky_characters.cgi`.

```ksh
#!/usr/bin/ksh
# funky_characters.cgi: CGI program called by haiku_contest.htm

# Convert the plus signs and %NN sequences into original characters.
function decode
{
  typeset result="${@// /+}"         # convert any spaces to + signs
  result=$(print -f "${result//(%)([A-F0-9][A-F0-9])/\\x\2 }")
    # space added so "%24f" xlates to "$f" instead of "0"
  result="${result// /}"             # remove spaces just put in
  print -r -- "${result//+/ }"       # + -> space
}


###########################################################################
# Program begins execution at next line.
# Write the necessary HTML header.
  print "Content-type: text/html"
  print
  print "<html>"
  print "<head><title>Thank You </title></head>"
  print "<body><h1><center>Your Entry Received</center></h1>"

# Read from standard input.
# Assign all of standard input to variable raw_input.
  raw_input=$(cat -)

# Clip raw_input, just in case there are some superfluous
# characters at the end.
  name_value_pair=${raw_input:0:$CONTENT_LENGTH}

  the_raw_poem=${name_value_pair#"poetry="}

# The poem is encoded; let's decode it.
  decoded=$(decode "$the_raw_poem")
  print "$decoded" >> haiku_repository
  print "<p>Your poem has been stored in our haiku repository."

# Now print the HTML trailer.
  print "</body>"
  print "</html>"
```

Executing This Script

To run this CGI script, tune your browser to the following URL:

```
/cgi-bin/haiku_contest.htm
```

Your browser should display a Web page. After entering a haiku, here's what my browser looked like:

Write an Anonymous Haiku

Enter a haiku inside the box.

```
The rain is so pure.
The ocean so clear and blue.
Why is tap so brown?
```

Clear   I'm so Proud

When finished with your haiku, press I'm so Proud, and the CGI program will run. The CGI program will generate a simple Web page acknowledging your submission. Now look for a file named haiku_repository. The most recently entered haiku should be at the end of this file.

Environment Variables Passed by the Web Server

Before invoking a CGI script, the Web server sets values for several environment variables. Two of these CGI environment variables—**QUERY_STRING** and **CONTENT_LENGTH**—are deservedly famous and often are seen frolicking about in South Beach and Cannes, driving fancy cars and popping up at chic parties. In addition, hordes of lesser known environment variables—jealous, petty things, wracked with self-doubt—also get passed to your CGI program. Some of the CGI environment variables describe the Web server, some the browser or user making the request.

The exact list of the variables passed to your CGI program depends on which version of the CGI protocol your Web server is using. As of this writing, most Web servers are using CGI Version 1.1, although a standards committee currently is haggling over the final contents of CGI Version 1.2. After a few more expensive meals, they should have it all nailed down. For a complete list of environment variables in the different CGI versions, browse on over to:

```
http://www.w3.org/CGI
```

Table 17-1 summarizes the CGI environment variables available in CGI Version 1.1. All these variables likely will be in CGI Version 1.2 as well.

Table 17-1. Environment Variables Passed to CGI Scripts

Environment variable	What it holds
AUTH_TYPE	The kind of scheme used to authenticate this user. The most common authentication scheme is HTTP basic authentication in which the user enters a username and password.
CONTENT_LENGTH	The length (in bytes) of the name-value pairs the client has posted.
CONTENT_TYPE	The mime type of the information that the client is attaching. For example, when using the post method, the browser attaches the name-value pair gathered by the form and sets the **CONTENT_TYPE** to application/x-www-form-urlencoded.
GATEWAY_INTERFACE	The version of the CGI protocol; for example, CGI/1.1.
HTTP_ACCEPT	The comma-separated list of mime types that this browser will accept.
HTTP_USER_AGENT	The kind of browser that made this CGI request.
HTTP_*	The client can pass an enormous variety of header information to the server. The Web server assigns the value of each header to a CGI environment variable named **HTTP_***header*. For example, if the client passes the **COOKIE** header to the Web server, the Web server passes the value of the **COOKIE** header as the CGI environment variable **HTTP_COOKIE**.

Table 17-1. (Continued.)

Environment variable	What it holds
PATH_INFO	Extra path information at the end of a URL.
PATH_TRANSLATED	The physical pathname corresponding to the virtual pathname of PATH_INFO.
QUERY_STRING	In a get method, the name-value pairs containing form input.
REMOTE_ADDR	The IP address (such as 255.255.255.255) making the request.
REMOTE_HOST	The hostname (such as juggler.openmarket.com) making the request.
REMOTE_IDENT	The sort of authenticated username. If the user has been authenticated using RFC931 identification, then REMOTE_IDENT holds the user's name.
REMOTE_USER	The authenticated username. That is, if the user has been authenticated through basic authentication (typed the correct username and password), then REMOTE_USER holds the username.
REQUEST_METHOD	This is usually either "GET" or "POST" although a few more obscure request types are possible.
SCRIPT_NAME	The name (not the complete pathname, just the filename) of the script being executed.
SERVER_NAME	The identity of the server, expressed as its IP address or as its domain name (such as, www.chic_parties.com).
SERVER_PORT	The port number (such as 80) the client requested.
SERVER_PROTOCOL	Protocol that server and browser use to communicate.
SERVER_SOFTWARE	The name and version number of the Web server.

Redirects

As noted earlier, not all CGI scripts generate HTML. For instance, many CGI scripts generate a command to redirect the user's browser to a particular URL. For example, to redirect a user's browser to http://www.awl.com, a CGI script would provide the following three lines of code:

```
print "HTTP/1.1  302 Moved"
print "Location: http://www.awl.com"
print      # Blank line
```

Browserless Browsing

Let's conclude the chapter by moving away from CGI programming and into another kind of Internet programming, namely, how to write a KornShell script that acts as a client of a Web server. As you'll soon see, you don't necessarily need a browser to contact your favorite Web site. This is so beyond cool that it is practically cryogenic.

A KornShell can connect to a Web site by issuing an **exec** statement of the format:

> **exec** *n*<> **/dev/tcp/**hostname**/**port_number

where:

n	is an integer symbolizing the stream you are creating.
hostname	the DNS name of the Web server you are contacting, for example, www.noodnick.com.
port_number	the port number on which the Web server is listening. Most Web servers listen on port 80. The port number for secure connections is typically 443.

For example, the following KornShell script uses an **exec** statement to connect to the Addison-Wesley Web site. Then, the script writes the HTML contents of a particular Web page on that Web site to standard output:

```
USAGE="usage: browserless_browsing.ksh"  # download a Web page

# This script reads the HTML file stored at
#  http://www2.awl.com:80/cseng/titles/0-201-310180-X/weather_table.htm

# Establish a two-way connection to http://www2.awl.com:80
 exec 3<> /dev/tcp/www2.awl.com/80
# 80 is the default port for HTTP connections.

# Send the Web server an HTTP request that means,
# "get me the Web page at this pathname"
 print -u3 'GET /cseng/titles/0-201-31018-X/weather_table.htm'

# Read the Web page line-by-line and write it to standard output.
 while read -u3 line
 do
   print "$line"
 done

# Close the connection.
 exec 3<&-
```

Executing This Script

```
$ browserless_browsing.ksh
<html>
<head>
<title>Weather Data on a day in July, 1998</title>
... Lots and lots of lines omitted for space reasons
</HTML>
```

Assuming this worked, you might very well be thinking, "So what? I'd rather use my browser to display the home page than try to plow through all that raw HTML." Suppose, however, that you frequently use your browser to access a certain very lengthy Web page that, because of the sheer volume of HTML and the number of images it contains, takes a solid 60 seconds to display in its entirety. Adding insult to injury, you really could care less about most of the information in this Web page. In fact, you are interested in only one essential fact located about half way down this Web page. Instead of fuming about the wasted time, why not write a KornShell script that can pick out the one important fact and write it to standard output, or store it in a file at 9:00 every night, or send it as e-mail, or do whatever you want with it.

The trick in writing such a script is in determining how to pluck out the information you need. Many times, the information you are seeking will be the only line in the Web page that matches a certain pattern. In other Web pages, the key fact is always located at a fixed line number. For example, the data for Boston is located on line 11 of the output. Therefore, the code to write only line 11 of the Web page is:

```
while read -u3 line
do
    (( line_counter++ ))
    if (( line_counter == 11 ))
    then
      print "$line"
    elif (( line_counter == 12 ))
    then
        break
    fi
done
```

Often, the data you retrieve is encased in HTML tags. For example, line 11 is:

```
<tr> <td>Boston</td> <td>78</td> </tr>
```

You can use KornShell search and replace operations to strip out these HTML tags. For example, to print only the temperature, you can use the following code:

```
t=${line##*'<td>'}
temperature=${t%'</td>'*}
print "$temperature"
```

BEWARE: Moral Concerns

Browserless browsing presents a sticky moral issue. Many Web sites depend on advertising for revenue, but browserless browsing makes it very easy to side-step these advertisements. (Are you really going to download the ads?)

So, is this the moral equivalent of getting up from the couch when a television commercial comes on, or are you ruining a nice arrangement?

Browserless Browsing for GIFs

When you run `browserless_browsing.ksh`, you'll quickly notice that although the **<img>** tags from the Web site do appear in the output, the GIF images themselves do not get copied to your site. To get a GIF image, you have to request it specifically, as in the following example:

```
USAGE="usage: get_a_gif.ksh"  # reeling in a GIF

# This script gets the GIF image at:
#  http://www2.awl.com:80/cseng/titles/0-201-310180-X/one_july_day.gif

# Establish a two-way connection to http://www2.awl.com:80
 exec 4<> /dev/tcp/www2.awl.com/80

# Get a particular GIF image at this site.
 print -u4 'GET /cseng/titles/0-201-31018-X/one_july_day.gif'

# Duplicate stream 4 so that stream 0 (standard input)
# is temporarily synonymous with stream 0.
 exec 0<&4

# Write the GIF file to my_copy.gif
 cat - > my_copy.gif

# Close stream 4, which ends the connection to world.std.com.
 exec 4<&-
```

Executing This Script

To execute this script, type the following at the KornShell prompt:

```
$ get_a_gif.ksh
```

Nothing visible will happen, but if this script successfully connected, a file named `my_copy.gif` will be created. Use any GIF viewer to display `my_copy.gif`.

BEWARE: When Browserless Browsing Fails

Quite a few circumstances can make browserless browsing fail.

If you can't connect, perhaps the problem is at your end. Is there a firewall at your site that requires requests to pass through some sort of proxy server?

Perhaps the Web server is refusing this kind of request. Some Web servers reject requests when the client does not identify itself with the proper HTTP client headers.

Perhaps you can connect, but the organization of the information that comes back on Tuesday isn't what you got back on Monday. Ah, there's the rub; you don't control the Web server, so when it changes, your script has to be smart enough to adapt.

A   Statement and Alias Quick Reference

alias [-pt] [*name*=['*value*']]

-p   print the word *alias* in front of each alias definition.

-t   establish a tracked alias between *name* and the program at pathname *value*. Most users can ignore this option. The KornShell can find *value* faster if it is a tracked alias than if it is not a tracked alias. You can establish a tracked alias only if 1) the trackall option is on (use **set -h** to turn it on) and 2) the directory in which *value* is stored is part of your **PATH**.

name   the name of the alias. If you do not supply a value, `alias name` displays the definition of *name*.

value   any string. Usually, *value* is the name of an operating system command or a KornShell statement.

Use **alias** to create aliases or to display a list of all known aliases. An alias is a nickname (or shorthand) for *value*. For details, see "Aliases" on page 204.

```
$ alias        # list names and values of all aliases
2d='set -f;_2d'
autoload='typeset -fu'
command='command '
...
z='ls -aRl'

$ alias z # print the definition of the alias named z
z='ls -aRl'

$ alias input='read -r'  # create alias named input

$ alias this='print "Dir is $PWD"; ls -l' # create alias named this

$ alias -t mygame='$HOME/mygame'  # create tracked alias named mygame
```

autoload *[function]*

> *function*   the name of the function to be autoloaded. The function must be in a
>   directory listed in **FPATH**. If you do not supply a function, **autoload** lists
>   all the currently autoloaded functions.

Use **autoload** to get the KornShell to load *function* into the KornShell. In
essence, *function* becomes an extension of the KornShell. For details, see "Autoloaded Functions" on page 185.

> **autoload** is an alias for **typeset -fu**.

bg *[job_name]*

> *job_name*   the job you want to restart. See "job_name" on page 386. If you do not
>   specify job_name, **bg** lists all background jobs that you have started.

Use **bg** to resume execution of a stopped (suspended) job. The resumed job
will run in the background. For an explanation of the background, see "Background and Foreground" on page 309.

```
$ payroll  # Run a program in foreground
<CONTROL-Z>  # Send the program a stop signal
[1] + Stopped                   payroll
$ bg %1    # Now resume the program, but run it in the background
[1]      payroll&
$ jobs     # Make sure the bg statement really worked
[1] + Running                   payroll
```

break *[number]*

> *number*   number of nested (enclosing) loops to which **break** applies. Default
>   value of *number* is 1.

Use **break** within loops only. Use it to leave the current loop (if *number* is 1) or
the current loop plus any enclosing loops (if *number* is greater than 1). For examples of **break**, see "Using break to Leave a Loop" on page 109 and "The break
Statement Within a Nested Loop" on page 121.

```
break    # leave current loop
break 1  # same as above
break 2  # leave current loop and loop enclosing current loop
```

builtin [-s] [-d *function***] [-f** *shared_library] [function]*

-d *function*	delete *function* from the list of built-in statements the KornShell can access. You cannot delete any special KornShell functions. You can delete any nonspecial KornShell functions or any KornShell extension functions that you provide.
-s	display special built-in KornShell functions, which cannot be deleted.
-f *shared_library*	search for function in this shared library.
function	is the name (minus the leading b_) of a KornShell extension function defined in *shared_library.* For example, if you wrote in C a KornShell extension function named b_onion, then you would set function to onion.

Use **builtin** without any arguments to list all statements and KornShell extension functions supported by your KornShell. You can also use it to load a KornShell extension function into the KornShell; see "Extending the KornShell by Writing C Functions" on page 187.

case *value* **in**
    *pattern1***)** *[command1*
          ...
         commandN] **;;**
    *pattern2***)** *[commandN*
          ...
         commandN] **;;**
   ...
    *patternN***)** *[command1*
          ...
         *commandN]***;;**
esac

value	is any value. Typically, you specify the *value* of a variable.
pattern	is any constant, pattern, or group of patterns. Use the | symbol to separate individual patterns within a group of patterns.
command	is the name of any program, shell script, or KornShell statement.

Use **case** to compare a *value* to one or more *patterns.* If *value* matches a *pattern,* the KornShell executes *command1* through *commandN.* Compare **case** to **if.** For more details and examples, see Chapter 6.

```
case $string in    # compare value of string to three patterns
  [a-z]*) print "$string starts with a lowercase letter."
          print "It yearns for something higher.";;
  [A-Z]*) print "$string starts with an uppercase letter.";;
  *) print "$string does not start with a letter.";;
esac
```

cat

Some versions of KornShell provide the UNIX **cat** command as a KornShell statement (thus improving its performance). The KornShell version of **cat** has the same features as the standard UNIX version of **cat**.

cd [-LP] [*dir_name*]
cd [-LP] -

-L is ignored unless *dir_name* contains a double dot (. .). If *dir_name* contains a double dot, **-L** directs **cd** to assume that the double dot refers to the *logical* parent of the specified directory.

-P is ignored unless *dir_name* contains a double dot (..). If *dir_name* contains a double dot, **-L** directs **cd** to assume that the double dot refers to the *physical* parent of the specified directory.

dir_name is the pathname of any directory. If you specify an explicit pathname, then the KornShell attempts to change the current directory to *dir_name*. If you specify an implicit pathname, then **cd** uses the directory list of **CDPATH** to find the appropriate current directory; for details, see "PATH, CDPATH, and FPATH—Search Directories" on page 294. By the way, a *dir_name* that begins with . . means the directory above the current one.

- is equivalent to **cd $OLDPWD; pwd**. That is, the – puts you back into the previous directory and then prints the name of the new current directory.

Make *dir_name* the current directory. Specifying **cd** without any arguments is equivalent to specifying **cd $HOME**.

```
$ pwd            # what is the current directory?
/udir/bina
$ cd /udir/per/programs   # change current directory
$ pwd            # what is the current directory now?
/udir/per/programs
$ cd -           # go back to previous directory
/udir/bina       # cd - automatically prints new directory

$ ln -s /udir/bina/under/the/sea  ocean      # make a link
$ cd ocean       # change current directory
$ pwd            # what is the current directory now?
/udir/bina/under/the/sea
$ cd -L ..       # go up to parent.
$ pwd            # but which way is "up"?
/udir/bina

$ cd ocean       # go back down
$ pwd            # here we are again
/udir/bina/under/the/sea
$ cd -P ..       # go back up to parent
$ pwd            # now the physical path is the way "up"
/udir/bina/under/the
```

cd *change_this to_this*

> *change_this*   is a string within the current directory name that you want to change.
>
> *to_this*   is the string you want to change *change_this* to.

Use this form of **cd** to change the current directory by changing *change_this* to *to_this*. After making the change, **cd** prints the new current directory.

```
$ pwd                  # what is the current directory?
/usr/users/roger/programs
$ cd roger nancy   # change current directory and print new location
/usr/users/nancy/programs
```

chmod

Some versions of KornShell provide the UNIX **chmod** command as a KornShell statement (thus improving its performance). The KornShell version of **chmod** has the same features as the standard UNIX version of **chmod**.

command [-pvV] *a_command* [*arguments_to_a_command*]

> **-p**   when searching for *a_command*, use the default value of **PATH** (usually, /bin:/usr/bin) instead of the current value of **PATH**.
>
> **-v**   do not execute *a_command*, but indicate what category *a_command* falls into. If *a_command* is a KornShell statement, command -v merely echoes the name of that statement. If *a_command* is an alias, command -v echoes the name of that alias but puts the alias name inside a pair of special markers. If *a_command* is an executable program, command -v writes the pathname at which this program is stored.
>
> **-V**   same as **-v**, except in a more verbose, less cryptic format.
>
> *a_command*   is any KornShell statement, KornShell script, or operating system command. Basically, *a_command* could be anything you could put on a KornShell command line.
>
> *arguments_to_a_command*   are the arguments to *a_command*. For example, if *a_command* is cat, then *arguments_to_a_command* probably would be one or more filenames.

The confusingly named **command** statement runs *a_command* or reports the category to which *a_command* belongs. A typical situation for using **command** is when you have written a function that has the same name as a KornShell statement, KornShell script, or operating system command. In this situation, by default, if you invoke *a_command*, the KornShell will invoke your function. If you want the

KornShell to invoke the KornShell statement, KornShell script, or operating system command instead of your function, then use **command**.

```
USAGE="cmd_ex.ksh"  # demonstrates the command statement

function date
{
    print "I'll pick you up at 8."
}

date           # invoke the date function
command date   # invoke the date statement
```

Executing This Script

```
$ cmd_ex.ksh
I'll pick you up at 8
Thu Dec  4 10:10:59 EST 1997
```

continue *[number]*

> *number*   number of nesting loops to which **continue** applies. The default value
>   of *number* is 1, meaning the containing loop only.

Use **continue** only within loops. If *number* is 1, **continue** skips the current iteration of loop. If *number* is greater than 1, **continue** skips the current iteration of the loop and *number* enclosing loops.

```
continue    # skip rest of current iteration of innermost loop
continue 1  # same as above
continue 2  # skip rest of current iteration of innermost loop and
            # loop surrounding it
```

cp

Some versions of KornShell provide the UNIX **cp** command as a KornShell statement (thus improving its performance). The KornShell version of **cp** has the same features as the standard POSIX version of **cp**.

cut

Some versions of KornShell provide the UNIX **cut** command as a KornShell statement (thus improving its performance). The KornShell version of **cut** has the same features as the standard POSIX version of **cut**.

date

   Some versions of KornShell provide the UNIX **date** command as a KornShell statement. The KornShell version of **date** has the same features as the POSIX version of **date**.

disown *[job_name1 ... job_name2]*

   job_name   the job(s) you want to disown. See "job_name" on page 386. If you do not specify a *job_name*, the KornShell disowns all background processes.

   Use **disown** to prevent the KornShell from killing *job_name* when the user who started this job logs out.

```
$ payroll.ksh > results 2> bad &    # run a script n the background
[1]     18582
$ disown %1      # disown the script
$ exit           # log out, but payroll.ksh continues to run
```

do

   Use **do** to mark the beginning of the body of a **for, while, select,** or **until** statement.

done

   Use **done** to mark the end of the body of a **for, while, select,** or **until** statement.

echo

   echo is an old Bourne shell output statement. It is still supported for backwards compatibility; however, you should use the **print** or **printf** statement instead of **echo.**

elif

   Use **elif** to precede the second through Nth conditions of an **if** statement. See "if" on page 385.

else

   Use **else** to introduce the default actions of an **if** statement. In other words, if all previous conditions are false, the KornShell executes the commands between **else** and **fi**. See "if" on page 385.

esac

Use **esac** to mark the end of a **case** statement. See "case" on page 371.

escape sequences

\a	ring bell
\b	output backspace character
\c	suppress printing *text* following **\c**
\f	output formfeed
\n	output newline
\r	output carriage return
\t	output horizontal tab
\v	output vertical tab
****	output one backslash character
\0*number*	output character whose octal ASCII value is *number*

The **print** and **printf** commands both take escape sequences as optional arguments.

eval [*arg1... argN*]

arg   any value

eval is short for "evaluate." This statement works in three steps: **1)** The Korn-Shell expands *arg1* through *argN*. **2)** The KornShell catenates the results of Step 1 into a single command. **3)** The KornShell executes the command formed in Step 2.

```
$ x=10; y=12; z=8                        # assign values to a few variables
$ read mystery_variable?"What variable would you like to examine: "
What variable would you like to examine: y
$ eval print '$'$mystery_variable    # execute the command print $y
12
```

exec *numberaction target*

number	a nonnegative integer. Enclose numbers greater than 9 within braces; for example, {12}. The KornShell reserves *number* 0 for standard input, *number* 1 for standard output, and *number* 2 for standard error. Values greater than 2 are for user-defined streams.
action	an I/O redirection operator.
target	the pathname of a file, the *number* of another stream, or a minus sign (-).

Use **exec** to open, close, or copy a stream.

Don't put any white space between *number* and *action*. See page 245 for complete syntactic details on **exec**.

```
$ exec 3< data # open file data for reading, assign it stream number 3
$ exec 4<& 3    # open stream 4 as a redundant copy of stream 3
$ read -u3 line # read first line of data
$ exec 3<&-     # close stream 3; stream 4 is still open
$ read -u4 line # read second line of data
```

exec [**-c**] [**-a** *name*] *program [args]*

-c	before running *program*, clear all environment variables deposited by the current KornShell process.
-a *name*	when running *program*, the KornShell assigns *name* to positional parameter **$0**.
a_command	the pathname of a KornShell script, program, or operating system command.
args	arguments to *program*.

Use this version of **exec** to replace the current KornShell with *program*, and do so such that *program* occupies the process space now occupied by the KornShell.

```
$ exec down.ksh  # run down.ksh in KornShell's process space
```

exit [*number*]

number	integer that will serve as the exit status. The KornShell will assign the exit status to the reserved variable **$?** in the caller's environment. If you do not specify *number*, the KornShell sets the exit status to the current value of **$?**.

Use **exit** to leave a KornShell script or to quit a KornShell session.

```
exit 2  # terminate script; assign 2 to $? of caller
```

export [-p] *[name = [value]]*

    -p   if *name* is not specified, display the name of each exported variable pre-
                       ceded by the word **export**.

    name   the name of the variable to be exported.

    value   the starting value assigned to variable *name*.

Use **export** to make variable *name* and its *value* accessible to children of the current process. If you specify **export** inside the body of a function, *name* won't be a local variable. If you specify **export** and don't specify *name*, the KornShell lists the names of all exported variables.

```
$ export       # list all exported variables
CC=/bin/cc
CMDLINE=WIN
...
myvar=17.2
$ export x     # allow children of current process to access variable x
$ export x='hello' # same as above, but initialize x to 'hello'
```

false

Use **false** to create a condition that always evaluates to false.

fc

fc is the old-fashioned version of **hist**. In KornShell 93, you should use **hist** instead of **fc**.

fg *[job_name]*

    job_name   the job you want to restart. See "job_name" on page 386. If you do not specify *job_name*, **fg** resumes execution of the job that was most recently stopped.

Moves a background job to the foreground, where it will resume execution.

```
$ longwinded.ksh &   # run a job in the background
[1]    7765
$ fg %1    # now run this job in the foreground
```

fi

Use **fi** to mark the end of an if statement. See "if" on page 385.

float *[variable[=value]]*

> *variable*   the name of a variable.
>
> *value*   the starting value assigned to *variable*.

    Use **float** to declare a *variable* as a float. That is, once declared as a **float**, *variable* can only hold a floating-point value. If you do not specify *variable*, **float** returns a list of all variables declared as floats.

    float is an alias for **typeset** **-E**.

```
float normal=98.6 # declare and initialize float variable normal
```

for *variable* [**in** *list*]
do
  command1
  ...
  commandN
done

> *variable*   is any variable name.
>
> *list*   is one or more strings, numbers, or filenames. If *list* contains any Korn-Shell wildcards, the KornShell expands the wildcards into filenames before beginning the loop.
>
> *command*   is the name of any program, any shell script, or any KornShell statement.

    Use **for** to loop through all the elements of *list*. The first time through the loop, **for** assigns the first item in *list* to *variable*; the second time through the loop, **for** assigns the second item in *list* to *variable*, and so on, until all the elements in *list* are used up. For example, if *list* contains five items, the KornShell executes the commands between **do** and **done** five times.

    The **in** *list* portion of the syntax is optional. If you omit it, then the first time through the loop, **for** assigns **$1** to *variable*; the second time through the loop, **for** assigns **$2** to *variable*, and so on, until all positional parameters are used up. For example, if there are eight positional parameters, the KornShell executes the commands between **do** and **done** eight times.

    You can nest a **for** loop (or any other kind of loop) inside another **for** loop.

    For more details, see page 124.

```
# Print a list of all objects in current directory that start
# with the letter b.
for object in b*
do
  print "$object"
done
```

```
# Catenate all files named on the command line.
for cla
do
   cat "$cla" > compendium
done
```

for ((*[expr1]*; *[expr2]*; *[expr3]* **))**
do
 command1
 ...
 commandN
done

expr1	is any program, shell script, or KornShell statement. Typically, *expr1* is an assignment statement.
expr2	is any program, shell script, or KornShell statement. Typically, *expr2* is a statement that compares two values.
expr3	is any program, shell script, or KornShell statement. Typically, *expr3* is a statement that increments or decrements a variable.
command	is the name of any program, shell script, or KornShell statement.

Use this version of **for** to create a C-style **for** loop. This **for** loop begins by executing *expr1*. Then, if *expr2* evaluates to true, the **for** loop executes *command1* through *commandN*. Following the execution of *commandN*, the **for** loop executes *expr3*. If *expr2* evaluates to false, the **for** loop terminates and the KornShell executes the line after **done**.

All three *expr*'s are optional. If you omit *expr2*, **for** assumes that *expr2* is always true, which creates a potentially infinite loop.

For more details, see page 123.

```
for (( x=0; x<=100; x+=10 )) # set x from 0 to 100 in steps of 10
do        # loop iterates 11 times
    print $x
done
```

function *name*
{
  body
}

name	is the name of the function.
body	is the body of a function. The body can contain any code that any other part of a KornShell script could contain. However, you cannot specify another function within the *body*; that is, you cannot nest functions. Recursive function calls are legal, though.

Use **function** to define a named routine that can be called from within the script in which it is defined. For details on the syntax of **function**, see page 195.

An autoloaded function is a function stored in a separate file. An autoloaded function can be called from the KornShell or from any KornShell script. For details on autoloaded functions, see page 185.

```
function triangle-area   # define a function named triangle-area
{
  base=$1      # $1 is the first argument (45) to triangle-area
  height=$2    # $2 is the second argument (63) to triangle-area
  (( area = (base * height) / 2 ))
  print "The area of the triangle is $area"
}

triangle-area 45 63   # call function and pass it two arguments
```

functions *[name1 ... nameN]*

name	the name of a function.

Use **functions** to print the definition of one or more function *names*. If you do not specify a name, **functions** prints the definitions of all active functions.

functions is an alias for **typeset** **-f**.

```
$ functions air  # what is the definition of function air?
function air
{
  print "You breathe it and it keeps you alive."
}
```

getconf *[config_param [pathname]]*

> *config_param*   the name of a configuration parameter. This is optional.
>
> *pathname*   a pathname. This is optional. For the vast majority of configuration parameters, **getconf** ignores the value of *pathname*. However, if a configuration parameter pertains to a list of pathnames, then the value of *pathname* potentially influences the value returned by **getconf**.

Use **getconf** to display the names and values of POSIX and X/OPEN configuration parameters. If you do not specify *name*, **getconf** displays information about all configuration parameters. If you do specify *name*, **getconf** displays information about that configuration parameter only.

getopts **[-a** *name]* *possible_switches var_name [data1...dataN]*

> **-a** *name*   assigns *name* to **$0**.
>
> *possible_switches* is a list of legal one-letter switch names, possibly including one or more colons. A colon : indicates that the preceding switch requires an argument. However, if a colon is the first character in *possible_switches,* the KornShell will respond to illegal command line switches by setting the value of *var_name* to ? and the value of **OPTARG** to the name of the undefined switch.
>
> *var_name*   is any variable name.
>
> *[data1... dataN]*   is one or more strings separated by white space. If you do not specify *data,* **getopts** will analyze the current set of positional parameters (usually set by the command line). If you do specify *data,* **getopts** will evaluate data instead of the positional parameters.

Use **getopts** to analyze command line switches. A command line switch is a + or - followed by a single letter.

```
# Handle the -l and -h switches.
while getopts lh argument
do
    case $argument in
        l) amplitude=10;;
        h) amplitude=25;;
    esac
done
```

hash

> **hash** is an alias for **alias -t --**.

head

> Some versions of KornShell provide the UNIX **head** command as a KornShell statement. The KornShell version of **head** has the same features as the POSIX version of **head**.

hist [**-e** *editor*] [**-lnr**] [*cmd_id_range*]

-e *editor*	specify pathname of *editor* to use when editing *cmd_id_range*. If you specify – for *editor*, **hist** will suppress editing of the command line and will simply re-execute *cmd_id_range*.
-l	list the commands in *cmd_id_range*, or, if *cmd_id_range* is not specified, list the 16 commands most recently issued.
-n	suppress command numbers in output listing.
-r	reverse the order in which **hist** displays or edits commands.
cmd_id_range	is the command or group of commands to which **hist** applies. If you specify a number for *cmd_id_range*, **hist** applies to that command number. If you specify two numbers for *cmd_id_range*, **hist** applies to all the commands from the first number to the second number inclusive. If you specify a string for *cmd_id_range*, **hist** applies to the most recently issued command whose name starts with string.

> Use **hist** to list recently issued commands, re-execute them, or edit a list of recently issued commands and then re-execute them.

> If you omit **-e** *editor*, **hist** uses the command line editor stored at variable **HISTEDIT**. If **HISTEDIT** is not set, **hist** uses the editor stored at variable **FCEDIT**. If neither **HISTEDIT** nor **FCEDIT** is set, **hist** uses the editor stored at /bin/ed.

> For more details on **hist**, see Chapter 16.

```
$ hist 45        # edit, then re-execute command number 45
$ hist 45 48     # edit, then re-execute commands 45, 46, 47, and 48
$ hist f         # edit, then re-execute the most recent command
                 # that starts with 'f'
$ hist -l 400 500 # list command numbers 400 to 500 inclusive
```

hist -s *change_this=to_this [cmd]*

-s	substitute, then re-execute *cmd*.
change_this	the string in *cmd* that you want to change.
to_this	the replacement string for the current string. If there are multiple occurrences of *change_this* in *cmd*, only the first occurrence of *change_this* will be replaced.
cmd	the command to which **hist** applies. If you specify a number for *cmd*, then **hist** applies to that command number. If you specify a string for *cmd*, then **hist** applies to the most recently issued command whose name starts with string. You cannot specify multiple command numbers because this form of **hist** only applies to a single command. If you omit *cmd*, **hist** applies to the most recently issued command.

Use this version of **hist** to perform a simple string substitution a recently issued command and then to re-execute that command.

This version is fairly limited; if you have more serious command line editing to do, you should use the **hist -e** option and edit *cmd* with vi or emacs.

```
$ typeset -F cake=3.14159  # a command to play with
$ hist -s cake=pi     # edit most recent command, changing cake to pi
typeset -F pi=3.14159  # here's the command that gets executed

$ hist -s 95  # re-execute command number 95
```

history

history is an alias for **hist -1**. Use it to display the last 16 commands you have issued on the KornShell command line. For details, see "Listing Previous Commands" on page 326.

if *condition*
then
  command1

  ...

  [commandN]
[elif *condition]*
  command1

  ...

  [commandN]

... *# you can specify multiple elif statements*

[else]
  command1

  ...

  [commandN]
fi

      condition   is usually a numerical comparison, string comparison, or object test; however, *condition* can be the name of any program, operating system command, or KornShell statement (except **if, then, elif,** or **else**).

      command   is the name of any program, shell script, or KornShell statement.

    Use **if** to evaluate one or more conditions and take an action depending on the outcome.

    For more details and examples on the **if** statement, see Chapter 6.

```
if (( x > 0 ))
then
  print "$x is positive."
elif (( x == 0 ))
  print "$x is zero."
else
  print  "$x is negative"
fi
```

in

    Use **in** as a modifier within a **for** or **case** statement. See **for** and **case**.

integer *[variable[=value]]*

> *variable*   the name of a variable.
>
> *value*   the initial value to assign to *variable*.

Once declared as a **integer**, *variable* can hold only an integer value. If you do not specify *variable*, **integer** returns a list of all variables declared as **integer**.
integer is an alias for **typeset -i**.

```
integer perfect=10
```

job_name

The **bg, fg, kill,** and **wait** statements all require a *job_name* as an argument. The *job_name* can be the PID (process identifier) of the job. In addition, if the job was invoked from the KornShell (as opposed to being invoked from inside a script), you also can specify *job_name* as any one of the following:

> **%%**   the current job.
>
> **%+**   another way of specifying the current job.
>
> **%-**   the previous job.
>
> **%***number*   the job with this number. (When you invoke a background job, the KornShell returns the job number within square brackets; for example, [1].)
>
> **%***string*   the job whose invocation command begins with this string.
>
> **%?***string*   the job whose invocation command contains this string

jobs [-lnp] *job_name*

> **-l**   list all jobs and their PIDs.
>
> **-n**   list stopped or exited jobs only.
>
> **-p**   list PIDs only (omit all other job information).

Use **jobs** to get information on background and foreground jobs.

```
$ jobs      # list all jobs
[2] + Running                    sysmon >> monitor_log &
[1] - Running                    payroll > /dev/null &

$ jobs -l # same as previous, except show PIDs as well
[2] + 3659        Running              sysmon >> monitor_log &
[1] - 3348        Running              payroll > /dev/null &

$ jobs %sys # just report on job beginning with letters "sys"
[2] + 3659        Running              sysmon >> monitor_log &
```

kill *[-s signal_name]* *[-n signal_number] job_name*
kill -l
kill *[-l signal_name]* *[-l signal_number]*

-s *signal_name*	send the named signal (for example, **INT** or **TERM**) to *job_name*.
-n *signal_number*	send the numbered signal (for example, 2 or 15) to *job_name*.
job_name	the job you want to send a signal to. See "job_name" on page 386.
-l	list all signal names and numbers.
-l *signal_name*	list the signal number corresponding to *signal_name*.
-l *signal_number*	list the signal name corresponding to *signal_number*.

Use **kill** to send a signal or to get a list of signals. (See also **trap**.) For details and examples on **kill**, see Chapter 15.

```
$ kill -l         # list names of all legal signals on this system
HUP
INT
...
USR2
$ kill -l INT     # what signal number corresponds to signal name INT?
2                 # signal number 2
$ kill -s INT %1  # send an INT (interrupt) signal to job number 1
$ kill -n 2 %1    # same as above
```

let *expr*

The **let** statement arithmetically evaluates *expr*. Use **((...))** instead of **let**.

mkdir

Some versions of KornShell provide the UNIX **mkdir** command as a KornShell statement. The KornShell version of **mkdir** has the same features as the POSIX version of **mkdir**.

nameref *[nameref_variable_name=regular_variable_name]*

nameref_variable	the nickname for *regular_variable_name*.
regular_variable	the name of a variable.

Use **nameref** to establish a synonym, such that whatever happens to *regular_variable* also will automatically happen to *nameref_variable*. For details, see "Declaring **nameref** Variables" on page 33.

The nameref statement is an alias for **typeset -n**.

newgrp

Some versions of KornShell provide the UNIX **newgrp** command as a Korn-Shell statement. The KornShell version of **newgrp** has the same features as the POSIX version of **newgrp**.

nohup *command [args_to_command]*

command	a KornShell statement, KornShell script, program, or operating system command to run. The standard output and standard error.
args_to_command	arguments (options, filenames, and so on) to be used by *command*.

By preceding *command* with **nohup**, you tell the KornShell to continue running *command* even after you log out. If you do not redirect standard output or standard error, **nohup** writes both standard output and standard error to pathname ./nohup.out. If you do not have write permission on the current directory, **nohup** writes both standard output and standard error to pathname $HOME/.nohup.out.

```
$ nohup ls -Rl / &
$ exit   # logout, but the ls command will continue to run
```

print [-nprRs][--] [-u*number*] [-f *format_string*] *text*

-n	suppress printing a carriage return after printing *text*.
-p	redirect *text* to co-process (instead of standard output).
-r	interpret the backslash (\) literally instead of as the escape character.
-R	interpret (\) and - literally (except for the - in the **-n** option).
-s	redirect *text* to history file (instead of standard output).
--	interpret the minus sign (-) literally rather than as a character that starts an option.
-u*number*	redirect *text* to stream symbolized by *number*. Setting *number* to 1 sends text to standard output; setting *number* to 2 sends *text* to standard error; setting *number* to some value greater than 2 sends *text* to a user-defined stream. See "exec" on page 377 for more information on opening streams.
-f *format_string*	use the **printf** syntax, where *format_string* is a **printf** style string. (See "printf" on page 389.) If you specify **-f**, **print** does not apply any **-n**, **-r**, or **-R** options you supply.
text	the *text* you want to output. You can optionally enclose *text* within a pair of single or double quotes. The *text* can consist of any combination of variable names, literal values, and escape sequences. (See "escape sequences" on page 376.)

Use **print** to output *text*. See also **printf**. See also the approximately one gazillion examples of **print** that appear throughout the book.

```
print "hi\t$x"    # text consists of a literal value, an escape
                  # sequence, and the value of a variable
```

printf *format_string* [*arg1 ... argN*]

format_string	a string encased in a pair of quotes. The string can contain any combination of plain text, conversion specifiers, and escape sequences (see "escape sequences" on page 376).
arg	anything that the KornShell can evaluate. Typically, *arg* is a variable name, but it also could be a constant or a mathematical expression.

Use **printf** to output *format_string*, substituting *arg1* for the first conversion specifier in *format_string*, *arg2* for the second conversion specifier in *format_string*, and so on. For examples of **printf**, see "Getting Fancy Output with the printf Statement" on page 224. For details on **printf** syntax, see page 250.

pwd [-LP]

  -**L**   display the logical pathname of the current directory.

  -**P**   display the physical pathname of the current directory.

Use **pwd** to print the name of the current (working) directory.

The logical and physical pathnames are identical *unless* a **cd** command took advantage of a link to a directory. In that case, the -**L** option tells **pwd** to display the pathname via the link, but the -**P** option ignores the link.

```
$ pwd              # what is the current directory?
/udir/tsvi

$ ln -s /udir/tsvi/deep/blue ocean       # make a link
$ cd ocean         # change current directory

$ pwd -L           # what is the current logical directory?
/udir/tsvi/ocean

$ pwd -P           # what is the current physical directory?
/udir/tsvi/deep/blue
```

r

r is an alias for **hist** -**s**. Use **r** to repeat a previously issued command. Think of **r** as an abbreviation for "repeat" or "re-execute." For examples of **r**, see "Re-Executing Previous Commands" on page 327.

read [-A *array*] [-d*c*] [-prs] [-t*sec*] [-u*number*] [*var?prompt*] [*var1...varN*]

  -**A** *array*   assign each input token to the next element of *array*. You must leave white space between -**A** and the name of the array.

  -**d***c*   stop reading input when character *c* is encountered. If you do not specify the -**d** option, **read** will gather an entire line of input.

  -**p**   read input from co-process (instead of standard input).

  -**r**   turn off the special meaning of a backslash (\) at the end of a line.

  -**s**   store a copy of the inputted values inside the history file.

  -**t***sec*   limit user to *sec* seconds in which to enter input.

  -**u***number*   read input from stream symbolized by *number*. See "exec" on page 377.

  var   assign input to this variable (or variables).

  prompt   print *prompt* before gathering input from user. Enclose *prompt* within single or double quotes.

Use **read** to gather input and assign it to one or more *variables*. The **read** statement uses the **IFS** variable to split input into tokens. The KornShell then assigns the first token to *variable1*, the second to *variable2*, and so on. If there are more

tokens than *variables,* the KornShell assigns remaining tokens to *variableN.* For a
more complete description of **read**, see page 246.

```
$ read x              # gather input and assign it to variable x
tofu on the barby     # assign "tofu on the barby" to variable x

$ read y z            # assign first token to y and all other tokens to z
tofu on the barby     # assign "tofu" to y; assign "on the barby" to z

$ read value?"Enter a value: "    # prompt, then assign input to value
Enter a value: 17                 # assign 17 to value

$ read -A ar
dog rat ox            # assign dog to ar[0], rat to ar[1], ox to ar[2]
```

readonly *variable=value*
readonly [-p]

-p print the word **readonly** in front of each variable name when dis-
        playing the list of **readonly** variables.

variable=value the name and value of a variable you wish to declare as a constant.

Use **readonly** to declare constants. Once assigned, you cannot change the
value of a constant.

If you specify **readonly** without specifying *variable=value,* the KornShell displays the names and values of all constants.

```
$ readonly x=7 # declare x as a constant
$ x=0          # wrong; causes a KornShell error because x cannot change
```

redirect

The **redirect** statement is an alias for command exec.

return [*number***]**

number (integer) value returned to caller. The default value of *number* is the cur-
          rent value of **$?**.

Use **return** to leave a function and return to the caller. If you specify a *number,*
that number is returned to the caller as the value of **$?**.

If you specify **return** outside of a function, **return** is equivalent to **exit**.

```
return 2   # leave callee and return to the caller; pass 2 back to $?
```

select *variable* [**in** *list*]
do
  command1
  ...
  [commandN]
done

variable	any variable name.
list	a list of strings, numbers, or filenames. If the list contains any KornShell wildcards, the KornShell expands the wildcards into filenames before beginning the loop. If you do not specify **in** *list*, **select** uses "$@" as the list.
command	usually a **case** statement but it could be any program, shell script, or KornShell statement.

Use **select** to create a menu. See Chapter 8 for examples.

```
select language in espanol francais english
do
    case $language in
        espanol)  load_spanish;;
        francais) load_french;;
        english)  load_english;;
    esac
done
```

set [**-A** *name*][**-s**][**--**][*arg1 ... argN*]   ]

-A *name*	create an array called *name*.
-s	**-sA** *name* sorts the values being assigned to array *name*; **-s** (without **-A** *name*) sorts the positional parameters.
--	unsets all the positional parameters. If you use this option, do not specify any *args*.
arg	zero or more numerical constants, string constants, or string patterns. The KornShell will try to glob wildcards into object pathnames.

Use **set** to assign and/or sort positional parameters or array values. You also can use **set** to unset positional parameters. If you don't specify **-A** *name*, the KornShell uses the *args* to set the positional parameters. If you do specify **-A** *name*, the KornShell sets the cells of array *name* with *args*.

```
$ set -A nums 97 85 92 # create array named nums; assign 97
                       # to nums[1], 85 to nums[2], and 92 to nums[3]

$ set -As nums 97 85 92  # create array named nums; assign 85 to
                         # nums[1], 92 to nums[2], and 97 to nums[3]
```

```
$ set 97 85 92          # assign 97 to $1, 85 to $2, and 92 to $3
$ set -s 97 85 92       # assign 85 to $1, 92 to $2, and 97 to $3
$ set *   # expand to names of all objects in current directory
          # and then make each object a positional parameter
$ set --   # unset positional parameters
```

set *[option1 ... optionN]*

    where *option* is one or more of the following:

±o **allexport** or ±a	export the value, data type, and attributes of every variable.
±o **bgnice**	run background jobs at a lower priority than foreground jobs.
±o **emacs**	run **emacs** as the command line editor; does not influence **FCEDIT**.
±o **errexit** or ±e	issue an **ERR** trap if a command ends with a nonzero value of **$?**.
±o **gmacs**	run **gmacs** as the command line editor; does not influence **FCEDIT**.
±o **ignoreeof**	an end-of-file character won't kill the current KornShell session.
±o **markdirs**	append (/) to directory names resulting from wildcard expansion.
±o **monitor** or ±m	print a completion message after a background job finishes. The KornShell waits until the next prompt to display this message. **-o monitor** is the default for the KornShell command line.
±o **noclobber** or ±C	suppress overwriting of existing files caused by > redirection operation.
±o **noexec** or ±n	don't execute the script, just check it for syntax errors.
±o **noglob** or ±f	suppress expansion of patterns into pathnames.
±o **nolog**	suppress storing function definitions in history file.
±o **notify** or ±b	print a message as soon as a background job ends. If you do not supply this option, the KornShell waits until the next prompt before printing the job completion message.
±o **nounset** or ±u	suppress expansion of unset variables; print error message.
±o **privileged** or ±p	suppress execution of $HOME/.profile login script. Use /etc/suid_profile as the environment (**ENV**) file.
±o **trackall** or ±h	create tracked aliases for all subsequently executed binary objects that are stored in one of the directories in your **PATH.**

±o verbose or **±v**	echo all commands (without expanding them) to standard error as they are executed.
±o vi	run **vi** as the command line editor; does not influence **FCEDIT**.
±o viraw	run **vi** in single-character-at-a-time mode (as opposed to line mode).
±o xtrace or **±x**	run in debug mode. Expand all commands and echo them to standard error as they are executed. Precede each expanded command by value of **PS4** variable.
±o	report status (on or off) of above options.

Use **set** to turn on or off certain attributes of the KornShell. These attributes influence the KornShell command line or KornShell scripts. The minus sign turns the attribute on and the plus sign turns it off.

The syntax for the **set** statement is a bit weird. To turn on an attribute, you can specify either **-o** followed by a full word (such as **xtrace**) or you can specify a one-letter switch (such as **-x**). Be careful—the name of the one-letter switch is not always the first letter of the full word. For example, the abbreviation for **-o trackall** is not **-t**.

```
$ set -o allexport    # export subsequently defined variables
$ x=7                 # variable x will be exported
$ set +o allexport    # turn off allexport feature
$ y=5                 # variable y will not be exported
```

shift [*number*]

    number   (integer) the number of positional parameters to eliminate. (Default is 1.)

Use **shift** to reduce the quantity of positional parameters by *number*. **shift** slides all remaining positional parameters to the left by *number*. For details, see "Processing Positional Parameters with shift" on page 147.

```
$ set a b c d e  # assign $1, $2, $3, $4, and $5
$ shift          # left shift all positional parameters one position
$ print $*       # print all positional parameters ($1 through $4)
b c d e
$ shift 2        # left shift all positional parameters two positions
$ print $*       # print all positional parameters ($1 through $2)
d e
```

sleep *n*

> *n*   the number of seconds that the current process should pause.

> Use **sleep** to pause the current process for *n* seconds.

```
$ sleep 7.5; print "\a"  # sound an alarm after 7.5 seconds
```

stop *job_name*

> *job_name*   see "job_name" on page 386.

> Use **stop** to halt a running job. Once halted, you can use the **bg** or **fg** statements.

```
$ ls -Rl / > /tmp/good 2> /tmp/bad &  # run ls in the background
[1]      15718
$ stop %1    # stop the ls command
$ fg %1      # continue running the ls command, but in the foreground
```

test *expression*

> **test** is an old Bourne shell statement that evaluates *expression,* returning true or false. You should use **[[...]]** or **((...))** instead of **test.**

then

> See "if" on page 385.

time *command*

> *command*   an operating system command (such as **ls**), a user program (such as **a.out**), a KornShell statement, or a KornShell script. The command also could contain one or more pipe operators (|). If it does, **time** applies to the entire pipeline, not just its first element.

> Use **time** as a stopwatch; **time** tells you how long it took to run *command.* Actually, **time** returns three pieces of information:

- **real** indicates the elapsed time it took for *command* to complete. This would be the time you would get if you pressed *go* on a real stop watch when you invoked *command* and then pressed *stop* when *command* finished.

- **user** indicates how long *command* was actually running inside the CPU.

- **sys** indicates how much time the operating system required on behalf of *command.*

The value of **real** will often be larger than the sum of **user** and **sys,** with the missing time belonging to other processes running at the same time that *command* ran.

```
$ time myscript      # how long does it take to run myscript?
real        0m1.76s  # actual time
user        0m0.15s
sys         0m0.35s
```

trap *[response] [event]*

response   a command enclosed in single quotes, or an empty string, or -. If you specify a command, the KornShell executes that command in response to an event. If you set *response* to an empty string, the KornShell ignores *event*. If you set response to -, the KornShell restores the original *response* to the *event*.

event   the name of a system signal (for example, **INT**) or the name of a special KornShell signal (for example, **ERR, DEBUG,** or **EXIT).**

Use **trap** to execute a *response* to an *event.* For more details about the syntax of **trap**, see page 322.

```
trap 'wrap_up_script' QUIT  # run wrap_up_script upon
                            # receipt of a QUIT signal
```

true

   true is an alias for the colon (:) statement. Use it to create a condition that always evaluates to true.

```
while true   # create an always-true loop
```

type *name*

name   the name of any file, KornShell statement, function, or alias.

   type is an alias for **whence -v**. See "whence" on page 404.

typeset [-f] [±ft] [fu] *[function_name1 ... function_nameN]*

-f	display the code for *function_name*. If you don't specify *function_name*, then **-f** displays the code for all accessible functions.
-ft	turn on debug mode within *function_name*. (**typeset -ft** is equivalent to **set -x.**)
+ft	turn off debug mode within *function_name*. (**typeset +ft** is equivalent to **set +x.**)
-fu	tell the KornShell that *function_name* is externally defined; that is, the code for *function_name* is located in another file. Use **-fu** to tell the KornShell that *function_name* is to be autoloaded.
function_name	is the name of the function(s) to which the option applies.

Use **typeset -f** to research functions or to set certain attributes within them.

```
$ typeset -f     # display names and contents of all accessible functions
$ typeset -f funk   # display name and contents of function funk
$ typeset -ft funk # go into debugging mode whenever funk is called
$ typeset +ft funk # don't go into debugging mode when funk is called
$ typeset -fu carambola   # tell KornShell that carambola is the name
                          # of a function that is defined externally
$ autoload carambola      # same as above
```

typeset [±AHlprtux] [±EFLZi[number]] *[variable_name[=value]]*

±A	declare *variable_name* as an associative array.
±E	declare *variable_name* as a floating-point number having ten significant digits.
±E*number*	declare *variable_name* as a floating-point number having *number* significant digits.
±F	declare *variable_name* as a floating-point number having 10 digits past the decimal point.
±F*number*	declare *variable_name* as a floating-point number having *number* digits past the decimal point.
±H	the KornShell ignores this option if you are working on the UNIX operating system. If you aren't, **-H** converts the value of *variable_name* to a format consistent with pathnames on your system. The conversion formula is built into your KornShell implementation; you cannot change it.
±i	declare *variable_name* as an integer.
±i*number*	declare *variable_name* as an integer and specify that the value of *variable_name* will always be printed in base *number*.

±l	whenever the KornShell expands *variable_name*, the KornShell temporarily changes any uppercase letters in *value* to lowercase.
±p	displays information in a way that makes it convenient to copy and paste into a start-up file.
±L[*number*]	left-justify *variable_name*. The optional *number* specifies the field width.
±LZ[*number*]	left-justify *variable_name* and strip leading zeros from its value. The optional *number* specifies the field width.
±r	make *variable_name* into a constant. That is, after setting the value of *variable_name*, you cannot change it.
±R[*number*]	right-justify *variable_name*. The optional *number* specifies the field width.
±RZ[*number*]	right-justify *variable_name* and strip trailing zeros from its value. The optional *number* specifies the field width.
±t	has no meaning to the KornShell. You can use this to "tag" *variable_name* for your own purposes.
±u	whenever the KornShell expands *variable_name*, the KornShell temporarily changes any lowercase letters in *value* to uppercase.
±x	export *variable_name* to children of the current process.
variable_name	the name of the variable you are declaring. If you don't specify *variable_name*, the KornShell will display the names of all variables declared with the given attribute.
value	the string, integer, or floating-point number that will be the initial contents of *variable_name*.

Use **typeset** to declare the data type and/or attributes of *variable_name*. By default, all variables are automatically strings and you do not have to declare them before you use them. If you specify **typeset** *variable*, *variable* will be declared as a string. Using **typeset** within the body of a function gives *variable* function scope.

Specifying a minus sign (-) in front of an option turns on the feature; specifying a plus sign (+) turns off the option.

Specifying **typeset** without any options (or with the **-p** option) generates a list of all variables created with a **typeset** statement or one of its aliases.

For more details on **typeset** and data types, see Chapter 3. For details on the **-L** and **-R** options, see "Left Justification" on page 257.

```
$ typeset      # list variables declared with typeset or its aliases
export TZ
export MSGVERB
export PATH
...

$ typeset -i  # list all integer variables
```

```
HISTCMD=362
LINENO=1
MAILCHECK=600
...

$ typeset -E pH=7.5 # declare variable pH as a float and set its
                    # initial value to 7.5
```

ulimit [-HS] [-a]
ulimit [-HS] [[-cdfmnstv] [*number* | **unlimited**]]

-a	display the soft limits of all resources. If preceded by **-H**, display the hard limits of all resources.
-c *number*	set the size limit of a core dump at *number* blocks.
-d *number*	set the size limit of the data area at *number* Kbytes.
-f *number*	set the size limit of files created by child processes at *number* blocks. (This may prevent a child process from inadvertently filling up the disk.)
-H	set or display the hard limit. The hard limit, once set on a resource, cannot be changed.
-m *number*	set the size limit of physical memory that this process can access at any one time at *number* Kilobytes.
-n *number*	set the number of streams that this process can open.
-S	set or display the soft limit. The soft limit can change; however, the soft limit never can exceed the hard limit.
-s *number*	set the size limit of the stack at *number* Kilobytes.
-t *number*	set the real time limit of *number* seconds that any process can use.
-v *number*	set the limit on the amount of virtual memory that this process can use to *number* Kilobytes. This might be a useful limit to establish during the debugging phase of programming, particularly in programs that do a lot of recursion.
unlimited	indicates that you don't want a limit on the designated resource. Note that operating system or hardware limitations still may come into play even if you set an attribute to **unlimited**. For example, the operating system probably maintains its own limit on the number of streams that a process can open. Setting **-n** to **unlimited** still will not allow Korn-Shell processes to exceed the limit established by the operating system.

Use **ulimit** to set or display KornShell resources. If you specify *number*, then the KornShell sets a limit. If you don't specify *number*, the KornShell displays the current limit. If you specify **unlimited**, the KornShell will not maintain a limit on the specified resource. If you don't specify an option, the default is **-f**.

The options supported by **ulimit** vary between KornShell implementations. In other words, your version of the KornShell may support different **ulimit**

options than those listed. In addition, some KornShell implementations prevent
you from changing certain limits.

```
$ ulimit -a        # display all resource limits
time(seconds)          unlimited
file(blocks)           204800
data(kbytes)           524288
stack(kbytes)          65536
memory(kbytes)         1541448
coredump(blocks)       0
nofiles(descriptors)   200
vmemory(kbytes)        524288
$ ulimit -Ht 100    # set process time limit to a hard 100 seconds
$ ulimit -St  50    # set process time limit to a soft 50 seconds
$ payroll           # run a process that takes longer than 60 seconds
exceeded CPU time limit
$ ulimit -St  70    # since 50 wasn't enough, better bump up to 70
$ payroll           # no problem running payroll now
$ ulimit -St 200    # can't increase soft limit past hard limit
ksh93: ulimit: 200: limit exceeded [Not privileged]
$ ulimit -Ht 200    # can't increase hard limit
ksh93: ulimit: 200: limit exceeded [Not privileged]
```

umask [*mask*]

> *mask*　　　　　is a three-digit octal number or a four-digit octal number.
>
> If a three-digit octal number, the first digit represents the user's permis-
> sions, the second the group's permissions, and the third all other's per-
> missions.
>
> If a four-digit octal number, the first digit represents various system
> information, the second the user's permissions, the third the group's
> permissions, and the fourth all other's permissions.

Use **umask** to set or display the default protections for all files and directories
that the current process creates. If you do not supply a *mask*, **umask** displays the
default protections. If you do supply a *mask*, **umask** sets the default protections.

The **umask** statement often is confused with the **chmod** command. The Korn-
Shell uses the value of **umask** to determine an object's initial permissions; the
chmod command changes the permissions of an object that *already* has been created. The **chmod** command often is issued from the command line; the **umask**
statement is rarely issued from the command line. (The **umask** statement usually
is placed inside a start-up file.)

If you specify a *mask* of all zeros as follows:

```
$ umask 000
```

then all created directories will give user, group, and others complete protections. Furthermore, all created files will give user, group, and others read and write permission, but not execute permission.

If you specify a mask other than 000, various starting permissions disappear. Each digit represents a different permission. The first digit indicates which permission to remove for the individual owner (the user) of the file, the second digit is for the group owner of the file, and the third digit is for everyone else. A value of 4 means shut off reader permissions, a value of 2 means shut off write permissions, and a value of 1 means shut off execute permissions. For example, setting the *mask* to a very unlikely 421 as follows:

```
$ umask 421
```

means shuts off read permission for the user, write permission for the group, and execute permission for others.

You can shut off multiple permissions by adding the 4, 2, and 1 in various combinations. For example, the following statement:

```
$ umask 037
```

shuts off write and execute permissions for the group, and shuts off all permissions for others.

umask -S [*WhoOperationPermissions*] ...[*WhoOperationPermissions*]

Who	is a **u** (user), **g** (group), or **o** (others), or any combination of **u**, **g**, and **o** (for example, **ug**). If you omit *Who*, **umask** assumes **ugo**.
Operation	is an **=** (assign these permissions), a **+** (add these permissions), or a **-** (remove these permissions).
Permissions	is an **r** (read), **w** (write), **x** (execute), or any combination of **r**, **w**, and **x** (for example, **rx**). If you omit *Permissions*, **umask** assumes that you mean no permissions at all.

In KornShell 88, **umask** supported only the octal number syntax. The KornShell 93 version of **umask** still supports the octal syntax, but supplements it with a textual syntax based on simple abbreviations. For UNIX oldtimers out there, the textual syntax is identical to the textual syntax of chmod. If you omit the **-S** option, the KornShell assumes the octal syntax. If you specify the **-S** option, the KornShell assumes the textual syntax.

By setting the **umask** as follows:

```
$ umask -S ugo=rwx
```

directories will be created with full permissions for everyone, and files will be created with read and write permissions for everyone (sorry, there's no way to have **umask** give files execute permission).

By setting the **umask** as follows:

```
$ umask u=rw g=r o=
```

directories and files will be created with read and write permissions for the user, read permission for the group, and no permissions for others.

unalias [-a] *alias_name*

-a	delete all aliases.
alias_name	the name of an alias.

Use **unalias** to delete *alias_name* from the list of aliases or to delete all aliases.

```
$ alias doit='ls -alR'  # create alias named doit
$ unalias doit # cancel alias doit
$ doit        # causes an error because doit no longer means anything
```

unset [-fvn] *name1 [... nameN]*

-f *name*	to unset function *name*.
-v *name*	to unset variable *name*.
-n *name*	to unset **nameref** variable *name*.
name	the name of a function, variable, or **nameref** variable.

Use **unset** to remove variables or functions from the KornShell's list of set objects. You cannot unset constants (variables declared as **readonly**).

To unset an alias, use the **unalias** statement.

```
$ str="Hello"  # create a variable named str
$ unset str    # delete str from list of variables
$ print "$str" # print a blank line because str is no longer set
```

until *condition*
do
  command1
  ...
  commandN
done

     condition   usually a numerical comparison, string comparison, or object test; however, *condition* can be the name of any program, operating system command, or KornShell statement (except **while, do,** or **done**).

     command   the name of any program, any shell script, or any KornShell statement.

    Use **until** to create a loop. The loop will execute as long as *condition* is false. For example, the following loop will write the numbers 1 through 5 inclusive to standard output:

```
integer count=1
until ((count > 5)) # create loop to count from 1 to 5
do
    print $count
    ((count = count + 1))
done
```

wait [*job_name1 ... job_nameN*]

     job_name   the job or jobs you want to wait for. If you don't specify any *job_names,* the KornShell waits for all the background jobs invoked by the current KornShell. See "job_name" on page 386.

    Use **wait** when you need to hold off executing a command until one or more *jobs* finish running.

```
$ myscript1 &                   # run myscript1 in background
$ myscript2 &                   # run myscript2 in background
$ wait myscript2; myscript3 & # when myscript2 finishes,
                                # run myscript3
$ wait; print "All jobs done!" # print a message when
                                # all jobs complete

$ pay1 &                        # run pay1 in background
$ pay2 &                        # run pay2 in background
$ wait pay1 pay2; pay3 &     # when pay1 and pay2 both finish, run pay3
```

wc

    Some versions of KornShell provide the POSIX **wc** command as a KornShell statement. The KornShell version of **wc** has the same features as the POSIX version of **wc**. The –**l** option of **wc** returns the number of lines in standard input and is heavily used in pipelines.

whence [-afpv] *name*

-a	list all occurrences of *name*.
-f	if *name* is a function, suppress listing it.
-p	if *name* is a statement, alias, or function, suppress listing it.
-v	list the occurrence of *name* that will be invoked. Describe the category (function, built-in, alias, tracked alias) to which *name* belongs.
name	the name of any file, KornShell statement, function, or alias. If a file, *name* will be detected only if the file is stored in a directory assigned to **PATH**.

Issuing **whence** *name* (without any options) returns a pathname, a string, or nothing. If a pathname is returned, *name* is a file. If a string other than a pathname (that is, a string that does not start with a slash) is returned, *name* is a Korn-Shell statement, alias, or function. If nothing is returned, *name* does not exist.

The -**v** option is particularly helpful where *name* could mean several different objects and you aren't sure which one the KornShell will invoke. For example, suppose you create a function named okra and an alias named okra. When you type okra, will the KornShell invoke the function or the alias? Use the -**v** option to answer that question. Note that **whence** -**v** is similar (but slightly more intelligent) than the whereis UNIX command.

```
$ whence grep     # returns a pathname; thus, grep is a file
/bin/grep

$ whence for       # returns a word; thus, for exists but is not a file
for

$ whence unicorn  # returns nothing; thus, unicorn does not exist

$ whence -a test  # list all occurrences of test
test is a shell builtin
test is a tracked alias for /bin/test

$ whence -v test  # if I invoke test, which occurrence is invoked?
test is a shell builtin
```

while condition
do
   command1
   ...
   [commandN]
done

condition	is usually a numerical comparison, string comparison, or object test; however, *condition* can be the name of any program, operating system command, or KornShell statement.
command	is the name of any program, shell script, or KornShell statement.

Use **while** to create a loop. The loop will iterate as long as *condition* is true. For details on **while**, see page 122.

```
x=5;
while (( x < 10 ))
do
  (( y = (x * x) + 2 ))
  print $y
  (( x++ ))
done
```

B Just Enough HTML

By now, a lot of you know HTML (Hypertext Markup Language) and can safely skip this appendix.

For the rest of you laggards, what are you waiting for? Three shelves of my local bookstore are devoted solely to HTML books; Shakespeare only gets one shelf. Oh, wait, I get it. You're one of those artsy types who feel they "know" HTML because they've created some Web pages with some wamby-pamby HTML editor. Well, bucko, when you're lying head first in a CGI core dump, FrontPage is not going to save your hide. DO YOU UNDERSTAND ME?

All right, I've taken a few deep breaths. Let's move along, shall we?

The next few pages are designed to give you just enough HTML to understand the CGI scripts that appear in Chapter 17. HTML is a vast and expanding universe, and it would take approximately five billion pages to describe every nuance properly. Nevertheless, in just a few pages, you can learn enough HTML to book a hotel or order a charming meal.

HTML describes the way that a Web page should look. HTML files consist of some combination of tags and text. *Tags* are directives placed inside a pair of angle brackets; for example, `<ul>` and `<h1>` are two different tags. *Text* is, well, words and stuff. Basically, text is anything that doesn't appear inside a pair of angle brackets.

Most tags need to be paired; that is, you have to specify both a start tag and a stop tag. A stop tag looks just like a start tag except it has a slash (/) right after the opening angle bracket <. For example, `<ul>` is a start tag and `</ul>` is its stop tag. Some stop tags are optional.

Essential HTML Tags

Table B-1 contains the essential HTML tags, those that appear in nearly every Web page.

Table B-1. Essential HTML Tags

Tag	What it does	Where to put it
`<html>`	Starts and ends every HTML file.	Put **<html>** at the start of every Web page; put **</html>** at the end of every Web page.
`<head>`	Marks the borders of the preface of an HTML file.	Put **<head>** right after **<html>**; put **</head>** just before **<body>**.
`<title>`	Marks the title of this Web page. The browser usually displays the title in the window banner; also, the title is used in bookmarks.	Usually, you put **<title>** just after **<head>**, and put **</title>** just before **</head>**
`<body>`	Marks the start of the nonprefatory parts of this HTML file.	Put **<body>** just after **</head>**; put **</body>** just before **</html>**
`<p>`	Marks the start and end of a paragraph.	Just about anywhere in the body of an HTML file.

The following HTML file, first.htm, demonstrates all these HTML tags.

```
<html>

<head>
<title>HTML Requirements: The Boring Stuff</title>
</head>

<body>
<p>"Originality is when you forget your sources."</p>
<p>I forgot who said that.</p>
</body>

</html>
```

If you direct your browser to open `first.htm`, you'll see something like the following:

> "Originality is when you forget your sources."
>
> I forgot who said that.

Here are some general things to note about HTML:

- Start tags do not have to appear at the beginning of a line, and stop tags do not have to appear at the end of a line. I just put them there to make them easier to spot.

- Tags are case-insensitive; that is, **\<head\>**, **\<HEAD\>**, and **\<Head\>** all have the same meaning to a browser.

- Browsers generally ignore blank lines, although a blank line does form an implicit stop tag for certain tags, such as **\</p\>**. In general, you should use blank lines to make your HTML source easier to read.

- Browsers generally ignore the newline character. For example, you could eliminate all newlines from `boring.htm`, put the entire contents on one physical line, and the Web page still would come out looking the same.

- Most modern browsers no longer require the **\<html\>**, **\<head\>**, and **\<body\>** tags, but you should use them anyway, because...well, just because it's the right thing to do, that's why.

- Many stop tags, such as **\</p\>**, are optional.

Headings

HTML allows you to sprinkle headings liberally in Web pages. The highest level heading, a head level 1, is marked with the start tag **<h1>**. An **<h2>** indicates a second-level head, an **<h3>** a third-level head, and so on. The following Web page, heads.htm, contains an **<h1>** at the top and a bunch of **<h2>** and **<h3>** tags.

```
<html>

<head>
<title>Heads in HTML</title>
</head>

<body>
<h1>The Old Hacker</h1>
<p>The old programmer plunged his debugger into the heart of the
algorithm.  The algorithm was a worthy opponent and the old
programmer loved it.</p>

<h2>How He Loved It</h2>
<p>"Go home old man," Jose, the project leader warned.</p>
<p>"I cannot go home yet, young one," the old man replied. "For
I love strong data typing like a brother."</p>

<h3>What He Thought of His Brother</h3>
<p>The old man had a brother, but they hadn't seen each other
since the brother moved to Cupertino. "A PERL programmer," said
the old man, spitting in disgust. </p>

<h2>Somber Algorithms</h2>
<p>"I had a beautiful algorithm once," reflected the old man.  "But it
is vanished. Like some forgotten PDP/11, it is gone.</p>
</body>
</html>
```

Here's how this Web page (heads.htm) looks on my browser:

The Old Hacker

The old programmer plunged his debugger into the heart of the algorithm. The algorithm was a worthy opponent and the old programmer loved it.

How He Loved It

"Go home old man," Jose, the project leader warned.

"I cannot go home yet, young one," the old man replied. "For I love strong data typing like a brother."

What He Thought of His Brother

The old man had a brother, but they hadn't seen each other since the brother moved to Cupertino. "A PERL programmer," said the old man, spitting in disgust.

Somber Algorithms

"I had a beautiful algorithm once," reflected the old man. "But it is vanished. Like some forgotten PDP/11, it is gone.

You can use the **<center>** tag to center nearly anything on a Web page. For example, the following line causes the top-level header to be centered between the left and right sides of the browser window:

```
<center><h1>The Old Hacker</h1></center>
```

Lists

You can create three kinds of lists in HTML:

- Unordered (bulleted) lists

- Ordered (numbered) lists

- Definition lists, which often are used to create glossaries

The following HTML file illustrates unordered and ordered lists:

```
<html>
<head><title>Lists in HTML</title></head>
<body>
<h1>Ian Fleming: The Tech Writing Days</h1>
<p>Blofeld, you won't get away with it for the following reasons:</p>
<ul>
<li>My Walther PPK (when installed with optional bullet attachment, which
should only be used AFTER reading the manual in its entirety) is
pointed directly at you.</li>
<li>I'm having an outstanding hair day.</li>
</ul>

<p>Bond, in order to defeat me, you must perform
the following steps:
<ol>
<li>Destroy my satellites.</li>
<li>Blow up this installation.</li>
<li>Close with a double entendre.</li>
</ol>
</body>
</html>
```

This HTML file, lists.htm, generates the following Web page:

Ian Fleming: The Tech Writing Days

Blofeld, you won't get away with it for the following reasons:

- My Walther PPK (when installed with optional bullet attachment, which should only be used AFTER reading the manual in its entirety) is pointed directly at you.
- I'm having an outstanding hair day.

Bond, in order to defeat me, you must perform the following steps:

1. Destroy my satellites.
2. Blow up this installation.
3. Close with a double entendre.

Character Tags

When you specify a **<p>** tag, the browser, by default, writes the paragraph's text as "Roman" text, which means the resulting text will have no adornments like boldfacing or italicizing. To dress up plain old Roman text, HTML provides quite a few character tags, including the popular ones shown in Table B-2.

Table B-2. Popular HTML Character Tags

Tag	What it does
<strong>	Strengthens the text, usually by putting it in bold.
<em>	Emphasizes the text, usually by putting it in italics.
<code>	Displays in a fixed-width font, as if the text were typed on a typewriter. Useful for displaying program code.
<small>	Makes the font smaller than it was.
<big>	Makes the font bigger than it was.

The preceding tags are all just hints to the browser. For example, if you tag text with **<em>**, you are asking the browser to emphasize this text but you are not specifying what emphasis means; it is up to the browser to decide. As it happens, all current versions of Netscape and Microsoft browsers italicize text marked as **<em>**. The following HTML file, `characters.htm`, show off some of these tags.

```
<html>
<head><title>Concept Font Tags</title></head>
<body>
<h1>Characters Font Tags</h1>
<p>Certain writing styles (and I am <strong>not</strong> making this up)
are so <big>instantly recognizable</big> that alert readers,
<small>such as Dave Beckedorff of Hackerville, Massachusetts,</small>
write in to tell us about them.  It seems that in Massachusetts
(motto: <em>"We're all legally insane."</em>), angry tech writers are
<big><big><strong>ripping off</strong></big></big> award winning
humor writers.</p>
</body>
</html>
```

And here's how this HTML file looked on my browser:

Characters Font Tags

Certain writing styles (and I am **not** making this up) are so **instantly recognizable** that alert readers, such as Dave Beckedorff of Hackerville, Massachusetts, write in to tell us about them. It seems that in Massachusetts (motto: *"We're all legally insane. "*), angry tech writers are **ripping off** award winning humor writers.

Hyperlinks

Click on a hyperlink and be transported to another URL. To create a hyperlink, use the **<a href="***destination***">** tag, where *destination* is a URL. For example, the following Web page, hyperlinks.htm, contains a hyperlink to another Web page (marge.htm).

```
<html>

<head><title>Hyperlinks</title></head>
<body>
<h1>Homer's Odyssey</h1>
<p>Sing in me, oh <a href="marge.htm">Marge</a>,</p>
<p>and through me tell the story</p>
<p>of that wanderer, uncomprending Homer,</p>
<p>Whose breath could launch a thousand ships.</p>
</body>
</html>
```

And here is the target of the hyperlink:

```
<html>

<head><title>Marge</title></head>
<body>
<h1>About Marge</h1>
<p>Daughter of Menelaus and Athena, blue-haired Marge</P>
is beloved as the Patron Muse of Underachievers.</p>
<p><a href="hyperlinks.htm">Return to Home</a>.</P>
</body>
</html>
```

When viewed through my browser, hyperlinks.htm looks as follows:

Homer's Odyssey

Sing in me, oh <u>Marge</u>,

and through me tell the story

of that wanderer, uncomprending Homer,

Whose breath could launch a thousand ships.

Clicking on the <u>Marge</u> hyperlink should transport you to the `marge.htm` home page, which looks like the following:

About Marge

Daughter of Menelaus and Athena, blue-haired Marge

is beloved as the Patron Muse of Underachievers.

Return to Home.

Images

Q: What would the Web be without images?
A: Fast.

Images are the Sirens of Web pages, attracting users by their beauty, only to drive users insane from the interminable download wait.

To put images up on a Web page, use the **<IMG>** tag. The **<IMG>** tag supports a boatload of arguments, all but one of which is optional. The sole required option is **src**, which you use to specify the pathname of the image you want to display.

In theory, most browsers can be set up to display images encoded in just about any imaginable graphics format. In practice, most current graphical browsers are guaranteed to support only the following two graphics formats:

- GIF

- JPEG

The following HTML file, `graphics.htm`, displays a simple GIF image:

```
<html>
<head><title>Graphics in HTML</title></head>
<body>
<h1>Worth a Thousand Words</h1>
<p>Here's an attractive pattern:</p>
<p><center><img src="stars.gif"></center></p>
</body>
</html>
```

Here's the way it looks on my browser:

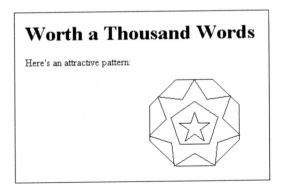

By the way, some CGI scripts can create graphic images on the fly, typically by calling special graphics creation utilities. For instance, a CGI program might gather a bunch of input data, then call a program that creates a bar graph in GIF format.

Bibliography

Bolsky, Morris, and David Korn. *The New KornShell Command and Programming Language.* Upper Saddle River, New Jersey: Prentice Hall, 1995.

Musciano, Chuck, and Bill Kennedy. HTML: *The Definitive Guide (Nutshell Handbook).* Cambridge, Mass.: O'Reilly and Associates, 1997.

Nemeth, Evi, Snyder, Garth, and Scott Seebass. *UNIX System Administration Handbook.* Englewood Cliffs, New Jersey: Prentice Hall, 1989.

Pendergrast, J. Stephen. *Desktop KornShell Graphical Programming.* Reading, Mass.: Addison Wesley Longman, 1995.

Robbins, Arnold. *KORN SHELL REFERENCE.* Seattle, Washington: Specialized System Consultants, 1995.

Stein, Lincoln. *How to Set up and Maintain a Web Site.* Reading, Mass.: Addison Wesley Longman, 1997.

Stevens, W. Richard. *TCP/IP Illustrated, Volume 3.* Reading, Mass.: Addison Wesley Longman, 1996.

Index

Symbols

! in wildcards 60
!! operator 86
!( ) wildcard 67
!= operator 84
" (double quotes) in strings 21
(substring deletion) operator 264
   vs. ## operator 267
#! in CGI scripts 345
(substring deletion) operator 267
$ prompt 296
$ variable value 16
$! variable 307
$# variable 144, 145
$$ variable 307
$(< filename) operator 260
$(...) operator 171
$(command) operation 241
$* variable 148
$? variable 196, 288
   functions 171, 172
   life of 173
   range of 171
   trapping 319
$@ variable 148
$_ variable 302
   mail file 293
${string:+expr} operator 277
${string:=expr} operator 277

${string:?expr} operator 277
${string:-expr} operator 277
${string_var/#search_pattern/
      replacement_string} operator 261
${string_var/%search_pattern/
      replacement_string} operator 261
${string_var//search_pattern/
      replacement_string} operator 261
${string_var/search_pattern/
      replacement_string} operator 261
$0 variable 144, 302
$1 variable 143
   within functions 167, 168
% (substring deletion) operator 265, 268
   vs. %% 268
%% (substring deletion) operator 268
%= (assignment) operator 55
%d conversion specifier 224
& (background) operator 309
<&- (close stream) operator 240
& wildcard modifier 58
&& operator 86
&= (assignment) operator 55
((...)) math container 44, 75
* wildcard 62
   in a case statement 88
*( ) wildcard 65
*= (assignment) operator 55
+ (debug mode prompt) 20

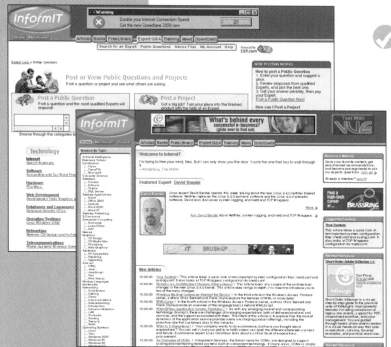

Register
Your Book
at www.aw.com/cseng/register

You may be eligible to receive:
- Advance notice of forthcoming editions of the book
- Related book recommendations
- Chapter excerpts and supplements of forthcoming titles
- Information about special contests and promotions throughout the year
- Notices and reminders about author appearances, tradeshows, and online chats with special guests

Contact us

If you are interested in writing a book or reviewing manuscripts prior to publication, please write to us at:

Editorial Department
Addison-Wesley Professional
75 Arlington Street, Suite 300
Boston, MA 02116 USA
Email: AWPro@aw.com

Addison-Wesley

Visit us on the Web: http://www.aw.com/cseng